'TOTALLY UN-EN

CW00566987

BRITAIN'S INTERNMEN
ALIENS' IN TWO WORLD WARS

THE YEARBOOK OF THE RESEARCH CENTRE FOR GERMAN AND AUSTRIAN EXILE STUDIES

7

INSTITUTE OF GERMANIC AND ROMANCE STUDIES UNIVERSITY OF LONDON

Editorial Board

Charmian Brinson, Richard Dove, Anthony Grenville, Marian Malet, J.M. Ritchie, Jennifer Taylor, Ian Wallace

Amsterdam - New York, NY 2005

'TOTALLY UN-ENGLISH'?

BRITAIN'S INTERNMENT OF 'ENEMY ALIENS' IN TWO WORLD WARS

Edited by

Richard Dove

The paper on which this book is printed meets the requirements of
'ISO 9706: 1994, Information and documentation - Paper for documents -
Requirements for permanence'.

ISSN: 1388-3720
ISBN: 90-420-1658-2
Editions Rodopi B.V., Amsterdam - New York, NY 2005
Printed in The Netherlands

Table of Contents

Acknowledgements   7

Introduction

'A matter which touches the good name of this
country'   11
Richard Dove

A Marginalized Subject? The Historiography of
Enemy Alien Internment in Britain   17
Panikos Panayi

Internment in the First World War

Prisoners of Britain: German Civilian, Military
and Naval Internees during the First World War   29
Panikos Panayi

Behind the Wire: the material culture of civilian
internment on the Isle of Man in the First World
War   45
Yvonne Cresswell

Die Bedeutung der Musik für 26.000 internierte
Zivilisten während des Ersten Weltkriegs auf der
Isle of Man   63
Jutta Raab Hansen

Civilian Internment in Scotland during the First
World War   83
Stefan Manz

Internment in the Second World War

'Loyal to the Reich': National Socialists and Others
in the Rushen Women's Internment Camp   101
Charmian Brinson

'Wer sie nicht erlebt hat, der begreift sie nie.' The
Internment Camp Revue *What a life!*   121
Richard Dove

'Something to make people laugh'? Political
content in Isle of Man Internment Camp Journals
July-October 1940   139
Jennifer Taylor

The Internment of Italians 1940-1945   153
Lucio Sponza

After the Prison Ships: Internment Narratives in
Canada   165
Nicole M. T. Brunnhuber

The Dunera Boys: Dramatizing History from a
Jewish Perspective   179
Birgit Lang

Exile, Internment and Deportation in Norbert
Gstrein's *Die englischen Jahre*   193
J. M. Ritchie

Index   205

Acknowledgements

The editors would like to thank *German Life and Letters* for generous financial support for the production of this volume. Grateful thanks are also due to Manx National Heritage and to the Imperial War Museum for permission to reproduce images used in this publication. Finally we are indebted to David Newton for the technical expertise without which none of it would have happened.

Introduction

'A matter which touches the good name of this country'

Richard Dove

The internment of 'enemy aliens' by the British government in two world wars is a subject which remains largely hidden from history. British historians of the two world wars have treated the subject – if at all – as a regrettable minor episode, a footnote to the main narrative of Britain at war. Academic interest in internment has been sporadic, often responding to external stimuli. There are two major reasons for this. Firstly, historical research has been handicapped by the culture of secrecy of the British government, which appears to have successfully survived even Freedom of Information. For many years the records of government departments relating to internment in 1940 were unavailable for public scrutiny. In the 1980s and 90s much material was released, but access to other documents is still denied or severely restricted, while it has also become apparent that some material has simply been destroyed. The second reason is related to the first. Internment in both world wars was a confused and shabby policy, which is difficult to reconcile with the accepted historical narrative of 'Britain at War': an epic story of unity, courage, endurance and final victory.

Historians are united in considering internment in both wars as an unjust and largely unnecessary measure, calling it variously 'an intolerant act' (Panikos Panayi), 'monstrously unjust' (François Lafitte) or 'a disreputable story' (Peter and Leni Gillman). The introduction of wholesale internment in May 1940 has nonetheless also sharply divided historical opinion. Some have excused the measure as a panic response to the threat of imminent invasion, and its later reversal as a wrong finally righted, a reassertion of British belief in justice and fair play; others have seen it as the inevitable result of traditional British intolerance towards foreigners and immigrants which is embedded in various Aliens Acts.

There are in fact significant differences (as well as similarities) in both government policy and the popular response to it, in the two world wars, which are indicative of the changing social climate. In the 'Great War', Britain interned some 30,000 German nationals, most of whom had been resident in the country for a number of years; many were arrested and interned in May 1915 in the outbreak of spy-mania which followed the sinking of the liner *Lusitania*. In the prevailing atmosphere, distorted by orchestrated patriotism and Germanophobia, the policy of internment seemed both logical and justifiable, and was not widely questioned. Those, like the Quakers, who tried to bring spiritual and material solace to the internees were decried as 'Hun coddlers'. In fact, internment was a policy which brought little discernible benefit to Britain, but which cruelly damaged the lives and livelihoods of those detained, breaking up families and disrupting social networks. It resulted in the destruction of German communities in Britain, which suffered a blow from which they never recovered.

During the Second World War, the situation was both more differentiated and more chaotic. When war broke out in September 1939, some 60-70,000 German and Austrian refugees, the great majority of whom were Jewish, had sought asylum in Britain. The British government had actually considered the question of internment before the outbreak of war, reviewing the policy pursued during the First World War and concluding that it had been essentially futile. It therefore rejected wholesale internment as unnecessary, resorting to a system of tribunals, the task of which was to grade refugees according to the degree of risk they were judged to represent. This was abruptly replaced in May 1940 by the introduction of wholesale internment.

Contrary to the situation in the First World War, the policy of mass internment outraged some sections of the British intelligentsia, including such figures as the Oxford classical scholar Professor Gilbert Murray, the Bishop of Chichester, George Bell, the author H. G. Wells and the MPs Colonel Josiah Wedgwood and Eleanor Rathbone. It was the subject of persistent criticism in the House of Commons. Introducing a debate which lasted nearly six hours, on 10 July 1940, the young Conservative MP, Major Victor Cazalet, called the internment of refugees 'totally un-English'. In a second debate on 22 August he declared that he would not be happy until 'this bespattered page of our history has been torn up and re-written', causing the stolid Home Secretary, Sir John Anderson, to concede that it was indeed 'a matter which touches the good name of this country' (Hansard Vols. 362 and 364 (1939-40), 10 July and 22 August). By then, the policy had already gone into reverse.

Differences in public attitudes and awareness are evident in the changing vocabulary of internment. During the 'Great War' little attempt was made to distinguish civilian from military prisoners: in the official terminology of the time, combatant and civilian detainees alike were referred to as 'prisoners of war'. Although the government usually chose to separate military prisoners from civilians, this was largely for administrative reasons. Among the memorabilia produced by civilian internees on the Isle of Man is a panoramic view of Knockaloe Camp, containing the inscription

'Kriegsgefangenenlager Knockaloe'. Some of the camps, such as Stobs, were referred to as 'concentration camps', a term which subsequently acquired a resonance making its use impossible in 1939/40.

No account of internment can overlook the Isle of Man, which became the place where the majority of internees in both world wars were held. An offshore island in the Irish Sea, the Isle of Man is a dependency of the British Crown, but is not part of the United Kingdom. Nonetheless, in times of war, it has asserted its loyalty to the Crown, twice serving the British state as the major location for internment. An historian of the island during the First World War has written that by 1916 'the Isle of Man had become one huge enemy prison camp' (Margery West, *Island at War*, 1986). Indeed the island's isolated location and rugged topography seemed to offer an ideal place to detain those deemed a threat to British security. While a few prisoners did manage to escape from the camp, none ever succeeded in escaping from the island.

The present volume is quite consciously interdisciplinary, drawing on expertise from different quarters and disciplines. It is introduced by Panikos Panayi's outline historiography of internment which summarizes the fluctuations of interest in the subject – and the reasons for them. Thereafter, the book is structured chronologically. Panayi has also contributed a comprehensive review of civilian and military internment in the First World War, referring *inter alia* to the phenomenon of 'barbed wire disease' which afflicted so many prisoners. Many sought to alleviate it through meaningful activity, such as arts and craft work, as portrayed in Yvonne Cresswell's essay on craftwork in Knockaloe Camp. Music was also a significant source of relief, as exemplified in Jutta Raab Hansen's account of the extensive programme of concerts and musical events in camps on the Isle of Man. This section also includes Stefan Manz's case study of the Scottish internment camp at Stobs, near Hawick, which concludes that internment policy in Scotland was driven by the same prejudices as in the rest of the United Kingdom.

Internment in the Second World War has generally attracted greater attention from historians, though a few specific aspects have remained under- or totally un-researched. For example, although some 4,000 women were interned on the Isle of Man, the topic of women's internment remains under-researched. Charmian Brinson's essay on women internees (Nazis and others) who were 'loyal to the Reich' opens up consideration of an area which has hitherto been largely ignored. The volume also includes my own essay on the production of the musical revue *What a Life!* – one of the legendary (but hitherto un-researched) cultural events of internment, which harnessed the talents of the film director Georg Höllering and the composer

Hans Gál. Among the most notable features of internment life were the camp journals, which served a vital function as both notice-board and sounding-board. Jennifer Taylor's article considers the question of censorship, and the bounds of acceptable content, in the case of such journals as *The Camp*, the *Central Promenade Paper* and the *Onchan Pioneer*.

One distinguishing feature of internment policy in World War II was the deportation of several thousand men to the 'Dominions'. Nicole Brunnhuber's pioneering article considers some of the literary responses to deportation and internment in Canada, such as those of Carl Weiselberger and Henry Kreisel, both of whom went on to establish a literary reputation there. Of four ships which set sail to take deportees to Canada, only three arrived, the ill-fated *Arandora Star* being torpedoed and sunk by a German submarine, with the loss of some 650 lives. Only one ship, the *Dunera*, went to Australia, the gross mistreatment of refugees on board by the crew and the military escort causing such a scandal that the captain and other crew members were eventually brought to trial. Birgit Lang's article focuses on the representation of this experience in the Australian TV docu-drama *The Dunera Boys*, which used the conventions of Jiddish theatre to frame the episode as an essentially Jewish experience.

Internment and deportation have also served as a subject of fiction, the best-known example being Richard Friedenthal's *Die Welt in der Nussschale*. A more recent example is Norbert Gstrein's successful novel *Die englischen Jahre*: J. M. Ritchie's article addresses the novel's portrayal of internment and deportation. (Gstrein actually visited the Isle of Man in the course of his research, gaining the overriding impression that the Manx population had long ago suppressed all but residual memories of internment.)

Among those interned and/or deported there were also some four thousand Italians, who had been transformed overnight into 'enemy aliens' by Mussolini's belated and opportunistic declaration of war in June 1940. While most Germans and Austrians had been released by the end of 1941, many Italians were interned until Italy's surrender in 1943, while some remained behind barbed wire until the end of the war.

One of the Italians interned by the British was the young Eduardo Paolozzi, later to become known as the father of British 'pop art' and later still to be knighted. An astonishing number of those whom Britain imprisoned as 'enemy aliens' in 1940 went on to make outstanding contributions to British society, particularly in education and the public services, in science and the arts. To name only a random selection of those who lived into the twenty-first century and have only recently died: the academic Keith Spalding, the judge and international arbitrator Sir Michael

Kerr, the bio-chemist and Nobel prize-winner Max Perutz, the conductor Peter Gellhorn and the violinist Norbert Brainin, a founder member of the Amadeus Quartet, three of whose four members actually met in internment. The published obituaries of all these figures contained brief reference to their internment in 1940, restoring, however briefly, historical awareness of the episode.

The internment of 'enemy aliens' probably still remains outside mainstream historiography. However, history is too important to be left entirely to historians. In his recent book *Bloody Foreigners* (2003), written as a popular history of immigration into Britain, the journalist Robert Winder includes a spirited account of internment in 1940. Even more recently, the television presenter David Baddiel has published *The Secret Purposes* (2004), a novel based on the experiences of his grandfather who, as a German-Jewish refuge from Königsberg, was interned on the Isle of Man in 1940. Whatever their academic credentials, both books have reached a wide readership, helping to insinuate the theme into collective memory. The present volume does not aspire to such a wide audience, but it does aim to shed more light on this still submerged aspect of British history. The British government's recent use of detention without trial emphasizes the contemporary relevance of the topic: internment and its administrative variants, remain 'a matter which touches the good name of this country'.

A Marginalized Subject? The Historiography of Enemy Alien Internment in Britain

Panikos Panayi

During the two World Wars, Britain interned tens of thousands of 'enemy aliens', mostly of German origin. This policy faced significant criticism, for differing reasons, during both conflicts. Although books appeared on the Great War incarceration in the two decades which followed its conclusion, a silence about this episode in British history remained until the 1980s. Since then, a new wave of historians and literary scholars has increasingly brought internment into critical interpretations of the home front during both World Wars.

During the two World Wars, the British state embarked upon a policy of civilian internment of enemy aliens, which affected tens of thousands of people. As the Wars themselves progressed, much attention focused upon the internees and the policy of internment itself. In the case of the Great War, a Germanophobic press and right-wing MPs constantly demanded a tightening of internment, so that the procedure remained operational throughout the war, covering all male enemy aliens of military age after May 1915. In contrast, internment during the Second World War lasted for just over a year for most of those who became victims, as public opinion took a more enlightened view of most of those behind barbed wire, particularly because of their Jewish origins.

Despite the numbers interned during both Wars, and the level of contemporary focus, scholars devoted relatively little attention to the experiences of internees and the policy of incarceration itself until the final decades of the twentieth century. This outline of the historiography of internment will attempt to explain this delay and the reasons for the recent growth of attention to the subject.

During the Great War, incarceration of enemy aliens represented part of the campaign against Germany, as the eradication of German control and influence from Britain became central to a state saturated with Germanophobia. With a few notable exceptions, the attention devoted towards internees and the policy which demanded their internment, especially in parliament and in the press, remained overwhelmingly negative, despite the fact that male enemy aliens of military age (17-55) within Britain found themselves behind barbed wire after general internment for this group became operational in May 1915.[1] A couple of interesting accounts of life behind barbed wire did actually appear in German from individuals who had endured incarceration and then repatriation before 1918.[2]

Shortly after the end of the First World War two volumes were published, from completely different perspectives, which brought home the policy of internment. In the first place, the Society of Friends, one of the few organizations which actually made any efforts to assist enemy aliens, published an account of its work during the conflict, including its efforts to help internees, which gave insights into the reality of life behind barbed wire, especially on the Isle of Man.[3] Three years after the appearance of this volume, a German author, C. R. Hennings, published a book about the history of Germans in England, which included a scathing attack upon the treatment of this minority during the Great War, including the policy of internment.[4]

The interwar years also saw the publication of a series of personal experiences of internment in Britain, although, as most of those imprisoned were soldiers, the majority of such volumes came from combatants.[5] But a couple of recollections appeared from civilian internees. One of these, Pal Stoffa, had spent time in Alexandra Palace and on the Isle of Man, and provided some interesting insights into aspects of life in these two camps.[6] Paul Cohen-Portheim unquestionably wrote the best personal account of civilian internment during the First World War. This artist, who visited England every summer, found himself behind barbed wire for nearly four years. He provides a brilliant and moving description of the life of an internee, especially in the camp in Lofthouse Park, near Wakefield, where he spent much of the conflict. The book is, in fact, an outstanding description of incarceration *per se*, which deserves a reissue.[7]

First World War internment then remained a forgotten subject from the publication of Cohen-Portheim's work in 1931 until the 1980s. This is despite the fact that the German anarchist Rudolf Rocker gave an account of his experiences in Alexandra Palace, in his recollection of his time in London, published in 1956.[8] Since the 1980s the history of First World War internment has really come to life as historians have turned their attention to this episode, partly prompted by the research on the Second World War episode. The starting point for renewed attention towards developments during the Great War was J. C. Bird's 1986 volume, which looked at official policy towards enemy aliens during the conflict, including internment.[9] Five years later there followed my own account of Germans in Britain during the First World War, based on my 1988 Ph.D thesis on the same subject. It essentially consists of a study of hostility towards German enemy aliens during the Great War, with two chapters on internment, one dealing with the evolution of this policy and another examining life behind barbed wire.[10] At around the same time as the publication of my own work, Stella Yarrow published an article on the way in which hostility impacted upon Germans in Britain between 1914 and 1918.[11] The collection of essays on internment edited by David Cesarani and Tony Kushner,[12] while deriving from a conference held to commemorate the fiftieth anniversary of Churchill's decision to introduce this policy in 1940, also carried an article I had written on the First World War,[13] as well as an extract from Cohen-Portheim's *Time Stood Still* in a section on 'Internment Testimonies'.[14] After this 1993 volume there then appears something of a gap until Stefan Manz turned his attention to the Germans of Glasgow between 1864 and 1918; his book *Migranten und Internierte* includes a chapter on the First World War.[15] Manz has also produced an essay on the internment camp in Stobs which held both civilian and military prisoners.[16]

We therefore now have a reasonable historiography of internment in Britain during the First World War. The main gap actually consists of a study of military prisoners, despite the fact that they counted far larger numbers than civilians.[17] In addition, we have very little on either Ottoman or Habsburg internees.

When we turn to the Second World War we find a similar chronology of attention to that which occurred for the Great War. Some publications appeared during the conflict itself. Thus, we have a few personal accounts of life behind barbed wire, although on this occasion they appeared in English, rather than German, and were clearly aimed at quite a different audience.[18] Whereas the recollections of the Great War had a sympathetic German audience in mind, those of the Second World War could clearly not appeal to such a constituency. As well as these accounts, an attack on internment policy by François Lafitte also appeared as a 'Penguin special', shortly after the implementation of wholesale internment in 1940. Lafitte traced the steps which had led to this decision and then went on to outline the experience of the prisoners. A reissue of the volume in 1988 provided details of the subsequent fate of some of those incarcerated.[19] At the same time as the original publication of Lafitte's volume, there also appeared the anonymously authored *Anderson's Prisoners*, the title referring to Sir John Anderson, the Home Secretary of the time, whose department oversaw the implementation of the policy.[20]

In the introduction to their edited volume marking the fiftieth anniversary of the implementation of internment, Kushner and Cesarani pointed out that after the event occurred, 'the refugees did not want to dwell on the episode', which they explain by pointing to three factors. 'First and perhaps foremost was the desire not to appear ungrateful – Britain had provided these individuals with asylum'. Second, 'their position was still vulnerable', as they were uncertain about their fate after the end of the War. 'The third point is that alien internment in the Second World War was, for the majority, a short-lived experience'.[21]

Kushner and Cesarani point to the fact that, after the war, the internment episode remained largely forgotten – until the end of the 1970s. In the intervening years, the Association of Jewish Refugees had commemorated the events of 1940, but had 'sanitized' them 'into a jolly jape'.[22] In any case, the readership of their journal, the *AJR Information*, remained confined to Jewish refugees from the Nazis. Amongst the Italian community internment also remained forgotten, as far as historians were concerned, and suppressed amongst the community itself because of the 446 Italian deaths on the *Arandora Star*, which was sunk taking internees to Canada in July 1940.[23] Nevertheless, one autobiography from 1966 did refer to the episode.[24]

Kushner and Cesarani partly explained the gap in internment studies by pointing to the continuing gratitude of the German Jewish internees, epitomised by the 'Thank-Offering to Britain Fund', presented to the British Academy, and by the fact that the 1940 episode 'did not fit into the image' of 'Britain Alone', fighting for 'democracy and freedom against totalitarianism'.[25] We can also suggest other reasons for the lack of attention which internment received in the three decades following the end of the War, linked with both British and international historiography. Firstly, if we want to see the story of internment as part of British history, then we need to contextualize it against the background of a relatively sparse history of immigration into Britain, as this field did not really begin to take off until the 1980s and 1990s.[26] Similarly, we can also view the internment episode as part of the history of the Holocaust – had the refugees not escaped to England, they would almost certainly have perished as a result of Nazi racial policy during the Second World War. The study of their experience in Britain therefore coincides with the increasing attention which the Holocaust has received since the 1970s. Up to that time, the murder of European Jewry did not form part of mainstream historiography.[27] Despite the publication of Raul Hilberg's *The Destruction of the European Jews* in 1961, a more important turning point was Lucy Dawidowicz's *The War Against the Jews*, which appeared in 1975. Since that time the stream of works which have followed on all aspects of the Nazi persecution of European Jewry, including a focus upon those who escaped, has remained fairly constant.[28]

The historiography of internment in Britain during the Second World War therefore takes off at the very end of the 1970s and the beginning of the 1980s. The starting point finds partial explanation in the growth of interest in the Holocaust, as well as in the increasing attention which migrants in Britain began to attract, as we can see particularly from the appearance of works by Colin Holmes, the pioneer in this field.[29] This, in turn, can be said to reflect the increasing multiculturalization of British society, even if German Jewish refugees do not easily fall into this process. At the same time, the romantic memory of the War began to fade, as the brutal realities, especially connected with the Holocaust, began to surface in mainstream historiography.

Against this background a series of books dealing with internment appeared in a very short space of time, which means that they probably did not influence each other. Some of these focused purely upon this subject, while others covered it as one aspect of the German refugee experience in Britain. The first work to deal with internment was Bernard Wasserstein's *Britain and the Jews of Europe, 1939-1945*, which, as its title suggests, covers a broader theme. The implementation of internment comes in a chapter on 'The Home Front'.[30] In the following year there followed the more focused *'Collar the Lot'*, written by two journalists, Peter and Leni Gillman. This work provides a thorough and readable account of the internment episode, as well as the deportations which followed, looking at the experience of both Jews and Italians, based on newly-released Home Office files, together with interviews.[31] The same year saw the publication of Ronald Stent's *A Bespattered Page?* Written by a former internee, it is a narrative which begins with the migration of the 1930s and continues until the end of the War.[32] We also need to mention the books by Miriam Kochan, Eric Koch and Connery Chappell, which take a variety of approaches,[33] as well as a short account of internment in a volume edited by Gerhard Hirschfeld on refugees from the Third Reich in Britain.[34]

Much of the work actually formed part of the construction of a German Jewish historiography in Britain, although, as Kushner and Cesarani have pointed out, in the 'major collection of academic articles on German-speaking Jews in the United Kingdom published in 1991, which concentrated on the arrivals from Nazi Germany, not one piece was devoted to internment amongst the 36 offerings'.[35] This quote refers, of course, to *Second Chance*, edited by a team led by Werner E. Mosse. Significantly, the overwhelming majority of the essays in this volume were written either by Jews (English or German or both), or Germans, including several who were either refugees themselves, or descended from refugees.[36] In fact, the ethnic make-up of the contributors to this book reflects that of the authors of the major volumes on the history of German Jewry: they almost invariably consist of English or German Jews (often refugees or descendants of refugees) or Germans, often residing in Britain. Scholars of Second World

War internment and German Jewry in Britain therefore write about subjects close to their heart.[37]

Although the 1980s therefore saw the development of a historiography of the 1940 internment episode, Kushner and Cesarani, writing in the early 1990s, identified a couple of significant problems with the new work. 'First, the very fact of rediscovery led to a potential for sensationalism'. At the same time, the bulk of attention focused upon German and Austrian Jews, rather than Italians,[38] due to the ethnic backgrounds of most of those writing about internment.

The publication of the collection of essays edited by Kushner and Cesarani in 1993 therefore represents an important turning point in the historiography. Emerging from the May 1990 conference to commemorate the fiftieth anniversary of the decision to intern enemy aliens, in which both academics and Italian and German Jewish internees participated, the book covered a wide variety of topics. Italians received attention from the two emerging specialists in this field, Terri Colpi[39] and Lucio Sponza,[40] while the volume also included contributions about the First World War[41] and anti-alienism before 1940.[42] It concluded with 'Internment Testimonies' from both World Wars.

In fact, the conference and subsequent volume brought together the work of people working in the growing area of the history of immigration in Britain. This particularly applies to the contributions on Italians, where Lucio Sponza and Terri Colpi played the pioneering roles. Both these scholars proudly display their Italian origin: the former was an immigrant himself and the latter described herself as a 'third generation Italian Scot'.[43] Their work on internment formed part of broader studies on the history of Italians in Britain, with Sponza producing a volume on the experience of Italian civilian and military internees during the Second World War.[44] In addition, other scholars, again mostly of Italian origin, have also looked at internment, largely as an episode in longer-term histories, although often focused upon a specific community.[45]

As far as the historiography of German Jewish internment is concerned, we can see two developments since the 1980s. In the first place, a radical approach has emerged, exemplified by Tony Kushner and David Cesarani, as part of a reinterpretation of the experience of Anglo-Jewry initially inspired by the work of Colin Holmes.[46] These historians contextualize Second World War internment within British official and unofficial attitudes towards Jews during the 1930s and 1940s, which they view negatively,[47] despite the fact that Britain accepted more refugees from Nazi persecution than any other European state.[48] On the other hand we have seen the emergence of a less critical and more literary school of Second

World War internment studies revolving around the University of London Research Centre for German and Austrian Exile Studies. The *Yearbook* of the Centre has brought together much of this work, while several books have appeared under its aegis, with contributions on internment.[49] The present volume brings together many of the scholars and traditions of internment studies which have emerged over the past two decades, focusing upon both World Wars.

The classic accounts remain those which appeared in the early 1980s. More recent work has filled the gaps and offered new interpretations.[50] The study of internment in Britain therefore appears healthy in the sense that a significant historiography now exists on both World Wars covering a variety of themes, approaches and ethnic groups. However, the 1993 article by Kushner and Cesarani mentioned 'the continued reluctance of historians of Britain in the War, especially those concerned with political developments, to even mention internment'.[51] We therefore need to ask whether the more recent work has seeped into mainstream historiography. Certainly, most books published about Britain in the First World War during the last decade make some reference to my work.[52] Similarly, general studies of World War Two which have appeared over recent years have certainly not ignored the events of 1940-1, usually as part of a wider debate on the position of 'aliens'.[53] These developments reflect the questioning of traditional myths about British society during the Second World War, as well as the increasing impact of immigration upon British historiography. Nevertheless, there is a limit to this reinterpretation. Robert Mackay, for instance, can still write that 'the internment episode reflected more credit than shame upon British society', because what began 'as a dangerous and near-hysterical rush towards the police state ended in a reassertion of tolerance and calmness'.[54]

At the start of the twenty-first century, our knowledge of Britain's history during the previous hundred years, and the centrality of War within it, now includes an acknowledgement of internment. However, Britain has not simply used this policy during the two World Wars, but also during the two Gulf Wars and the so-called 'War against Terror', in which Britain has exercised its right to hold people without trial simply on suspicion that they may help the enemy, a clear continuation of the polices of the two World Wars, when innocents faced imprisonment. Certainly, media attention, at least in the liberal press, recognized the plight of these prisoners without trial.[55] Following their release, we can only hope that this most recent episode will soon be the subject of scholarly attention.

Notes

[1] Panikos Panayi, *The Enemy in Our Midst: Germans in Britain during the First World War* (Oxford: Berg, 1991), pp. 70-98.

[2] Hans Erich Benedix, *In England Interniert* (Gotha: F. A. Perthes, 1916); Adolf Vielhauer, *Das Englische Konzentrationslager bei Peel (Insel Man)* (Bad Nassau: Evangelische Blättervereinigung für Soldaten und kriegsgefangene Deutsche, 1917).

[3] Anna Braithwaite Thomas, *St Stephen's House: Friends Emergency Work in England* (London: Emergency Committee for the Assistance of Germans, Austrians and Hungarians in Distress, 1920).

[4] C. R. Hennings, *Deutsche in England* (Stuttgart: Ausland und Heimat Verlag, 1923).

[5] The best of these are: L. Bogenstätter and H. Zimmermann, *Die Welt hinter Stacheldraht: Eine Chronik des englischen Kriegsgefangenlagers Handforth bei Manchester* (Munich: Piloty und Loehle, 1921); and Fritz Sachse and Paul Nikolaus Cossmann, *Kriegsgefangen in Skipton: Leben und Geschichte deutscher Kriegsgefangenen in einem englischen Lager* (Munich: Ernst Reinhardt, 1920).

[6] Pal Stoffa, *Round the World to Freedom* (London: John Lane, 1933).

[7] Paul Cohen-Portheim, *Time Stood Still: My Internment in England, 1914-1918* (London: Duckworth, 1931).

[8] Rudolf Rocker, *The London Years* (London: Robert Anscombe, 1956).

[9] J. C. Bird, *The Control of Enemy Alien Civilians in Great Britain, 1914-1918* (New York: Garland, 1986), pp. 45-168.

[10] Panayi, *Enemy*, pp. 70-131.

[11] Stella Yarrow, 'The Impact of Hostility on Germans in Britain, 1914-1918', in *The Politics of Marginality: Race, the Radical Right and Minorities in Twentieth Century Britain*, ed. by Tony Kushner and Kenneth Lunn (London: Frank Cass, 1990), pp. 97-112.

[12] David Cesarani and Tony Kushner, eds, *The Internment of Aliens in Twentieth Century Britain* (London: Frank Cass, 1993).

[13] 'An Intolerant Act by an Intolerant Society: The Internment of Germans in Britain During the First World War', in *ibid.*, pp. 53-75.

[14] *Ibid.*, pp. 219-24.

[15] Stefan Manz, *Migranten und Internierte: Deutsche in Glasgow, 1864-1918* (Stuttgart: Franz Steiner, 2003), pp. 231-87.

[16] Stefan Manz, 'New Evidence on Stobs Internment Camp', *Hawick Archaeological Society Transactions* (2002), 59-69. Footnote 1 of this article points out that the Stobs camp previously received attention in the *Hawick Archaeological Society Transactions*.

[17] But see: Robert Jackson, *The Prisoners, 1914-18* (London: Routledge, 1989), pp. 134-50; and Panikos Panayi, 'Normalität hinter Stacheldraht: Kriegsgefangene in Großbritannien', in *Kriegsgefangene im Europa des Ersten Weltkrieges, ed.* Jochen Oltmer (Paderborn: Schöninghaus, 2005).

[18] Tony Kushner and David Cesarani, 'Alien Interment in Britain during the Twentieth Century: An Introduction', in Cesarani and Kushner, *op. cit.*, p. 20, note 17, mentions accounts by Alfred Lomnitz, Alfred Perlès and Livia Laurent.

[19] François Lafitte, *The Internment of Aliens* (London: Libris, 1988).

[20] Judex, *Anderson's Prisoners* (London: Victor Gollancz, 1940).

[21] Kushner and Cesarani, *op. cit.*, pp. 5-6.

[22] *Ibid.*, p. 7.

[23] Terri Colpi, *The Italian Factor: The Italian Community in Great Britain* (Edinburgh: Mainstream, 1991), p. 99.

[24] Peppino Leoni, *I Shall Die on the Carpet* (London: Frewin, 1966).

[25] Kushner and Cesarani, *op. cit.*, pp. 7-8.

[26] Panikos Panayi, 'The Historiography of Immigrants and Ethnic Minorities: Britain Compared with the USA', *Ethnic and Racial Studies*, 19 (1996), 825-9.

[27] See Dan Stone, *Constructing the Holocaust: A Study in Historiography* (London: Valentine Mitchell, 2003).

[28] As an introduction to the emigration of Jews from the Third Reich see, for instance, Juliane Wetzel, 'Auswanderung aus Deutschland', in *Die Juden in Deutschland: Leben unter Nationalsozialistischer Herrschaft*, ed., Wolfgang Benz (Munich: Beck, 1993), pp. 413-98; Walter Laqueur, *Generation Exodus: The Fate of Young Jewish Refugees from Nazi Germany* (London: I. B. Tauris, 2004). The standard work on emigration to Britain is now Louise London, *Whitehall and the Jews, 1933-1948: British Immigration Policy and the Holocaust* (Cambridge: Cambridge University Press, 2000).

[29] Colin Holmes, ed., *Immigrants and Minorities in British Society* (London: Unwin Hyman, 1978); Colin Holmes, *Antisemitism in British Society, 1876-1939* (London: Edward Arnold, 1979). The year 1982 also witnessed the launch of the journal *Immigrants and Minorities*, edited by Holmes and his former doctoral student, Kenneth Lunn.

[30] Bernard Wasserstein, *Britain and the Jews of Europe, 1939-1945* (Oxford: Oxford, University Press, 1979, 1988), pp. 82-108.

[31] Peter and Leni Gillman, *'Collar the Lot': How Britain Interned and Expelled Its Wartime Refugees* (London: Quartet, 1980).

[32] Ronald Stent, *A Bespattered Page? The Internment of His Majesty's 'Most Loyal Enemy Aliens'* (London: Deutsch, 1980).

[33] Miriam Kochan, *Britain's Internees in the Second World War* (London: Macmillan, 1983); Eric Koch, *Deemed Suspect: A Wartime Blunder* (Toronto: Methuen, 1980); Connery Chappell, *Island of Barbed Wire: Internment on the Isle of Man in World War Two* (London: R. Hale, 1984).

[34] Michael Seyfert, '"His Majesty's Most Loyal Internees"', in *Exile in Great Britain: Refugees from Hitler's Germany*, ed. by Gerhard Hirschfeld (Leamington: Berg, 1984), pp. 163-93.

[35] Kushner and Cesarani, *op. cit.*, pp. 9-10.

[36] *Second Chance: Two Centuries of German-Speaking Jews in the United Kingdom*, ed. by Werner E. Mosse *et al.* (Tübingen: J. C. B. Mohr, 1991).

[37] In fact, a large percentage of scholars who write about migrant groups in Britain have a connection with the minority about which they write.

[38] Kushner and Cesarani, *op. cit.*, p. 9.

[39] Terri Colpi, 'The Impact of the Second World War on the British Italian Community', in Cesarani and Kushner, *op. cit.*, pp. 167-87.

[40] Lucio Sponza, 'The British Government and the Internment of Italians', *ibid.*, pp. 125-44.

[41] Panayi, 'Intolerant Act'.

[42] David Cesarani, 'An Alien Concept? The Continuity of Anti-Alienism in British Society before 1940', in Cesarani and Kushner, *op. cit.*, pp. 25-52.

[43] Colpi, *Italian Factor*, p. 5.

[44] Ibid.; Lucio Sponza, *Italian Immigrants in Nineteenth Century Britain: Realities and Images* (Leicester: Leicester University Press, 1988); *Divided Loyalties: Italians in Britain during the Second World War* (Frankfurt: Peter Lang, 2000).

[45] See, for example: Paul Di Felice, 'Manchester's Little Italy at War, 1940-1945: "Enemy Aliens or Reluctant Foe?"', *Northern History*, Vol. 39 (2002), pp. 109-23; Colin Hughes, *Lime, Lemon and Sarsaparilla: The Italian Community in Wales, 1881-1945* (Bridgend: Seren, 1992); Anthony Rea, *Manchester's Little Italy* (Manchester: Neil Richardson, 1988).

[46] Holmes, *Antisemitism*.

[47] See, for instance: Tony Kushner, *The Persistence of Prejudice: Antisemitism in British Society during The Second World War* (Manchester: Manchester University Press, 1989); Colin Holmes, "British Justice at Work": Internment in the Second World War', in *Minorities in Wartime: National and Racial Groupings in Europe, North America and Australia during the Two World Wars*, ed. by Panikos Panayi (Oxford: Berg, 1993), pp. 150-65; London, *op. cit.*

[48] Michael Marrus, *European Refugees in the Twentieth Century* (Oxford: Oxford University Press, 1985), pp. 145-58.

[49] A good example is *Changing Countries: The Experience and Achievement of German-Speaking Exiles from Hitler in Britain from 1933 to Today* ed. by Marian Malet and Anthony Grenville, (London: Libris, 2002).

[50] See, for instance, Maxine Schwartz, *We Built Up Our Lives: Education and Community Among Jewish Refugees Interned by Britain in World War II* (London: Greenwood, 2001).

[51] Kushner and Cesarani, *op. cit.*, p. 9.

[52] See, for instance, Gerard J. DeGroot, *Blighty: British Society in the Era of the Great War* (London: Longman, 1996), pp. 158-9; G. R. Searle, *A New England? Peace and War, 1886-1918* (Oxford: Oxford University Press, 2004), pp. 772-4.

[53] See, for instance, Panikos Panayi, 'Immigrants, Refugees, the British State and Public Opinion during World War Two', in *War Culture: Changing Experience in World War Two*, ed. by Pat Kirkham and David Thoms (London: Lawrence and Wishart, 1995), pp. 201-9; Harold L. Smith, *Britain in the Second World War: A Social History* (Manchester: Manchester University Press, 1996), pp. 3, 10-12, 52-60; Mark Donnelly, *Britain in the Second World War* (London: Routledge, 1999), pp. 47-9; Robert Mackay, *The Test of War: Inside Britain, 1939-45* (London: UCL Press, 1999), pp. 96-101; Sonya O. Rose, *Which People's War? National Identity and Citizenship in Wartime Britain, 1939-1945* (Oxford: Oxford University Press, 2003), pp. 92-106; Juliet Gardner, *Wartime: Britain, 1939-1945* (London: Headline, 2004), pp. 215-38.

[54] Mackay, *ibid.*, p. 100.

[55] See, for instance, *Guardian*, 19 December 2004; *Independent*, 19 December 2004.

Internment in the First World War

Panikos Panayi

Prisoners of Britain: German Civilian, Military and Naval Internees during the First World War

During the First World War, hundreds of thousands of Germans found themselves interned in Britain. Although the vast majority initially came from the long-resident German civilian community, captured sailors and, more especially, soldiers, increasingly came to dominate the statistics in the latter stages of the conflict. The prisoners were interned in a large number of locations. While instances of mistreatment of internees remain largely absent, the experience of internment could involve years behind barbed wire away from families. The main problem the prisoners faced was actually boredom, which they tried to relieve in a variety of ways, most effectively by working.

During the course of the nineteenth century, a vibrant German community had developed in Britain which totalled 57,000 people by 1914. Although they may have regarded themselves as integrated and acculturated by the outbreak of War, much of British public opinion, encouraged by a Germanophobic press, did not share this view. As the conflict approached some manifestations of anti-German hostility impacted upon individual Germans, but they could not have imagined the fate about to befall them.[1] During the First World War British state and society became gripped by a Germanophobic intolerance, which ultimately aimed at eradicating the German community from Britain.[2]

A core part of the state campaign against enemy aliens consisted of the implementation of a policy of internment. By the end of the First World War the British state had responsibility for hundreds of thousands of prisoners of war, seized both within Britain, as well as further afield in the many battlefields of the First World War. Although the government put much effort into keeping civilian and military prisoners in separate internment camps, they faced similar experiences behind barbed wire.

Little planning had actually focused upon interment before 1914 but by September 1914 the Directorate of Prisoners of War had come into existence under the War Office.[3] At the beginning of the conflict the Directorate devoted most attention to civilians, as captured German soldiers remained few in number until the end of 1917, growing substantially following the failure of the German spring offensive and ultimate defeat of the Axis Powers the following year. After the anti-German hysteria of May 1915, following the sinking of the passenger liner *Lusitania* by a German submarine off the coast of Ireland, Asquith's government introduced a policy of wholesale civilian internment, demanded by extreme nationalists, which would affect all adult male enemy aliens between the ages of 17-55 and would remain in force until 1919.[4] In October 1916 a Prisoners of War Department had come into existence, headed by Lord Newton.[5]

An examination of the make up and numbers of prisoners of war in Britain demonstrates the importance of developments on French battlefields. The only constants in the period 1914-1919 were that Germans made up the overwhelming majority, joined by a small number of Austrians at the end of the conflict, and the fact that officers captured in France faced automatic removal to Britain.

Only 3,100 of the 13,600 internees held in Britain on 22 September 1914 had originated on the battlefields. Most of the remaining 10,500 came from the German civilian community in Britain.[6] The total figure of 13,600 included people captured by the British at sea, both civilians and naval personnel,[7] including Bruno Schmidt-Reder.[8] Gunther Plüschow, a wealthy German aristocrat and peacetime professional officer, was captured in the first year of the war when returning from neutral America aboard an Italian liner that was stopped in the Channel. After interrogation, the authorities took him to Dorchester.[9]

Numbers of captured naval and military personnel remained low throughout the early stages of the war. By 1 February 1915 'there were 400 officers (including a few Austrians), 6,500 soldiers and naval sailors, and between 19,000 and 20,000 merchant sailors and civilians (German and Austrian) interned'.[10] By November 1915, following the decision to intern all enemy aliens of military age, the number of civilian internees had reached 32,440.[11]

Military prisoners did not begin to increase until 1917 when the numbers of German soldiers captured in France grew. Thus, in that year, 73,131 combatants fell into British hands on French soil, followed by another 201,633 during 1918, the vast majority of them, 186,684, captured between 12 August and 9 December as the German armies faced defeat.[12] These figures translated into an increase in the numbers of military personnel held in Britain. Thus in December 1916 the figure stood at 876 officers and 24,251 men. Naval figures totalled 120 officers and 1,286 men, all but one of them Germans.[13] By 20 November 1917 79,329 people found themselves interned in British camps, including 29,511 civilians.[14] By November 1918 the British held a total of 207,357 prisoners of war throughout the world. The figure within Britain had reached 115,950, of whom 89,937 consisted of military staff (including 5,005 officers) together with 1,491 naval personnel.[15] By 5 July 1919 the British held responsibility for an amazing 458,392 internees globally. On home soil the figures had declined to 90,276 including 3,373 civilians, 2,899 naval personnel and 84,004 soldiers.[16] While the number continued to fall during the summer, 'general repatriation' began on 24 September and lasted until 20 November. During this time 4,161 officers and 73,118 German men went home. A further 3,624 prisoners, including 704 Austrians and Hungarians returned home between 26 November and 29 January. Finally, on 9 April 1920 3 officers and 9 other ranks (specially retained) completed the repatriation of Germans interned on British soil during the Great War.[17]

During the early stages of the war, military and civilian prisoners were housed in the same camps, although usually separated from each other within them. As the conflict progressed different camps evolved for the two groups. The fairly stable civilian population became overwhelmingly concentrated upon the Isle of Man, together with a few other locations on the mainland, notably Alexandra Palace, Stratford and Wakefield.

While a small number of locations housed a significant proportion of the naval and military prisoners during the War, a large number of camps evolved for such internees during the course of the conflict especially in 1918 and 1919 as the number of internees grew. Several sources point to the existence of more than 500 camps by this time.[18] A list from January 1918 gives the names of 566 places of internment. These cover a wide variety and size of locations, holding anything from a few individuals to thousands of prisoners. Many places were working camps which fed off the larger places of internment. At this stage even the smallest farm which employed prisoners of war counted as a place of internment. The list also included any number of hospitals which may have looked after a few individual German casualties.[19]

At the outbreak of war, when limited numbers of German prisoners found themselves in Great Britain, only a few camps existed. A publication from the end of 1914 claimed that 'In mid-October we held German prisoners of war at Blackdown, Camberley, Dyffryn Aled (North Wales), Douglas (Isle of Man), Frimley, Handforth, Lofthouse Park (between Leeds and Wakefield), Newbury, Queensferry, Templemore (Ireland), York and Olympia in London.'[20] Most of these catered mainly for civilians, including Handforth, Lofthouse Park, Douglas and Olympia.[21]

The first 'permanent POW camp' consisted of Dorchester, a 'hastily converted army camp', which opened in the middle of August 1914. As well as housing soldiers it also initially served as home to civilians and people captured on the high seas. The first military internees arrived on 27 August followed by others on 4 September and 18 October. On 8 October 450 civilians faced transfer to the Isle of Man. During the first few months of the War Dorchester held an average of 1,000 men, although by the start of 1915 this figure seems to have increased to over 2,000.[22] One detainee later wrote that the prisoners 'were extremely comfortable, as the food was good and plentiful, the treatment irreproachable, and there were many opportunities for sport'.[23] A report to the US Embassy in London (which looked after German interests in Britain until the USA entered the War) from 23 October 1914 wrote that 'the combatant prisoners of war are at present, in the main, interned at Frith Hill Camp'.[24] They quickly established their own control over the camp and set up their own institutions.[25] The camp at Newbury was actually established on the race course and the prisoners lived in horse boxes with neither heat nor light. In October 1914 it housed 1,200 people, including 200 wounded German soldiers. Newbury faced closure at the start of 1915 because of its unsuitability.[26]

At the start of 1915, due to the lack of accommodation for internees, the War Office made use of nine trans-Atlantic liners divided into three groups of three near Ryde, Gosport and Southend. The ships housed both civilian and military internees but seem to have ceased operating by summer 1915.[27] In the spring of that year several new camps housing military prisoners came into existence. D. W. Pult, captured in France, arrived on 10 March 1915 at a military hospital in a girls' school near Portsmouth, which held about forty wounded officers, where he remained until June.[28]

He then faced transfer to what would become one of the most important camps for military prisoners at Stobs, near Hawick in Scotland, which existed until 1919. This actually opened in November 1914 and held naval, military and civilian prisoners until July 1916 when the last group moved to Knockaloe on the Isle of Man.[29] One US embassy official described Stobs as follows: 'The camp is set on the side of a sloping hill and the camp has been in use for several years as a summer camp for manoeuvres and the training of Scottish Regiments.' In June 1915 Stobs held 2,377 prisoners made up of 1,098 civilians, 783 soldiers and 496 naval personnel.[30] By April 1916 a total of 4,592 prisoners lived in the camp including 1,821 soldiers and 502 sailors, all of them Germans. Stobs became one of the most established and sophisticated camps for prisoners of war with its own newspaper, *Stobsiade*, and much educational activity. It also acted as the supply centre to numerous working camps in Scotland and the north of England from 1917 including those at Catterick, Port Clarence and Crawford.[31]

The officers' camp at Donington Hall in Derbyshire also developed a sophisticated camp life. It attracted much negative attention in the House of Commons and the British press because of its allegedly luxurious conditions.[32] Coming into existence at the beginning of 1915, it 'was a large, old castle dating from the seventeenth century, surrounded by a lovely old park'.[33] In June 1916 it held '102 military officers, 39 naval officers, 50 military orderlies and 1 naval orderly, and 3 civilians, of whom 98 military officers and 38 naval officers were German, 4 military officers were Austrian, and 1 naval officer was a Turk. The civilians and orderlies were German'.[34] Other officers' camps existing from the early stages of the war included Holyport Castle near Maidenhead. When Pult lived there during 1915 it held 100 German officers and 40 orderlies and developed a sophisticated camp life.[35]

The civilian camps had become fully operational after the introduction of wholesale internment in May 1915. By far the most important of these lay on the Isle of Man. The first of these utilized the site of a former holiday camp in Douglas and held 2,300 prisoners, with a privilege camp, a Jewish camp and an ordinary camp. Much bigger was Knockaloe, on a site which had formerly acted as a base for 16,000 territorials and which would grow to hold 23,000 men, divided between four sub-camps. The two most important civilian camps on the mainland lay in Lofthouse Park, near Wakefield, on the site of an unsuccessful pleasure park, and Alexandra Palace in north London. The latter opened on 7 May 1915 and closed in May 1919 reaching a peak of 3,000 prisoners at any one time and housing a total of 17,000 individuals during the course of the war.[36]

A detailed description of the military camps which existed during the latter stages of the War would prove impossible because of the sheer numbers of places of internment which had sprung up. We can simply mention a few of the most important and best documented camps established from 1917. A list from January 1918 gave the following 'parent camps', which supplied labour for other smaller places of internment: Handforth, Blandford (Dorset), Dorchester, Leigh (Lancashire), Frognoch, Pattishall (Northants), Brocton (Staffordshire), Catterick (Yorkshire) and Shrewsbury. The officers' camps included Donington Hall, Holyport, Dyffryn Aled and others at Kegworth (Leicestershire), Sandhill Park (Somerset), Colsterdale (Yorkshire) and Southampton.[37]

Several accounts give details of some of these camps. Walther Scheller, for instance, spoke of 'das Paradies in Southampton'.[38] Wolff did not use such a complimentary phrase for Brocton, recalling that on arrival, 'all pockets, bags, boxes, valises and packets were exhaustively searched and many a thing was flung on the piles of prisoners' property.'[39] A report of January 1918 from the Swiss Embassy, which had taken over responsibility for looking after German interests in Britain after the USA had entered the War, stated that Brocton housed 4,715 prisoners of war 'of whom 4,423 belong to the German Army and 292 to the German Navy. These figures include the patients at present in Brocton Hospital.'[40]

The confinement of adult men within camps away from their families for periods which could total several years often proved a distressing experience, which, in some cases led to neurosis. In such circumstances the internees had to find ways to bring some sort of normality to their lives to alleviate depression and boredom caused by incarceration. The internees largely organized their affairs themselves by establishing camp committees and also managed to find other ways of killing time. The increase in numbers which occurred during the latter stages of the war coincided with labour shortages in the British economy which meant that the new prisoners found themselves employed in all manner of work, particularly agriculture. Those who did not work, including officers and the vast majority of civilians, found other ways to use their time such as education, theatre and music.

Little evidence exists to suggest that internees faced deliberate mistreatment. The most objective accounts, provided by American and Swiss Embassy observers in Britain, paint a generally positive picture. They immediately passed on any complaints they received from the prisoners, which happened on a regular basis, to the relevant British authorities. One of the only deliberate examples of the mistreatment of internees in Britain, during the early stages of the war, consists of 'the somewhat unfortunate decision...to place thirty-nine men captured on German submarines in confinement apart from ordinary prisoners of war'. However, following a month of negotiations through the American Embassy 'the British Government agreed to return the thirty-nine submarine prisoners to the ordinary officer's and men's camp'.[41]

Protection for prisoners of war came from various quarters. The Hague Convention of 1899 guaranteed the rights of prisoners, although during the course of the conflict the British and German governments reached agreements about various aspects of the treatment of captives, which essentially extended pre-War treaties.[42] Various mechanisms went into place to protect the position of captives, the most important being visits by staffs of neutral embassies.[43] Furthermore, the Prisoners of War Information Bureau, established in London in accordance with article 14 of the Hague Convention, tracked, maintained and distributed information on individual internees in Britain.[44]

As we have seen, internment camps included schools, hospitals, disused factories, tents, stables, farms and castles. The standard installation consisted of huts which simply resembled army barracks. As a rule, in the class-ridden societies which existed during the First World War, officers remained separate from their men, unless they used them as orderlies. Civilian internees also received preferential treatment if they could pay for it: in Wakefield prisoners paid ten shillings a week 'for the privilege of being there'.[45]

Stobs provides a good example of a location that might merit the description of a standard camp. An American Embassy official who visited Stobs on 15 June wrote:

> The prisoners are housed in huts 120 feet long by 30 feet broad. These are built for 60 men. I found, on an average, 33 men in each hut. There are doors at either end of these huts and four or five windows on each side, each window being about 3½ by 4½ feet.[46]

The Knockaloe camp was also constructed of the standard type of military barracks used at Stobs and elsewhere. One Swiss Embassy report noted that: 'Perhaps no complaints have been so persistent on the part of the prisoners as those in regard to the condition of the huts'.[47]

Camps which housed officers usually provided superior accommodation. A US Embassy report from December 1914 noted: 'Their quarters are comfortably furnished but without luxury.'[48] Public opinion in Britain focused upon Donington Hall as a camp where officers lived in apparent comfort.[49] Those who stayed there did not paint such a positive picture. Carl Spindler, for instance, who arrived in 1916, wrote that the 'camp was too small to accommodate the ever increasing number of prisoners.'[50] Other official accounts of officers' camps paint a positive picture. A Swiss Embassy report on Dyffryn Aled in Wales, in December 1917, for instance, left the impression that the 77 officers lived in luxury: 'This spacious and comfortable house offers every desirable convenience'. For instance, the dormitories 'are comfortable, well lit and well ventilated, and some of them have been newly papered'.[51] Overall, prisoners generally lived in decent accommodation, even if luxury was unusual.

An examination of the food rations the internees received also points to their fair treatment, although complaints surfaced about the quality of English fare. In 1914 the daily ration consisted of the following:

> Bread, 1lb. 8oz, or biscuits, 1lb.
> Meat, fresh or frozen, 8oz., or pressed, 4oz.
> Tea, ½oz. or coffee, 1oz.
> Salt, ½oz.
> Sugar, 2oz.
> Condensed milk, 1/20th tin (1lb).
> Fresh vegetables, 8oz.
> Pepper, 1/72oz.
> 2oz. cheese to be allowed as an alternative for 1g. butter or margarine.
> 2oz. of peas, beans or lentils, or rice.

In addition, prisoners could purchase 'tobacco, small luxuries, and other things' from canteens, throughout the war.[52] The above ration remained fairly constant, although there were some changes in the items served. In the latter stages of the war some items became scarce as a consequence of German submarine activity. In March 1918 meat was reduced to 4ozs. per day, and in July this was changed to 4ozs. of beef or horseflesh on 3 days per week, 13½ozs of Chinese bacon on two days, and 10 ozs. of cured or pickled herring on the remaining two days. An improvement took place during 1919. Prisoners who worked received higher rations.[53] Internees usually cooked their own food.[54] While the rations may have proved sufficient, prisoners did not find them especially appetizing. Plüschow described the food at Donington Hall as 'very good' but also mentioned that 'it was English, so that many did not like it.'[55]

The fair treatment and sufficient food which the German internees received did not hide other difficulties. One of the most significant problems, especially during the early stages of the war, when most captives did not work, as well as for officers and most civilians, who never worked, was boredom. Internees developed sophisticated methods to overcome the monotony. As Paul Cohen-Portheim recalled, time 'really had to be *killed*, for it was the arch-enemy, and everyone tried to achieve this as best he could'.[56]

A routine developed as outlined by Fritz Sachse and Paul Cossmann, interned in Skipton during 1918 and 1919: the trumpet sounded at 8am, the prisoners drank coffee at 9.15, at 10 they walked outside the camp, they returned at midday for their lunch; they received their post at 2 and they ate their supper at 7.30.[57] Plüschow also described the routine at the various camps in which he was interned. For instance, in Dorchester, 'Every afternoon 300 to 400 prisoners, of course closely guarded by English soldiers, were led out for their exercise'. In Holyport, 'The post was the Alpha and Omega of our existence. We divided our whole day according to its delivery, and the temper of the camp was regulated by it.'[58]

This collective mood existed in several camps and outside events determined it. For instance, the November 1918 armistice understandably had a negative affect upon prisoners.[59] This mood is summed up by the following quote describing the situation in Skipton:

> Als am Vormittag des 11. November, des Waffenstillstandtages, von draußen vor dem Lagertor der Laute der Jubel der englischen Wachmannschaften über den Stacheldraht klang und überall an den englischen Wohnbaracken die bunten Fähnchen im Winde flatterten, da stand der Schmerz und das Leid mit fast fremdartiger Härte in unserer deutschen Seele auf. Man sah ernste, starke Männer wie Kinder weinen.[60]

By the end of the war the concept of a prison camp psychosis had developed, an idea addressed by one of the inspectors from the Swiss Embassy in London, A. L. Vischer, who published a book on the subject. He actually spoke of a 'mental unity' amongst prisoners, although he recognized that 'there are many degrees' of 'barbed wire disease' from 'the easily excited to the introspective'. He claimed that 'very few prisoners who have been over six months in the camp are quite free from' it. Vischer put forward several causes of the disease including: complete absence of any chance of being alone; ignorance of the duration of the captivity; and irregularity of communication from home. Barbed wire served as the symbol of the prisoners' misfortune.[61] Personal accounts written after the war certainly reveal a consciousness of barbed wire psychosis. Franz Rinteln von Kleist claimed that several of those held at Donington Hall began to suffer from this problem.[62]

Prisoners of war devised a variety of ways of relieving their boredom, one of the main causes of 'barbed wire disease'. Education represented one of these so that several of the long-established camps developed substantial libraries and numerous courses. For instance, the first catalogue compiled at Handforth in autumn 1916 listed 2,522 books, which came from various German charities. By April 1917 the camp also ran 56 courses with 1,600 students.[63] Camp IV at Knockaloe possessed 18,080 volumes by 1919.[64] At Lofthouse Park, in Wakefield, a 'very thorough educational scheme' was organized 'on University lines' enrolling about 500 prisoners, one third of the total and beginning on 1 October 1917.[65]

Several camps had their own orchestras. For instance, Handforth had a band with between 25 and 30 players, while the internees in Skipton had performed 42 concerts by August 1919, with programmes that included everything from Weber to Wagner.[66] Theatre also became a common activity in many camps. Stobs, for instance, had several dramatic societies, which produced hundreds of plays during the course of the War.[67] Some internees spent their time producing items for sale or display, as described by an officer held at Donington Hall in a letter to his wife: 'We have a continuous display of things we have made' including oil-paintings, pastels, 'engine-construction' and 'carving work'.[68] Art and craft work also became part of everyday life at Wakefield and Alexandra Palace.[69]

Sport and other physical activity also helped to relieve the boredom of camp life. Stobs, for instance, held regular sporting festivals. Dyffryn Aled, a military camp in Wales, had a sports field separated from the camp by a river. 'The field is not fenced and the officers are placed on parole whilst at their sports. They take long walks every second or third day.'

The camps also held regular religious services. This applied, for instance, to Dyfrynn Aled.[70] Stobs developed an advanced Roman Catholic and Evangelical religious life. The latter held a Sunday service and, in the summer of 1916, established a choir. They used a hymn book from the YMCA entitled *Heimatlieder für die deutschen Kriegsgefangenen in Großbritannien.*[71]

The most dramatic development for German prisoners of war consisted of the decision by the government to make wholesale use of them for employment from the end of 1916. Until that time internees had carried out little work, partly due to trade union opposition and partly because of the level of Germanophobia which existed within the country which may have made it dangerous for 'small parties' of prisoners to work in the open. In addition, internees could only carry out unskilled labour and could therefore only fill some labour shortages. 'Some men were employed as bakers, tailors and shoemakers in the camps, but no work of national importance could be undertaken.' Until the end of 1916 no prisoners in Britain worked on the land.

In the autumn of 1916 the Prisoners of War Employment Committee was formed.[72] It dissolved following the Armistice 'and the allocation of prisoners of war to various forms of labour was vested in the War Office, which acted in close accord with the Department of Civil Demobilization and Resettlement of the Ministry of Labour.'[73]

The employment of prisoners of war represented a complex operation involving numerous rules and regulations. Firstly, only combatant men and non-commissioned officers became eligible. Furthermore, the internees could not work with 'civilian British or civilian Alien labour'. In addition, no application could be put forward 'until the resources of the local labour exchange have been exhausted'.[74] Employers who needed prisoners would have to make an application. The new employees could only work the same hours as local workers.

The numbers of working prisoners of war increased dramatically from the 3,832 of September 1916, especially following the general growth in the total of internees during 1917 and, more especially, 1918. In March 1917 the figure still stood at only 7,029 but had increased to 27,760 by December 1917 (including 1,782 civilians), 45,710 by June 1918 (including 2,360 civilians), reaching a peak of 66,853 (including 1,356 civilians) in December 1918. By August of the following year the figure had fallen to about 34,000.[75]

Prisoners found employment in a wide range of occupations, but agriculture dominated, fuelled by fears that the harvest of 1918 could not be gathered due to lack of labour. Although only 16.7 per cent of those employed worked in this area in February 1918, the figure had increased to 60.5 per cent by November 1918. The growing number of German prisoners employed in agriculture resulted from a series of conscious schemes to recruit them. While some lived in working camps, to which they returned at night, others found employment in 'migratory gangs' which lived on the farms where they worked. The prisoners certainly seemed to have proved valuable to farmers during 1918.[76] Apart from agriculture, internees found employment in a wide range of other activities. In July 1918 prisoners worked in aerodromes, quarries, timber production, shipyard construction, brick manufacture, cement making, road building and aluminium smelting.[77]

As we have seen, the employment of prisoners of war meant the opening of working camps dependent for their labour supplies on the established places of internment. A few examples illustrate working life for prisoners of war during 1917 and 1918. On 22 November 1917 a working camp opened in Monks Abbey in Lincolnshire, housing 220 prisoners in eleven huts who slept on mattresses on a waterproof sheet. 'Messrs Dick, Kerr and Co.' employed them for eight hours per day at between 1 and 2 pence per hour for bricklaying, drainage and general labouring.[78] Those prisoners held at Kilburn Hall in Derbyshire, dependent upon Brocton, found employment with 'the Tarmac Company Limited in breaking up slag for road making. They are paid 1½d. an hour, working on an average 48 hours a week. The tailor, shoemaker, clerk, cooks and 2 camp workers receive the usual wages'[79] Elsewhere, prisoners do not seem to have worked so conscientiously. An official report on a camp in Bramley, Hampshire, set up to house internees engaged in the construction of a permanent RAF depot described 'discipline and organisation' as 'deplorable'. The inspector claimed that the 'prisoners appeared to do pretty much what they liked, when they liked, and how they liked'.[80]

As the above extracts make clear, those prisoners who worked received payment, which averaged about 1½d. per day. They also obtained higher food rations. Thus, those not employed received 2,000 calories per day, while those who worked obtained 2,700 calories. The 'scientific adviser'' of the Ministry of Food also recommended that prisoners 'engaged on such work as quarrying, agriculture, land reclamation, and other similar work should receive a ration of not less than 3,300 calories'. Certainly, an increase took place in the quantity of food supplied at midday.[81]

An overall assessment of the life of internees in Britain between 1914 and 1919 would describe it as relatively comfortable. Instances of deliberate mistreatment seem rare. The British state seems to have fulfilled most of its obligations under the Hague Convention. But this relatively good treatment proved of little comfort to those incarcerated in a British prison camp. Isolated from their families, they had to find new temporary meaning for their lives, desperately looking forward to the end of their captivity. They tried to create a relatively normal lifestyle, as normal as it could be surrounded entirely by men of military age with little time for privacy. Most of them managed to keep themselves sane by educational, cultural, sporting and religious activity. When employment became the norm for soldiers in 1918, this group had more opportunity to take their minds off their surroundings. Once released, they would return to the chaos of post-war Germany.

Notes

[1] Panikos Panayi, *German Immigrants in Britain during the Nineteenth Century* (Oxford: Berg, 1995); Stefan Manz, *Migranten und Internierte: Deutsche in Glasgow, 1864-1918* (Stuttgart: Franz Steiner, 2003).

[2] Panikos Panayi, *The Enemy in Our Midst: Germans in Britain during the First World War* (Oxford: Berg, 1991).

[3] N[ational] A[rchives] H[ome] O[ffice] 11025/410118, Report of the Directorate of Prisoners of War, September 1920.

[4] Panayi, *Enemy*, pp. 70-98.

[5] NA HO 11025/410118, Report of the Directorate of Prisoners of War, September 1920; NA W[ar] O[ffice] 32/5376, Responsibility of the War Office for Questions Regarding Prisoners of War, November 1916; Lord Newton, *Retrospection* (London: John Murray, 1941), pp. 214-19.

[6] NA WO 32/5368, Internment of Alien Enemies, 1914.

[7] Robert Jackson, *The Prisoners*, 1914-18 (London: Routledge, 1989), p. 234.

[8] Bruno Schmidt-Reder, *In England Kriegsgefangen! Meine Erlebnisse in dem Gefangenenlager Dorchester* (Berlin: Georg Bath, 1915).

[9] James Leasor, 'Escape', *Observer Magazine*, 27 October 1974, p. 30; Gunther Plüschow, *My Escape from Donington Hall* (London: John Lane, 1922), p. 161.

[10] *The Times History of the War*, Vol. 6 (London: The Times, 1916), p. 272.

[11] Panayi, *Enemy*, pp. 75-81.

[12] NA WO 394/20, Statistical Information Regarding the Armies at Home and Abroad, 1914-1920.

[13] NA WO 394/1, Statistical Abstract, December 1916.

[14] NA WO 394/5, Statistical Abstract, November 1917.

[15] NA WO 394/10, Statistical Abstract, 1 November 1918.

[16] NA WO 394/15, Statistical Abstract, 1 September 1919.

[17] NA WO 394/20, Statistical Information Regarding the Armies at Home and Abroad, 1914-1920.

[18] Hampden Gordon, *The War Office* (London: Putnam, 1935), p. 313, states that they reached over 500, while I[mperial] W[ar] M[useum], 'German Prisoners of War in Great Britain, 1914-1918', lists 584.

[19] NA WO 162/341, Report of the Prisoners of War Information Bureau.

[20] Tighe Hopkins, *Prisoners of War* (London: Simpkin, Marshall, Hamilton, Kent, 1914), p. 108.

[21] Panayi, *Enemy*, pp. 99-108.

[22] Jackson, *op. cit.*, p. 135; Schmidt-Reder, *op. cit.*, pp. 47, 52, 54; Plüschow, *op. cit.*, p. 163.

[23] Plüschow, *ibid.*

[24] *Correspondence between His Majesty's Government and the United States Ambassador Respecting the Treatment of Prisoners of War and Interned Civilians in the United Kingdom and Germany Respectively*, P[arliamentary] P[apers], Vol. XXXIV, 1914-16.

[25] *The Times History of the War*, Vol. 6, pp. 272-3.

[26] Panayi, *Enemy*, p. 100; *Die Eiche*, 3 (July 1915), p. 437.

[27] Panayi, *ibid.*, pp. 101-2.

[28] D W Pult, *Siebzehn Monate in englischer Kriegsgefangenschaft* (Siegen: Hermann Montanus, 1917).

[29] Panayi, *Enemy*, p. 104.

[30] NA F[oreign] O[ffice] 383/33, Reports on Visits made in June 1915 by US Embassy staff to various camps.

[31] *Reports of Visits of Inspection Made by Officials of the United States Embassy to Various Internment Camps in the United Kingdom*, PP, Vol. XV, 1916; *Stobsiade*, May, June, August 1917.

[32] See, for instance, *Hansard* (Commons), fifth series, vol. 70 (1915), 557-560.

[33] Plüschow, *op.cit.*, pp. 178-9.

[34] *Reports of Visits of Inspection Made by Officials of the United States Embassy to Various Internment Camps in the United Kingdom*, PP, Vol. XV, 1916.

[35] Pult, *op. cit.*, pp. 61, 62, 66, 72, 81, 85.

[36] Panayi, *Enemy*, pp. 100-13.

[37] NA ADM [Admiralty] 137/3868, List of All Prisoner of War Camps in England and Wales (with Postal and Telegraphic Addresses), 1 January, 1918.

[38] Walter Scheller, *Als die Seele starb: 1914-1918: Das Kriegserlebnis eines Unkriegerischen* (Berlin: Reuther und Reinhardt, 1931), p. 89.

[39] IWM 82/35/1, Transcript of E. Wolff entitled 'My Adventures in the Great War 1914/18'.

[40] NA FO 383/431, Inspection of Brocton, 16 January 1918.

[41] *Manchester Guardian History of the War*, Vol. 4 (Manchester: *Manchester Guardian*, 1916), p. 219.

[42] *An Agreement between the British and German Governments Concerning Combatant Prisoners of War and Civilians*, PP, Vol. XXVI, 1918.

[43] See *Die Eiche*.

[44] NA WO 32/341, Report of the Prisoners of War Information Bureau; Ronald F. Roxburgh, *The Prisoners of War Information Bureau in London: A Study* (London: Longman, Green, 1915).

[45] Paul Cohen-Portheim, *Time Stood Still: My Internment in England, 1914-1918* (London: Duckworth, 1931), especially pp. 64-5, 100, 104-9.

[46] NA FO 383/33, Reports on Visits of Inspection made in June 1915 by US Embassy Staff to Various Camps.

[47] Bundesarchiv R85 3118, report of Swiss Embassy visit, 11 September 1918.

[48] *Correspondence between His Majesty's Government and the United States Ambassador Respecting the Treatment of German Prisoners of War and Interned Civilians in the United Kingdom*, PP, Vol. LXXXIV, 1914-16.

[49] See, for instance, *Hansard* (Commons), fifth series, vol. 70 (1915), 559.

[50] Carl Spindler, *The Phantom Ship* (London: Collins, 1931), p. 192.

[51] NA FO 383/431, Swiss Embassy Report of a Visit to Dyffryn Aled of 19 December 1917.

[52] *Correspondence between His Majesty's Government and the United States Ambassador Respecting the Treatment of German Prisoners of War and Interned Civilians in the United Kingdom*, PP, Vol. LXXXIV, 1914-16.

[53] NA HO 45/11025/410118, Report of the Directorate of Prisoners of War, 1920.

[54] L. Bogenstätter and H. Zimmermann, *Die Welt hinter Stacheldraht: Eine Chronik des englischen Kriegsgefangenlagers Handforth bei Manchester* (Munich: Piloty und Loehle, 1921), p. 27.

[55] Plüschow, *op. cit.*, p. 180.

[56] Cohen-Portheim, *op. cit.*, p. 91.

[57] Fritz Sachse and Paul Nikolaus Cossmann, *Kriegsgefangen in Skipton: Leben und Geschichte deutscher Kriegsgefangenen in einem englischen Lager* (Munich: Ernst Reinhardt, 1920), pp. 92-7.

[58] Plüschow, *op. cit.*, pp. 166, 173.

[59] Bogenstätter and Zimmermann, *op. cit.*, p. 88.

[60] Sachse and Cossmann, *op. cit.*, p. 123.

[61] A. L. Vischer, *Barbed Wire Disease: A Psychological Study of the Prisoner of War* (London: John Bale, 1919), pp. 3, 50-1, 53-5.

[62] Franz Rinteln von Kleist, *The Dark Invader: Wartime Reminiscences of a German Naval Intelligence Officer* (London: Lovat Dickson, 1933), p. 240; Plüschow, *op. cit.*, p. 185.

[63] Bogenstätter and Zimmermann, *op. cit.*, pp. 165, 169.

[64] NA HO45 10947/266042/361, 'Final Report on the Internal Administration of the Prisoners of War Camp IV, Knockaloe'.

[65] Cohen-Portheim, *op. cit.*, pp. 92-3; Society of Friends Library, FEWVRC/CAMPS/2/3.

[66] Bogenstätter and Zimmermann, *op. cit.*, p. 232; Sachse and Cossmann, *op. cit.*, pp. 182-6.

[67] Hermann Pörzgen, *Theater ohne Frau: Das Bühnenleben der Kriegsgefangenen Deutschen 1914-1920* (Königsberg: Ost-Europa Verlag, 1933).

[68] NA ADM 137/3855, Translation of a letter from 'Von Pabst', Prisoner of War at Donington Hall to his wife, dated 14 October 1915.

[69] Panayi, *Enemy*, p. 124.

[70] *Stobsiade*, 19 September 1915; NA FO 383/431, Report by the Swiss Legation on Dyfrynn Aled, 7 January 1918.

[71] *Stobsiade*, October 1917.

[72] NA HO45 11025/410118, Report of the Directorate of Prisoners of War, September 1920; NA CAB [Cabinet] 42/20/7, Employment of Prisoners of War, 1916; NA ADM 1/889/109, Memorandum by the Secretary of the Admiralty, 16 December 1916; P. E. Dewey, 'Farm Labour in Wartime: The Relationship Between Agricultural Labour Supply and Food Production in Great Britain during 1914-1918, with International Comparisons' (University of Reading Ph.D thesis, 1978), p. 242.

[73] NA HO45 11025/410118, Report of the Directorate of Prisoners of War, September 1920.

[74] NA CAB 24/46/4087, Prisoners of War Employment Committee First Interim Report.

[75] NA HO45 11025/410118, Report of the Directorate of Prisoners of War, September 1920; NA CAB 42/20/7, Employment of Prisoners of War, 1916; NA WO 394/15, Statistical Abstracts, 1 September 1919.

[76] Dewey, op. cit., pp. 244, 253; NA HO45 11025/410118, Report of the Directorate of Prisoners of War, September 1920; *The Times*, 16 September 1918.

[77] NA NATS [Ministry of National Service] 51/571, Details of Prisoners of War, Week Ended 14 July 1918.

[78] NA FO 383/432, Report of a Swiss Embassy Visit of 19 February 1918 to Monks Abbey.

[79] NA FO 383/431, Report of a Visit of Inspection by the Swiss Legation to Kilburn Hall on 18 December 1917.

[80] NA NATS 1/569, Report on Prisoners of War Camp, Bramley, Hampshire, 2-5 September 1918.

[81] NA HO45 11025/410118, Report of the Directorate of Prisoners of War, September 1920; NA NATS 1/570, Rations for Prisoners of War, 1918.

Yvonne Cresswell

Behind the Wire: the material culture of civilian internment on the Isle of Man in the First World War

The internment of civilians in Britain and Germany during the First World War is one of the lesser known aspects of the period. This study will examine one aspect of the internment experience: craftwork and the wide variety of material culture produced by the internees and the role it played in their lives. Its most obvious function was to alleviate boredom, but it also provided mementoes for internees to keep and served as a form of camp currency, being either given as gifts or traded for extra provisions.

A common misconception is that the Isle of Man is little more than the sum of tail-less cats, kippers and fast motorbikes, but this stereotypical image masks historically significant chapters of Manx history that have lain forgotten within a wider British context. One such chapter was the use of the Island for the internment of almost 30,000 civilians, identified as 'enemy aliens', during the First World War.[1] This study will examine one specific aspect of the internment experience on the Isle of Man, that of craftwork and the resulting material culture produced by the internees.

The initial question following the outbreak of war and the introduction of internment was where to house the internees. During the first few months of the war, the solution was to use temporary accommodation such as horse boxes at Newbury race course and an old wagon works at Lancaster.[2] As part of this process, the Cunningham's Young Men's Holiday Camp at Douglas was converted from being tented and chalet holiday accommodation for 2,800 holidaymakers in the first week of August, 1914, into a civilian internment camp by 22 September 1914. The camp held a maximum of 3,300 in the early months of the war and then eventually stabilised at 2,600 internees.[3]

The unsuitable nature of these early camps for full-time permanent habitation soon became apparent as winter began, in particular due to their lack of adequate heating, lighting and sanitation. Even the Douglas Camp proved to be unsuitable, as it had only been built for short-term summer occupation by young male holidaymakers. The conditions and unrest amongst the internees at the Douglas Camp, led in November 1914 to a riot in the dining hall about the food, which left five dead after the military guards fired on the 'rioting' internees.[4]

The need to house an increasing number of internees led to the creation of a second internment camp on the Isle of Man, following a visit to the Island by members of the Destitute Aliens Committee in October 1914.[5] The new camp was planned for Knockaloe Mooar, a farm on the west coast of the Island that had previously been used as a temporary camp for 16,000 Territorial troops.[6] The initial plans were for Knockaloe to be a purpose-built camp with a capacity for holding 5,000 internees, but the policy of mass internment that followed the sinking of the *Lusitania*, led to it holding 10,000, then 15,000 and it finally reached a maximum of 23,000 internees by 1917.

Knockaloe Camp had an adequate infrastructure for the number of internees that it was originally planned to hold, but the constant increase in numbers meant that regardless of the degree to which the facilities of the camp were increased, they were never sufficient for the numbers that were held at any particular period.[7]

> We stood on the hillside beyond Greeba, in Man, surveying the whole stretch of Knockaloe Camp, the great and strange cosmopolitan town where the streets are formed of double-ribbed barbed wire, and where the compounds, for all their spaciousness, look like enormous cages without tops.[8]

By 1917, Knockaloe internment camp was made up of four individual camps, the largest of which was Camp IV. Each camp was comprised of a series of self-contained compounds. The 23 compounds were each 100 yards square and initially contained 5 sleeping huts (each holding 200 internees), a kitchen, a recreation room, a bath house and latrines.[9]

In contrast, the Douglas Camp was always a far smaller establishment, with only 2,700 internees. The camp comprised three separate groups with an Ordinary Camp, a Jewish Camp and a Privilege Camp.

Although concerns about the physical conditions in which internees were housed were relatively less critical than they had been in the early months of the war, there were still issues over the mental health and welfare of those interned. Adequate food and accommodation was seen as being insufficient, the problem of boredom being expressed by a junior officer as: "'You must give 'em something to do or let them go 'dotty'." It was crudely expressed, but one recognised a sad truth.'[10]

The condition of mental illness became known as 'Barbed Wire Disease' and was identified with a loss of interests, suspicious nature, delusions of persecution, hysteria and ravings and was felt to be solely the result of the internees having no work or means to occupy their time.[11] The condition was recognised by the internees themselves, though work in itself

Figure 1: A panoramic view of Knockaloe Camp (Courtesy of Manx National Heritage)

was not considered to be the solution but rather finding work that was both 'congenial and remunerative' for themselves.[12]

Those interned did not exist in a temporal or spatial vacuum, but developed an alternative society, with its own distinctive social systems and material culture. Considerable self-help was exercised by the internees, with the initial efforts at craftwork being instigated by the internees themselves, in particular sailors, who produced models and ornaments for sale.[13] The initial plans at Knockaloe had been that each compound was to be 'self-contained' and 'entirely dependent on discovering its own latent talent for the development of industrial and recreative activity'. An example of the problems faced by the internees was shown in Camp IV, where 'due to the kaleidoscopic assembly in each compound', the reality led to the creation in 1915 of a 'Central Camp Organisation' by the internees. The roles of the committee were to co-ordinate and oversee the wide variety of activities and resources required by the seven compounds.[14] The various activities and facilities were also developed in part with the aid and support of external agencies such the military administrators of the camps and the Society of Friends (Quakers) who provided humanitarian assistance. There were three forums for 'industrial' work in Camp IV; these included the principal workshop (used for making mail-bags, boots, brushes and tailoring), the auxiliary workshops (used for wood and metal handicrafts) and the internees' living space in the huts used for working on small-scale craft projects.[15]

A turning point for work in the Knockaloe and Douglas camps was the appointment in 1915 of James T. Baily as Industrial Advisor to the Manx camps, under the auspices of the Friends Emergency Committee.[16] Although forbidden to provide educational assistance, he was allowed to assist the internees in organising their own educational and industrial facilities and requests for materials and equipment increased dramatically, resulting in the Friends' Emergency Committee having their own, large, storage facilities at the camp.[17] During the first few weeks of his appointment, the priority was the production of items 'necessary for making living conditions bearable and to preserve health'.[18]

The impetus for the Friends' humanitarian aid in the Manx camps and others around Britain was recorded in J. T. Baily's journal as being 'I was sick and ye visited me. I was in prison and ye came unto me. In all ye do, do all the glory of God'.[19] Although the work done by the Friends' Emergency Committee in attempting to provide improved facilities for the internees was apparently appreciated by the military personnel of the camps and the Manx Government, it gained them the nickname of *Hun-coddlers* in the British press.[20] The contribution of the Friends' Emergency Committee was also seen as essential by the internees in terms of their support and supply of tools and materials for handicrafts.[21]

All manner of items could be made by recycling waste materials from the camp, but they were not the only source of raw materials since:

> The prisoner with means may purchase pretty well anything he likes [...] in the dry canteen, which has a branch in every compound [...] one can buy anything from a tin of anchovy paste to a length of Manx homespun, and the monthly turnover runs to £9,000.[22]

The compound canteens drew their stock from central stores which frequently held stock in excess of £100,000 in value and had at times a monthly turnover of £12,000.[23] A portion of the profits from the canteens and the Camp Gazette and Printing Office were used to provide funds for the burial of men who died during their time of confinement at Knockaloe.[24]

Although some handicrafts were made in the auxiliary workshops, much of the work of bone carving, wood carving and knitting of handbags was done by internees in their own huts as they only required small hand tools.[25]

The significance of the provision of workshops was not underestimated and it was recorded that on the Isle of Man 'not a single prisoner who was a regular handicraft worker, has been taken to the asylum'.[26] The importance of the workshops and their employment was emphasized when the war was over and the internees looked forward to their long-awaited release and as a result all the workshops and camp activities rapidly stopped. Unfortunately they did not realise that many of them would still be held in the camps for almost another year as the slow process of repatriation proceeded.[27]

A large archive of glass plate negatives survive of the Manx camps which help to illustrate life behind the wire, in particular the large number of interior views of the internees' living accommodation. At first glance these images appear to exemplify the homogeneity of the internment experience, but on closer inspection, a diversity and variety of self-expression can be identified within the internees' personal living spaces.

This initial impression of homogeneity is also apparently reinforced when one considers the material culture produced in the internment camps, such as the ubiquitous hand-carved bone-work 'rose' vases, the marquetry boxes and ship models. However the uniformity of these images and, in particular, that of craftwork is illusory, as may be seen by the diverse nature of the material produced in the internment camps.

One of the first crafts to become established, after the initial settling down period, was woodworking, with Baily receiving numerous requests for fretwork outfits, fretwood materials and designs. As a result the branches of *Hobbies* in Liverpool and Manchester received large orders for supplies, in particular job-lot bundles of assorted types of fretwood.[28] The initial popularity of fretwork as a pastime was probably a consequence of its pre-war popularity as a male hobby. In both circumstances, its popularity may be related to it requiring relatively little financial outlay in terms of equipment and materials. Also the equipment occupied little room and the technique was easily learnt by a beginner. As a result the major prerequisites required were time and patience, attributes which were in considerable supply for the internees.

The popularity of fretwork was not confined to amateurs and beginners but also to skilled workers; one of the internees, Kachmarck, designed his own fretcutting machine with a treadle drive for making toys to his own design. The most popular of these toys was 'a snake and a crocodile made up of segments (of wood) glued to a strip of tape which ran from head to tail' to make an articulated mobile toy. Although no distinguishing marks were meant to be put on craftwork made by internees, Kachmarck designed a trademark for his toys, the design being a kitten surrounded by a floral wreath lithographed onto stamps for the toys.[29]

Woodwork was not just confined to fretwork and toymaking; many boxes were also produced, in various shapes and sizes. These included money boxes, playing card boxes (decorated with the four ace designs) and various forms of cigarette boxes with mechanisms to dispense a cigarette automatically. Larger objects included jewellery and sewing boxes, complete with lift-out trays and small compartments. The items were decorated with a variety of techniques such as marquetry panels and hand-painted designs. Much of the work was somewhat simple and obviously the work of a novice or produced relatively quickly by a more accomplished worker. But there are many items which represent a greater degree of time and expertise being employed in their execution. Frequently these are items that are still treasured possessions within an ex-internee's family, having been made specifically for a member of the family. This is exemplified by an extremely ornate sewing and general purpose box that was made by an experienced joiner for his wife. The box is extensively decorated, both inside and out, with painted panels depicting Manx cats, the three legs symbol and a dove of peace.

Supplies were not a problem for the woodworkers since the canteen provided everything from the carving tools and veneers they required through to the oval mirrors for hand mirrors and the inside lids of jewellery boxes.

A larger scale of woodwork was shown by the wide variety of furniture that was made at Knockaloe Camp during the period 1915 to 1918. At the more extravagant end of the spectrum, the Scottish Arts and Crafts designer Charles Rennie Mackintosh designed and had several suites of furniture made in Knockaloe for the industrialist, W. J. Bassett-Lowke. The furniture was made under the supervision of Charles Matt, who before the war had been a foreman in charge of about 80 men at a London furniture factory. Whilst in Knockaloe, Matt gathered together a workshop of some of the finest professional cabinet-makers.[30] The furniture commission was part of the remodelling of 78 Derngate, Bassett-Lowke's new house in Northampton, and during 1916 several pieces were produced at Knockaloe internment camp.[31] One of the bedroom suites designed by Mackintosh is now on display in the Hunterian Gallery in Glasgow.

At a more utilitarian level, during the last year of the war, the internees produced furniture for the Friends' War Victims Relief Committee. The Committee had built temporary homes for French refugees who been made homeless during the war but they still required furniture for the homes. Baily, the Industrial Advisor, designed various items of furniture that could be folded and packed flat ready for shipping to France. These included dozens of large dressers and buffet-cupboards and 150 kitchen tables.[32]

Metalworking had originally begun as a utilitarian activity utilizing the surplus of 'bully beef' tins which were used to produce much-needed guttering for the Knockaloe huts, considered 'a much appreciated, camp-wide public service'. The surface water had previously drained away in open trench gulleys, and was felt to be highly dangerous for pedestrians at night.[33] Another use for the large number of 'bully beef' tins was considered to be extremely novel, when some men used the tins to create a series of 'field bakeries', built within the compounds but at some distance from the huts.

The tinsmiths found a variety of uses for old cans by flattening them to produce sheets to make:

> mugs, cake tins, patty pans, shallow baking pans, pastry cutters, funnels, scoops, many kinds of tin boxes, candlesticks, reflectors for lamps, ash trays etc. Some very ingenious scales were made for weighing letters, these were constructed on the principle of the lever and were quite accurate.[34]

The tinsmiths were also responsible for the manufacture of 'properties' for theatrical productions, using the cans to produce lighting effects, the stage footlights and even 'suits of armour' for medieval plays.[35] Baily described the use of the tins as being: 'marvellous to see the clever improvising of "waste" materials which the craftsmen had recourse to; food supplies meant a residue of tin containers, heaps of them.' [36]

But there were also potential scientific uses for the waste cans, as Otto Gross, a mechanical engineer and metallurgist, examined the possibility of 'salving the tin coating from the canisters' and as a result was given permission to conduct the necessary experiments at the Douglas Foundry.[37]

What is not known is whether the surplus of 'bully beef' tins was available throughout the war or was only available in large quantities in 1917 when food shortages resulted in tinned meat being used as a substitute for fresh meat. Unfortunately Baily does not provide dates in his journal, compiled after the war, as to when the tinsmiths were in primary operation.

One of the most distinctive, and readily identifiable, items to be produced in the internment camps were the carved bones. They were also unique as being some of the only craft items that are marked with the camp name and/or date as part of their design. They also appear to be unique in terms of their design and use of material. Although bone was used by Napoleonic prisoners of war for craftwork such as model-making and sailors traditionally incised bone and tusks for scrimshaw work, there appear to be no historical antecedents for this particular type of bone carving.

Bone carving was similar to tin-working in that it was a product of circumstance, since the raw materials were readily available and as a result it was a craft enterprise undertaken in all four camps at Knockaloe. Other examples are known from the Stobbs camp, Hawick, and from Lancaster, although it does not appear to have been practised at Douglas camp. The indication is that the first carved bones were produced by 'artistic craftsmen, some of them sculptors and carvers'.[38] The bones used by the internees came from the meat supplied to the 'cook-house kitchens' and tended to be long bones from cattle (beef shin bones), thereby providing the characteristic shape of the tall 'rose' spill vases.

A wide variety of carved bone items (fancy articles) were produced as both souvenir curiosities together with utilitarian items. The long bones were made into vases while the shorter lengths of bone were used to make pin cushions, vase tidies, ashtrays, match and cigarette stands, table cruets, paper knives, letter openers and napkin rings. The napkin rings were carved with initials and names using ornamental lettering and are usually found as lone examples so it is unknown whether they were originally made as sets or as single commemorative pieces. An example with the inscription 'Deo Gratias' (Thank God) may have been made by or for someone who was about to be repatriated either during the war or at the end of the war; whatever the occasion, the inscription and its sentiment would appear to have been heartfelt.

The bones were prepared for carving by being first boiled to remove the fat, marrow and gristle and then boiled again with soda or bleaching

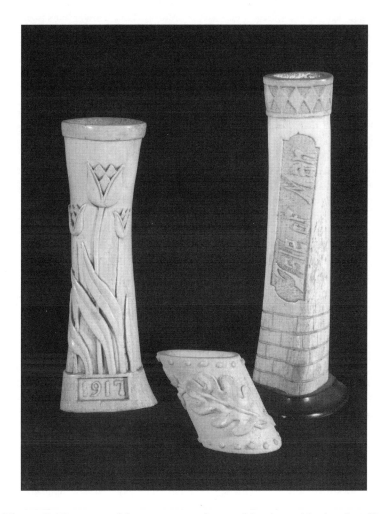

**Figure 2: Two carved bone vases and a napkin ring with simple tulip
and oak leaf designs (Courtesy of Manx National Heritage)**

powders to whiten the bones. The long leg bones were used to make flower vases; these were fitted with a dark hardwood base that was set with putty to make the vase watertight.[39] The vases were known as 'flower' vases because they were used to hold flowers in water but they also were carved with flower patterns, the most popular being roses and tulips. The designs were carved in relief, with the background deeply cut back leaving the flowers and lettering standing as raised bas-relief designs.

There appears to be a hierarchy of quality represented in the different designs used for the carved vases. These range from bones having simple flower designs, such as the outline pattern of a tulip with little detail shown, which may have been beginners' pieces or early practice pieces. A variety of rose designs can be found ranging from a single flower and stem through to several rose heads and leaves being carved onto a single bone. They may also show the roses as both buds and in full flower. The most complex and ornate of these designs were carved with folded leaves and petals and their stems cut back to make them free-standing, thereby producing an extremely delicate three-dimensional bone rose. As a result they were considered to be: 'the result of much ingenuity and patience [...] leaving the carving almost lifted away, with a few tendril connections to give stability.'[40]

The highest quality of carved bonework produced at Knockaloe was considered by J. T. Baily to be that produced by a member of the Lang family of Oberammergau Passion Play fame, who at the outbreak of war had been teaching at the Dublin School of Art. Baily considered himself to be highly honoured to see the pieces, which were rarely shown publicly and never to anyone British, in particular 'none of the military fraternity'. Lang made an exception for Baily because of the work that the Friends were doing for POWs and their families. The items were not made for sale but as personal mementoes for each member of his family.[41]

An examination of the surviving bone-work shows a wide variety in the colour of the bone from bleached white through to a heavily discoloured yellow. This may illustrate an inconsistency of quality in the bleaching techniques used at the time or may indicate that greater care and attention was consciously given to the bleaching of particular bones. Therefore the diversity of colours may indicate that there was poor quality control during the bleaching process or that the bones were produced in a variety of grades, depending on the length of time they had been boiled and bleached. As a result the perfectly bleached bones may have been reserved for the better quality carvers whilst the poorer bones may have been kept for use by the less experienced carvers. It is also possible that some discolouration of the bones has taken place over time and therefore the bones may have all been a standard white colour at the time they were initially carved.

The production of carved bone items appears to have been temporarily interrupted by the cutting of rations and the meat shortages in 1917.[42] The substitution of tinned meat meant that there were no bones available for carving; therefore this may be the point at which the production of material using meat tins was most extensive. The shortage was solved by J. T. Baily travelling to Liverpool and being put in contact with an importer of bones from the Argentine, hitherto presumably used to make bonemeal fertiliser. Baily purchased two tons of bones from a warehouse at the Liverpool docks and arranged for them to be packed in sacks and transported to Knockaloe. This allowed the production of carved bone to resume and was 'much to the relief of the bone carvers'.[43] The change of source of bone may also be another factor in the variety of colour of the bone in its finished, and aged, state. The discolouration therefore may be due to the time lapse between the bone being processed and carved and the initial butchery. The original Knockaloe bone would have been processed more quickly than the Argentinian bone which had been stored for an unknown period of time. Also of note is that a significant number of the carved bones that survive are dated 1917, even though morale and rations were at their lowest ebb at this time. One of the last designs to be produced by the bone workers was near the end of the war and was the introduction of toothbrush making, using machines designed by one of the internees, Otto Gross.[44]

As useful as the general craftwork was in providing some form of employment, the Friends' Emergency Committee also wanted to provide 'useful' employment. Although conscription had led to a reduction in the general British workforce, the use of internee labour was not viewed favourably by either the other traders who saw it as competing cheap labour or by the internees who saw it as Government exploitation of their labour for the British war effort. In addition any proposal had to be submitted in detail to the Home Office for scrutiny and approval.

One of the schemes proposed by the Friends that met with general approval was the establishment of a basket-making workshop. Although Knockaloe originally only contained three skilled basket-makers, these internees went on to train a hundred basket-makers, who were able to produce a wide variety of different sizes and types of baskets. The baskets produced included potato, vegetable and fruit hampers for export to England and later orders were received for laundry hampers, wicker suitcases, lounge chairs, clothes baskets and even a wicker side-car for a motorcycle was produced.[45]

Originally willow was imported from Lancashire and Nottingham but later the internees established an area at the Ballaugh Curraghs (wetlands) in the north of the Island to cultivate and harvest willow, not just for their immediate use, but also on a long-term basis.[46] The intention of James T. Baily, the Friends' Industrial Advisor, was that a fully established wicker industry would be set up after the war and it was hoped it would become a major local employer with Manx industry in succeeding years, using the expertise, stock and goodwill started by the internees.[47] The success of the venture could be seen in the scale of production with almost 65,000 baskets being made in the Knockaloe camp. Sadly, the plans of the Knockaloe Camp Commandant, Major Quayle-Dickinson and J. T. Baily were not pursued and the Curraghs were allowed to fall back into disuse until they were reclaimed and utilized in part as a Wildlife Park in the 1960s.[48]

The craftwork produced in the workshops illustrates not only great diversity of form but also of function since production served a variety of purposes. Their most obvious function was to provide a form of 'occupational therapy', a way to profitably occupy internees' time and to alleviate general problems of boredom, and, in more extreme cases, of mental illness. The variety of motives that internees might have for working was recognised at the time:

> [A] group of alien prisoners, attracted by the offer of reward and perhaps impelled by the monotony of camp life, were quarrying for stone[...] inside the huts we had already seen hundreds of deft craftsmen plying their trades. [49]

The subsequent sale of such items by the Society of Friends also raised funds to finance their work in providing facilities for the internees. The sale of the items was not however, always a simple procedure. At first the standard of workmanship was not always consistent and an individual's work was frequently one of their first attempts at a craft. In addition there were also the problems of finding sympathetic 'markets' through which the items might be sold. This was further exacerbated by the fact that conditions were set by the Camp authorities. If items were to be released for sale from the camp, they could not be publicly advertised or sold through any shop or firm. As a result items were sold through personal contacts with the general Camp Visitor taking cases of craft goods around Friends' meetings and to the Friends' House in London. Some items such as the wooden jointed toys and inlaid match cases sold easily but other items were far more difficult to sell: 'But boxes and bones we dreaded to see!'.[50] Other markets eventually became available and a large amount of material was sold in America via a

Prisoners of War Relief Committee in New York. In Sweden, an exhibition and sale of works was organized by the Crown Princess of Sweden to help prisoners of war in Russia and Germany.[51]

Craftwork also fulfilled less utilitarian necessities. It provided mementoes which the internees kept for themselves either to decorate their own living spaces or to send to their families in Britain and Germany.[52] They also served as a form of camp currency, being given as gifts to guards or civilian staff with whom friendships had developed, or sold or bartered for extra provisions. Many items remain within the families of ex-internees and camp staff as treasured family heirlooms.

Due to the large numbers of civilians interned on the Island during the First World War and their disparate origins, there is no individual internment experience which might be considered wholly characteristic and representative. The varied nature of an individual's experience of internment and the effect of 'barbed wire disease' upon the individual's perception of that experience was recognized in early accounts of internment.[53]

From businessmen, students on holiday, and merchant seamen in British ports at the Declaration of War, to settled immigrant tradesmen with British wives and families, the internees and their experiences were a diverse collection of biographies which became interwoven into the more complex and multifaceted chronicle that developed into the history of First World War internment.

For many ex-internees, their incarceration was an experience viewed, at best, with ambivalence. The intangible legacy of internment, the lost years and disrupted family relationships, were a part of ex-internees' lives which they had no choice but to retain. In contrast, the tangible legacy, the material culture of camp life, was an aspect that they could choose to either keep or destroy. It is therefore significant that many internees chose to keep the items that they made in the camps or that they had purchased as mementoes from fellow internees.

Many items made in the internment camps serve a mixture of functions, being both decorative and of practical use but also predominantly commemorative in nature. As a result the names *Knockaloe* and *Douglas*, with the date, frequently appear on objects, often with Manx symbols such as the three legs and a Manx cat. These items have become treasured heirlooms within families rather than cursed reminders of the war, although the memories of the hardship and trauma of internment have still been retained within the families' history together with the carved bones and wooden boxes.

The Kafkaesque nature of internment and the contrast of the individual internee's experience against society's experience of the First World War were summed up by Paul Cohen-Portheim:

> Compared to life at the front, life in a concentration camp was undramatic; there was no danger, there was no heroism, voluntary or forced. It was monotonous, it was drab, it was futile, and in that very futility lay its tragedy.[54]

Notes

I would like to thank the Director and Trustees of Manx National Heritage for the opportunity to research the archives and collections of Manx National Heritage for this work. I also wish to thank Dr Andrew Foxon, Head of Professional Services, Manx National Heritage for his suggestions and comments on this paper.

[1] Although at Government level, the precedent of civilian internment is well known, at a popular level 'alien internment remains a hidden feature of British history'. Civilian internment during the Second World War has become more well-known and increasingly the subject of research but civilian internment during the First World War is still relatively unknown and under-researched. Cf. Tony Kushner and David Cesarani, 'Alien Internment in Britain During the Twentieth Century: An Introduction' in *The Internment of Aliens in Twentieth Century Britain*, ed. by David Cesarani and Tony Kushner (London: Frank Cass, 1993), pp. 1-22 (pp. 2-3). See also John Clement Bird, *Control of Enemy Alien Civilians in Great Britain 1914-1918* (New York: Garland, 1986).

[2] Anna Braithwaite Thomas, *St Stephen's House: Friends Emergency Work in England 1914-1920* (London: Emergency Committee for the Assistance of Germans, Austrians and Hungarians in Distress, 1926), p. 46.

[3] Jill Drower, *Good Clean Fun – A History of Britain's First Holiday Camp* (London: Arcadia Books, 1982), pp. 40-50 (p. 45); B. E. Sargeaunt, *The Isle of Man and the Great War* (Douglas: Brown & Sons, 1920), pp. 58-97 (pp. 62-63).

[4] Bird, *Enemy Alien Civilians*, pp. 142-43.

[5] Panikos Panayi, 'An Intolerant Act by an Intolerant Society: The Internment of Germans in Britain During the First World War', in *The Internment of Aliens in Twentieth Century Britain*, pp. 53-75 (p. 65).

[6] Sargeaunt, *The Isle of Man and the Great War*, pp. 65-66.

[7] During the first year of the war, internment policy was dictated by the availability of accommodation and as a result each period of large-scale internment was followed by a period when some internees were released, only to be re-arrested shortly afterwards.
The problem of implementing internment policy was exacerbated by the differences of opinion between the Home Office and the War Office, who were originally jointly responsible for internment. The Home Office, who were subject to public pressure and opinion, advocated mass internment, whilst the War Office did not consider the internment of non-combatant alien civilians a high priority at a time when they wanted all available accommodation for

combatant military prisoners of war. See Bird, *Enemy Alien Civilians*, pp. 61-67; for an early description of Knockaloe Internment Camp in 1915 see Paul Cohen-Portheim, *Time Stood Still: My Internment in England 1914-1918* (London: Duckworth, 1931).

[8] George Leach, 'British Treatment of Enemy Prisoners' in *Manx Quarterly*, Vol. 17, No.3. (Douglas: S. K. Broadbent/ *Isle of Man Examiner*, 1916), pp. 71-74 (p. 71).

[9] Sargeaunt, *The Isle of Man and the Great War*, p. 78.

[10] Leach, 'British Treatment of Enemy Prisoners', p. 73.
The segregation of internees by social class and influence was a general policy throughout British Camps. In October 1914, the War Office instructed camp commandants to divide military and civilian prisoners into three groups: military officers, those able to pay for accommodation and rations and all others, who would be rationed and clothed by the state. See Bird, *Control of Enemy Alien Civilians*, pp. 145-46.
Whilst Douglas Internment Camp was known as a 'gentlemen's camp', together with Wakefield, Knockaloe had far greater social differences with only about 10% of the population having money in the Camp Bank, which they could withdraw at £1 per week. The rest of the camp population did not have any money and therefore had to find employment in the camp workshops or by working for other internees. Cf. Cohen-Portheim, *Time Stood Still*, p. 44.

[11] Braithwaite Thomas, *St Stephen's House*, pp. 52-53. The Society of Friend's Industrial Advisor described: 'The visitors to the Camps found themselves becoming increasingly concerned about the condition of the P.O.Ws; they found them degenerating physically and morally, a disease, which became known later as "barbed wirelitis", became more common bringing the threatened danger of insanity more prevalent.' James T. Baily, *Friends' Emergency Committee 1915-19 Isle of Man* Manuscript (Manx National Heritage Archives: n. d.), p. 4.

[12] Central Committee, *Half-Yearly Report on the Organisation, Functions & Activities of the Committees Formed by the Civilian Prisoners of War in Camp IV (English Edition)*. Typescript (London: Society of Friends, 1917), p. 6.

[13] Braithwaite Thomas, *St Stephen's House*, p. 61.

[14] Central Committee, *Half-Yearly Report on the Organisation* etc., p. 2.

[15] *Ibid.*, p. 6.

[16] 'It was […] August 1915 that I was invited by the F. E. C. to visit the Camps and report on conditions and to make recommendations for action. My report and recommendation we(re) received & accepted and I was then invited to implement the same, finally becoming resident representative in the Isle of Man as Industrial Advisor for Douglas and Knockaloe Camp, later becoming Industrial Superintendent to the latter camp under the IoMan Government.' James T. Baily, *Friends' Emergency Committee 1915-19*, p. 4.

[17] Braithwaite Thomas, *St Stephen's House*, pp. 68-69.

[18] James T. Baily, *Friends' Emergency Committee 1915-19*, p. 16. Baily's role became so essential to the running of the Knockaloe Camp, that he became Industrial Superintendent and was transferred to the Manx Government Service in 1918. See Leslie Baily, *Craftsman and Quaker: The Story of James T. Baily 1876-1957* (London: Allen & Unwin, 1959), pp. 86-107 (p.101).

[19] James T. Baily, *Friends' Emergency Committee 1915-19*, p. 4.

[20] Braithwaite Thomas, *St Stephen's House*, p. 44.

[21] Central Committee, *Half-Yearly Report on the Organisation etc*, p. 6.

[22] Leach, 'British Treatment of Enemy Prisoners', p. 73.

[23] Samuel Norris, *Manx Memories and Movements* (Douglas: Norris Modern Press, 1938), pp. 211-19 (p. 213). (Reprinted in 1994 by Manx Heritage Foundation.)

[24] Central Committee, *Half-Yearly Report on the Organisation etc*, p. 73.

[25] *Ibid.*, pp. 6-7.

[26] Braithwaite Thomas, *St Stephen's House*, p. 52.

[27] *Ibid.*, p. 76.

[28] James T. Baily, *Friends' Emergency Committee 1915-19*, p. 16.

[29] *Ibid.*, p. 17.

[30] Leslie Baily, *Craftsman and Quaker*, p. 102.

[31] Louise Campbell, 'A Model Patron: Bassett-Lowke, Mackintosh and Behrens', in *Journal of Decorative Arts Society*, 10 (1987), pp. 1-9 (pp. 2-4).

[32] Braithwaite Thomas, *St Stephen's House*, p. 73.

[33] James T. Baily, *Friends' Emergency Committee 1915-19*, p. 17.

[34] *Ibid.*, p. 18.

[35] *Ibid.*

[36] *Ibid.*, p.17

[37] *Ibid.*, p. 18.

[38] *Ibid.*, p. 19.

[39] *Ibid.*

[40] *Ibid.*

[41] *Ibid.*, pp. 19-20.

[42] The meat ration was reduced on 5 March 1917. See Central Committee, *Half-Yearly Report on the Organisation etc*. Typescript (London: Society of Friends, 1917), p. 5.

[43] James T. Baily, *Friends' Emergency Committee 1915-19*, p. 20.

[44] *Ibid.*

[45] Leslie Baily, *Craftsman and Quaker*, p. 105.

[46] *Ibid*, p. 104.

[47] Braithwaite Thomas, *St Stephen's* House, p. 72.

[48] Leslie Baily, *Craftsman and Quaker*, pp. 105-06.

[49] Leach, 'British Treatment of Enemy Prisoners', p. 71.

[50] Braithwaite Thomas, *St Stephen's House*, pp. 70-1.

[51] The amount of material sent to the New York Committee resulted in a surplus stockpiling, much of which had been damaged in transit. The material was finally repaired and sold in various towns by an interned German sea captain who was appointed by the committee.
The Society of Friends sent 33 cases of goods, valued at over £1,000, to the Stockholm exhibition which were sold within one to two hours. See Braithwaite Thomas, *St Stephen's*

House, p. 71. An unknown amount of this material probably still exists in America and Scandinavia awaiting discovery and identification as internee craftwork.

[52] The function of craftwork as a supplier of presents for family and friends seems to have been predominantly a factor in the early period of production for internees for whom craftwork, particularly fretwork, was a new and novel experience: 'but when the worker had supplied his family and friends there was but a limited sale for fretwork so we encouraged the use of the fretsaws to toymaking and this became a permanent feature in most of the Camp workshops as there soon came good orders from England, Sweden and USA.' James T. Baily, *Friends' Emergency Committee 1915-19*, p. 16.

[53] Braithwaite Thomas, *St Stephen's House*, p. 53; Cohen-Portheim, *Time Stood Still*, p. 34.

[54] Cohen-Portheim, *Time Stood Still*, p. 2.

Jutta Raab Hansen

Die Bedeutung der Musik für 26.000 internierte Zivilisten während des Ersten Weltkriegs auf der Isle of Man

Während des 1. Weltkrieges internierten die kriegführenden Nationen in Europa (nach 1917 auch die USA) zum ersten Mal Zivilisten. Rund 26.000 kriegstaugliche Männer wurden auf die Isle of Man in der Irischen See verbracht. In zwei von Stacheldraht eingezäunten und bewachten Lagern verwalteten die deutschen, österreichisch-ungarischen und türkischen Internierten weitgehend ihr Leben selbst. Eine besondere Rolle spielten dabei Theater und Musik. Sinfonieorchester, Lagerchöre, Kammermusik- und Tanzmusikensembles sorgten für die Umrahmung der Höhepunkte im Kreislauf des Jahres und halfen die Zeit des relativen Nichtstuns zu überbrücken. Musik beförderte den Patriotismus der Internierten, um der Zeit im Lager einen Sinn zu geben, diese als Dienst an der fernen Heimat darzustellen.

Der erste Weltkrieg dehnte sich in besonderer Weise auf die Zivilbevölkerung aus. War es bis 1914 bei vorangegangenen Kriegen Zivilisten, die sich bei Kriegsausbruch im Land eines Gegners befanden, erlaubt, ihre Dinge zu regeln und nach Hause zurückzukehren, so nahmen zum ersten Mal in der Geschichte alle kriegführenden Nationen Zivilpersonen in staatlichen Gewahrsam. Das waren im einzelnen: Touristen, Studenten, Geschäftsleute, Missionare, handelnde Seeleute, im Ausland lebende Einwohner, oder einfach kriegstaugliche Männer, die sich schlicht auf der falschen Seite befanden, als der Krieg ausbrach. Insgesamt waren davon 400.000 Menschen in Europa betroffen.[1] Die Internierungspolitik war von Land zu Land verschieden. Nachdem die USA 1917 in den Krieg eingetreten waren, gab es auch dort Internierungen.

Die Geschichte der britischen und deutschen Internierung im 1. Weltkrieg ist miteinander verzahnt. Kranke und für den Kriegsdienst unbrauchbare Männer wurden gegenseitig und nach einem bestimmten Schlüssel aus humanitären Gründen freigelassen.[2] Israel Cohen, britischer Journalist und selbst in Deutschland interniert, schreibt in seinem Augenzeugenbericht über das Gefängnis Ruhleben, dass das Verhältnis der Internierten 1916 im Verhältnis von 1:6,5 zugunsten der Deutschen lag.[3] Danach wurde auch der Austausch vollzogen, bei dem er aus dem Lager Ruhleben bei Berlin freigelassen wurde. In Großbritannien gab es 25.600[4] und in Deutschland demgegenüber 4.000 britische Internierte[5]. Mit der eigentlichen Kriegshandlung hatten die Internierten auf beiden Seiten nichts zu tun.

Isle of Man

Die Isle of Man, die sich in der Nordhälfte der Irischen See befindet, ist britisches Territorium, gehört jedoch nicht zum United Kingdom. Die Insel hat seit 979 das älteste Parlament der Welt mit dem keltischen Namen Tynwald mit einem gesetzgebenden Rat von zehn Mitgliedern und dem sogenannten House of Keys mit vierundzwanzig gewählten Vertretern. Obwohl im 13. Jahrhundert von Engländern und Schotten eingenommen, behielt die Insel ihre Selbständigkeit. Die Queen ist jedoch Lord of Man und wird vom Lieutenant Governor repräsentiert.[6]

Ungeachtet ihrer Eigenständigkeit hielten die Manx-Leute, wie sie sich selber bezeichnen, treu zur englischen Krone. Das Parlament verabschiedete nach Kriegsbeginn 1914, an „Act of the Imperial Parliament", der die Insel unter die geforderten Kriegsmaßnahmen stellte.[7] Bald hatte der Krieg auch die abgeschiedene Insel erreicht:

> The frequent interruption of the steamer communication with the Mainland in consequence of enemy submarine activity, the sound of guns at sea, the darkness of the streets as a result of the Extinction of Lights Order, the frequent landing in the Island of the crews of torpedoed vessels, and the recovery from the sea of bodies washed up around the coast, all helped to bring home to the residents of the Isle of Man the awfulness of the war.[8]

Die zahlreichen Begräbnisse von Seeleuten, Soldaten und Internierten taten ein übriges. Die Insel besaß auch eine strategische Bedeutung. Eine neue Funkstation diente als Ersatz für das Telefonkabel, damit in jedem Falle die Gefahr, die von Zeppelinen ausging, die das Festland bedrohten, weitergemeldet werden konnte.

Die Gefangenenlager auf der Isle of Man

Unter dem Befehl von Isle of Man-Chief Constable Lieutenant Colonel H. W. Madoc[9] übernahm die Regierung in London sofort ein Ferienlager in Douglas, der größten Stadt auf der Ostseite der Insel, baute es um und rüstete es entsprechend aus. Am 22. September 1914 kamen bereits die ersten zweihundert Gefangenen an.[10] Es folgten immer mehr, so dass am 19. November 1914 bereits 3.307 Österreicher and Deutsche hinter Stacheldraht lebten.[11] Genau an diesem Tag erschossen die Wachmannschaften fünf Gefangene, die – unzufrieden mit der Verpflegung und der Ausstattung – einen Aufstand angezettelt hatten.[12] Im Gegensatz zum Begriff „enemy aliens", der für Internierte im Zweiten Weltkrieg verwendet wurde, verwenden Autoren wie beispielsweise Margery West, die über den Ersten Weltkrieg in ihrer Publikation berichtet, durchgehend den Begriff „prisoner of war", also „Kriegsgefangener". Das führt zu Verwirrung, handelt es sich bei diesen Gefangenen doch ausschließlich um Zivilisten und nicht um Soldaten, für die ebenfalls die Bezeichnung „Kriegsgefangener" üblich ist. Im o. g. „Lager Douglas" wurden nach und nach die Zelte durch Hütten ersetzt. Nach seiner Fertigstellung waren darin etwa 2.600 Internierte[13] untergebracht. Ein überliefertes Foto aus diesem Lager zeigt eine belebte Geschäftsstraße. So gab es dort den „besten Frisör", einen Schneiderladen und ein Basar mit selbst hergestellten Nippsachen. Männer sind in gutsitzenden Anzügen und nicht in Häftlingskleidung abgebildet.[14] Eine einheitliche Lager-Kleidung gab es demnach offenbar nicht.

Da immer mehr „feindliche Ausländer" untergebracht werden mussten,[15] baute man ein weiteres Lager auf der Westküste in der Nähe von Peel in der Gemeinde von Patrick auf Knockaloe Moar, so der Name des Bauernhofes, zu dem das Land gehörte.[16] Danach erhielt dieses Lager seinen Namen. Für den Transport von Kohle und Verpflegung bauten die Internierten selbst eine zwei Meilen lange Eisenbahnstrecke vom Zentrum des „Knockaloe Camp" bis zum Hafen nach Peel.[17] Anfänglich für 5.000 Gefangene vorgesehen, waren dann nach mehreren Erweiterungen[18] rund 23.000 Gefangene in diesem Lager untergebracht.[19] Die internierten Zivilisten auf der Isle of Man – Deutsche, Österreicher und Türken – kamen aus verschiedenen Bereichen. Sie waren Hotelmanager, Küchenchefs berühmter Londoner Restaurants, Musiker,[20] Geschäftsleute, Friseure, Kellner, Seeleute und Vertreter vieler anderer Berufe.[21] Nach Angaben der Manx National Heritage Library waren insgesamt 25.600 Männer auf der Isle of Man interniert.[22]

Das riesige Lager „Knockaloe Camp" mit einem Umfang von drei Meilen[23] war folgendermaßen strukturiert: 1.000 Gefangene lebten auf einem von Stacheldraht umzäunten Compound[24] von etwa einhundert Quadratyards. Darauf befanden sich fünf Schlafhütten mit jeweils zweihundert Gefangenen, einer Küche, einem Unterhaltungsraum, einem Badehaus und Toiletten.[25] Das sind insgesamt 23 Compounds mit 1.000 Internierten.[26] Diese versorgten sich selbst. Nach den Erfahrungen der Briten mit Gefangenen Napoleons war Disziplin damit leichter zu erzielen und die Verteilung von Lebensmitteln auch einfacher.[27] Die Essensrationen wurden den Internierten direkt zugeteilt. So kochten die Männer ihre eigenen Gerichte und betrieben eine Kantine.[28] Das Brot hingegen wurde von einer zentralen Bäckerei geliefert. 1918, als Essen in England knapp wurde, strich die Lagerleitung den Internierten auch die Essenspakete.

Die Internierten nähten sich ihre Sachen selber und hatten deshalb eine Schneiderei gegründet.[29] Jedes der beiden großen Lager war mit Krankenhäusern und Isolierstationen ausgerüstet, da insbesondere zu Beginn

Geschlechtskrankheiten und Tbc grassierten.[30] Auf Sportplätzen spielten die Männer Fußball, Tennis und anderes.[31]

Das gesamte Lager auf der Isle of Man war in drei Kategorien eingeteilt: In die Bessergestellen, die Gewöhnlichen und die Juden. Als Bessergestellter musste ein Gefangener wöchentlich ein Pfund für die Einzelunterbringung bezahlen. Er bekam eine bessere Ausstattung, Essen und einen Diener aus dem Kreis der Gefangenen bzw. zwei Flaschen Bier oder eine Flasche Wein am Tag.[32] Für 500 Schillinge stand zwei oder drei Gefangenen ein Zelt oder eine Hütte allein zur Verfügung. Das „Jewish Camp", das auf 1.000 Insassen geschätzt wird,[33] erhielt koscheres Essen. Wie die Christen begingen auch die Juden ihre religiösen Feiertage.[34]

Alle drei Monate war ein Besuch erlaubt. Britischen und Frauen aus nicht feindlichen Ländern war es zudem gestattet, auf der Insel zu leben. Einmal in vierzehn Tagen durften sie in Anwesenheit eines Offiziers ihre Männer besuchen.[35]

2.500 Wachsoldaten, die außerhalb des Stacheldrahts lebten, bewachten die Gefangenen.[36] Manx-Zivilisten, z. B. Freiwillige bzw. auch nicht mehr zum Kriegsdienst geeignete Männer[37] versahen als „blue staff" ihren Dienst als Aufsicht im Lager. Immerhin wurden 345 Internierte wegen Fluchtversuchs vor Gericht gestellt und verurteilt.[38]

Das größte Problem für die Internierten war eine sinnvolle Beschäftigung bzw. auch die Möglichkeit, sich etwas Geld hinzuzuverdienen. Rechneten die „Zivilgefangenen", wie die Internierten sich auch nannten, zu Beginn noch damit, bald freigelassen zu werden, sah die Wirklichkeit jedoch anders aus. Dazu stellt in einer Lagerzeitung ein anonymer Autor fest:

> Nach fast dreijähriger Gefangenschaft sehen wir heute das Lagerleben ganz anders an, als wir es früher taten. Wir wissen heute, dass unsere Gefangenschaft kein k u r z e r Zwischenakt in unserem Leben ist, in dem wir die Zeit mit Skatspielen „totschlagen dürfen".[39]

Inzwischen hätten die meisten begriffen, dass das ein „Rückschritt" wäre und „mutig alle Arten von Arbeit neu begonnen und durchgeführt [...]. Die große Mehrheit arbeitet heute zielbewusst." Ende 1916 hatten bereits 85% der Gefangenen eine Anstellung gefunden. Etwa 150 von ihnen ersetzten die Bewacher, die nun zum Kriegsdienst eingezogen worden waren. Sie arbeiteten innerhalb der Lager auf der Post, als Lehrer und Bibliothekare. Mit den Jahren gab es einen reges Miteinander zwischen der Zivilbevölkerung und den Internierten: Die Internierung war so etwas wie eine eigenes Staatswesen auf der Insel, wovon auch die Inselbewohner profitierten. Sie bekamen Genehmigungen für neue Gewerke und Geschäfte mit Ausrüstungen für die Gefangenen.[40] Privatleuten war es gestattet, die zumeist arbeitswilligen Internierten für einen geringen Lohn zum Arbeiten heran zu ziehen. Die „Society of Friends", die Quäker, und das Internationale Rote Kreuz unterstützten die Internierten. Als Arbeitskräfte knapp wurden, stellten die Gefangenen sogar im Auftrag von englischen Firmen Artikel her oder arbeiteten in der in Verbindung mit dem Lager errichteten Bürstenfabrik. Sie verdingten sich bei Bauern, verbreiterten und vertieften den Fluss Sulby und stochen Torf in den Bergen.[41]

Über 1.000 Internierte besuchten Weiterbildungskurse mit Sprachen, Schreibmaschine und Kunst. Jeder Compound in Knockaloe besaß[42] sein eigenes Theater. Die Quellenlage anhand der Programmzettel und Lagerzeitschriften macht es hingegen schwer, das nachzuvollziehen.

Am 11. November 1918, als mit der Unterzeichnung des Waffenstillstandes der 1. Weltkrieg endete, befanden sich 24.450 Internierte im Knockaloe Camp. Nur sechzehn Prozent von ihnen durften weiter in Großbritannien leben. Alle anderen hatten in ihre Geburtsländer zurückzukehren. Die Anträge von Internierten, in Großbritannien zu bleiben, wurden von einem Regierungsgerichtshof, und erst nach nahezu einem Jahr, meist abschlägig beschieden. Obwohl einige Frauen von Internierten es ablehnten, England zu verlassen, wurde ihren Männern keine Ausnahmeregelung gewährt. Erst im Oktober 1919 verließen die letzten 175 Internierten das Lager.[43] Über zweihundert Gefangene, darunter elf Türken, waren in der Internierung gestorben und auf der Insel begraben worden. 1962 wurde ein deutscher „memorial cemetery" auf der Insel eingerichtet und nahezu sämtliche Gräber exhumiert.

Musikleben in den Lagern

In der Manx National Heritage Library in Douglas auf der Isle of Man sind einige Originalquellen erhalten, die Auskunft über das Musikleben geben. Es handelt sich dabei um Konzertprogramme, Lagerzeitschriften und einige Photographien. Ebenso heben die beiden von mir herangezogenen Publikationen ausdrücklich das lebendige Musikleben während der Internierung hervor: So schreibt B. E. Sargeaunt: „In the recreation huts were given most excellent concerts by orchestras composed entirely of prisoners, and high-class plays were not infrequently produced."[44] Und West denkt darüber nach, welchen Nutzen die Beschäftigung mit Musik hatte: „The prisoners made the best of being confined to camp. Concerts were an important feature of their life behind barbed wire. They were needed to keep up morale and were a necessary outlet for those alien prisoners with talent going to waste."[45]

Margery West verweist auf ein Konzert vom Oktober 1915, das auch der Lagerkommandant Colonel Madoc besucht habe. Ein Orchester von vierzig Musikern hatte dabei ein buntes Programm mit Orchestermusik, Rezitation, Tanz und dem „Porridge March", gesungen von einigen Gefangenen, dargeboten. Der Komponist des Marsches, Emil Gyoeri, leitete die Aufführung. Sie verweist darauf, dass es wahrscheinlich viele professionelle Musiker unter den Gefangenen gab. Am Theater von Compound No.1 habe ein Herr Sterbal[46] ein Orchester von vierzig Musikern betreut. Sterbal sei Mitglied des „Queen's Hall Orchesters"[47] und Dirigent der privaten Kapelle von Alfred Rothschild gewesen.[48] Außerdem habe er auch vor König Edward VII. gespielt.[49] In einer Konzertbesprechung äußert sich der Autor W. Baumfelder darüber, dass Sterbal ein Orchester aufgebaut habe, das ein gutes Konzert von zehn Nummern gab.[50]

Anhand von Musikkritiken, abgedruckt in den unvollzählig überlieferten Zeitschriften aus dem Camp Douglas und dem Knockaloe Camp[51], und durch überlieferte Programmzettel seit 1915[52] lässt sich das Musikleben bis zu einem gewissen Grade rekonstruieren. Danach ergibt sich folgendes Bild: Ein Konzert-Verein[53] organisiert Orchester- und Kammermusikkonzerte in den einzelnen „compounds". Die Orchester sind neben ihren Bezeichnungen an ihren Dirigenten zu unterscheiden. An erster Stelle muss hier Friedrich Gleitsmann-Wolf mit seinen kontinuierlichen Auftritten genannt werden. Im Januar 1917 begeht das Gleitsmann-Orchester sein einjähriges Bestehen. Als erste Komposition hatte Gleitsmann-Wolf Edward Elgars ersten Marsch aus „Pomp and Cicumstance" auf das Programm gesetzt. Das Konzert schließt mit dem „Krönungsmarsch" von Giacomo Meyerbeer. Offenbar lässt sich Gleitsmann-Wolf von der Freund-Feind-Situation wenig beeindrucken. Er spielt außerdem als Kammermusiker Violine und tritt als Hornist in Mozarts „Konzert für Horn und Orchester" in Es-Dur auf. Darüber hinaus instrumentierte er z. B. eine der beiden „Romanzen für Violine und Orchester" für die Beethoven-Feier zum 135. Geburtstag des Komponisten und hält dabei den Festvortrag. Außerdem leitet er ein Streichorchester.

Der bereits erwähnte Rudolph J. H. Sterbal taucht als Dirigent eines Orchesters auf, dass am 8. April 1917 zwei Jahre besteht. Dieses war aus einem Blasorchester hervorgegangen, das vorwiegend Marschmusik gespielt hatte. Dann seien Streicher hinzu gekommen und Rudolph J. H. Sterbal, der den Violinbogen mit dem Taktstock „vertauschte" und das Niveau des Ensembles angehoben hatte. Sterbal ist auch Dirigent des „Neuen Sinfonieorchesters". Am 17. Juni 1917 gab dieses Orchester ein Konzert im Knockaloe Camp Theater mit folgender Programmfolge:

Ludwig van Beethoven: Leonoren-Ouvertüre Nr. 3

Richard Wagner: „Liebestod" aus „Tristan und Isolde"

Felix Mendelssohn-Bartholdy: Schottische Sinfonie

Engelbert Humperdinck: Vorspiel zu „Hänsel und Gretel"

Peter Iljitsch Tschaikowsky: Suite „Casse-Noisette"

Franz Liszt: Ungarische Rhapsodie Nr. 1

Gioacchino Rossini: Ouvertüre zu „Wilhelm Tell"

Das 50. Sinfoniekonzert des Konzert-Vereins mit dem Lager-Chor dirigiert Alfred Mollwo, der auch als Liedbegleiter bei gemischten Programmen und Kammermusikkonzerten mitwirkt. Es gibt ein „Camporchester" mit dreißig Berufsmusikern, das ein Herr Döring leitet, ein Mandolinenorchester mit Herrn W. Lehmann, ein Wiener Salonorchester mit E. de Baneleur[54] und ein Sinfonie-Orchester des Lagers IV, dem ein Herr Winter vorsteht. Ein Th. Weinlich dirigiert z. B. am 27. April 1917 das dritte „Populäre Konzert" und tritt als Violin-Solist beim Pfingstkonzert des Lager-Chors auf. In Teillager 5 hat das Salonorchester von Hans Scheuffler[55] seinen Auftritt. Am Dirigentenpult stehen Herr Lauer oder A. Fleischmann. Eine Fotographie[56] zeigt ein Kammerorchester ohne Dirigenten, bestehend aus sieben Streichern und sieben Bläsern, das als „Knockaloe Camp Orchestra" (1915) bezeichnet wird. Das bedeutet, dass auch kleinere Besetzungen wie diese als „Orchester" bezeichnet werden. Heute, neunzig Jahre später, würde man ein solches Ensemble anders benennen.[57]

Verallgemeinernd lässt sich feststellen, dass die Orchesterkonzerte einen eindeutig unterhaltenden Charakter besitzen. Es werden bekannte Stücke wie Ouvertüren, Tänze, Märsche, Potpourris oder Marsch-Potpourris ausgewählt. Bei den meisten Konzerten dieser Art steht am Schluss des Programms ein Marsch als Zeichen des Patriotismus und der Verbundenheit mit der Heimat. Es finden sich „Unter dem Friedensbanner" von dem Lagerinsassen Karl Heber, „Festmarsch" von Helm, „Austria Marsch" von (wahrscheinlich Johann) Novotny, der Marsch „Alte Kameraden" und anderes mehr. Aber es gibt auch Ausnahmen, wie das zweijährige Jubiläumskonzert am 8. April 1917 mit Rudolph J. H. Sterbal, bei dem er als letztes Stück „Finlandia" von Jean Sibelius auf das Programm setzt. (Das wiederum verweist auf die politische Situation, denn Finnland erlangte 1917 seine Unabhängigkeit vom Kriegsgegner Russland.)[58]

Noch 1917 hatte der hier als Mottl-Schüler bezeichnete H. Winter aus München, früherer Dirigent der ‚Moody Manners Opera Company' in

England, ein Orchester mit 48 Mitgliedern, bestehend aus Berufsmusikern und Dilettanten, ins Leben gerufen. Sein Programm wiederholte er acht Mal in der ersten und zweiten Dezemberwoche 1917 in verschiedenen Teillagern.[59] Das deutet darauf hin, dass auch andere Orchesterbesetzungen in mehreren „Compounds" des großen Lagers Wiederholungskonzerte geben. Diese Konzerte standen offenbar allen Internierten offen. Es gab aber auch Konzerte, die demgegenüber einem bestimmten Kreis vorbehalten waren.

Chöre

Im Oktober 1916 beteiligten sich drei große Gesangsvereine mit dreihundert Sängern am Sängerfest im Knockaloe-Lager an einem Sängerwettstreit. Von Compound eins und sechs „Germania" unter Leitung von Herrn Haake, von Compound vier „Liederkranz" mit Herrn Schwenger und von Compound drei und fünf „Saxonia", geleitet von Herrn Wolf. Auch vereint als Massenchor traten die Chöre bei dieser Gelegenheit mit und ohne Orchester auf. Ein Festausschuss war eigens ins Leben gerufen worden, um das Ereignis, das den ganzen Tag andauerte, vorzubereiten. Der Männerchor „Sängerlust" oder der aus vierzig Sängern bestehende Gesangsverein „Harmonie", der 1917 zwei Jahre existiert, bietet auch Programme mit Salon-Orchester an. Alfred Mollwo leitet den „Lagerchor Isle of Man" und den „Douglas Lager Chor". Für ein Gesangs-Doppelquartett fühlt sich W. Goldberg zuständig. Der offenbar aus Ungarn stammende Geiger A. Csavojatz, ist Konzertmeister in einem Orchester, das Alfred Mollwo[60] anlässlich der 50. Veranstaltung des Konzert-Vereins zusammen mit dem Lager-Chor am 22. September 1918 leitet. Der Geiger verabschiedet sich in einem Solistenkonzert u.a. mit Kompositionen von Sarasate und Paganini Ende November 1918 aus dem Lager.

Österreicher und Ungarn veranstalten eigene Unterhaltungsabende. So wird eine ungarische Ansprache von u. a. ungarischer Zigeunermusik und ungarischen Volksliedern (instrumentiert von Emil Gyoeri) umrahmt. Beging man im August 1915 noch den 85. Geburtstag von Kaiser Franz Josef I. mit Feldgottesdienst und allgemeiner Feier mit Männerchören und Marschmusik, gedachten Österreicher und Ungarn dann im November 1916 des verstorbenen Kaisers und Königs in einer gemeinsamen Gedächtnisfeier. Lagerchor und Gleitsmann-Orchester sorgten für den feierlichen Rahmen. Am Ende der Feier stand selbstverständlich der Orchester-Marsch „Hoch Habsburg". Auch die Deutschen, ihrem Kaiser verbunden, veranstalteten gar ein Festessen zum Geburtstag Wilhelm II. mit Königs-Suppe, Sauerbraten, Kaiser Wilhem-Pudding und Kaffee sowie Kuchen. Zur 30. Wiederkehr der Thronbesteigung Wilhelm II. gab das Salon-Orchester Scheuffler am 16.

August 1918 ein Konzert, dem Märsche die entsprechende Ausrichtung gaben.[61]

Ensembles

Es existierten ein verstärktes Theaterorchester, eine ungarische Kapelle, die Orchester O. Lauer[62], Orchester Leopold[63], Orchester Hutmacher[64] und das Orchester Scheuffler.[65] Kammermusikbesetzungen sind ebenfalls reichlich vertreten: mit Streichquartett, Klavier vierhändig, Klaviertrio, Klavier und Violine, Klavier und Gesang bzw. Solisten (Klavier, Violine) und anderes mehr. Es gibt Hinweise darauf, dass Kammermusikkonzerte auch Kompositionen für Violine und Klavier von Bach, Beethoven, Schumann, Chopin, Dvořák, Wagner-Liszt (1. 7. 1917) enthalten. Bei sogenannten „populären Konzerten" stehen jedoch vorwiegend Operettenmelodien auf dem Programm. Auftrittsorte werden mit „großer Saal" oder z. B. Knockaloe Camp-Theater, Camp 1, Compound II bezeichnet. Unterhaltungskapellen schien es ebenfalls in größerer Anzahl gegeben zu haben.[66] Damit sind beispielweise ein Schrammel-Terzett, eine aus fünf Mitgliedern bestehende Schrammelkapelle, Zigeunermusik-Ensembles oder die Virtuosenkapelle von Herrn Hopf[67] gemeint. Zum Tanz spielt die 1914 im Lager gegründete Seemannskapelle, die aus Flöte, Handharmonika und Konzerthandharmonika sowie Tingeltangel[68] und Tamburin besteht.[69]

In der *Knockaloe-Lagerzeitung* von 1917 findet sich eine Würdigung der Kapelle Schubert-Banholzer, die ahnen lässt, welches Pensum die einzelnen Ensembles im Lager so bewältigten: Dieses Ensemble besteht aus acht Musikern, Dilettanten und Berufsmusikern. Ihr Leiter ist Josef Banholzer, der auch als Solo-Cellist genannt wird. Theo Schubert ist erster Konzertmeister und Herr Leimer Konzertpianist. Von November 1915 bis zum Januar 1917 gab die Kapelle folgende Aufführungen: 36 Abonnements- und andere Konzerte, 27 kombinierte Konzerte mit den Kapellen Kruse und Heber sowie verschiedenen Sängervereinen. Das Ensemble spielte bei acht Feiern z. B. wie Kaisers Geburtstag, an sieben Unterhaltungsabenden, bei 16 Hüttenkonzerten, war bei 88 Theateraufführungen für die Zwischenaktmusiken engagiert, wirkte mit bei 19 Kammermusikveranstaltungen, gestaltete sechs Freikonzerte populärer Natur und spielte vier Mal bei Tanzmusikabenden auf. Darüber hinaus „versucht die Kapelle, Trios, Quartette und sinfonische Werke unserer Tondichter in das Programm zu nehmen, um das Niveau anzuheben".[70] Das sind insgesamt 211 Auftritte in einem Jahr. Allein dieses Beispiel lässt erahnen, welch großen Stellenwert die Musik in den beiden Lagern auf der Isle of Man einnahm.

Konzerte waren einem bestimmten Komponisten wie beispielweise Richard Wagner am 22. Mai 1916 mit dem Orchester des Knockaloe Camp-Theater, geleitet von Rudolph J. H. Sterbal gewidmet. Ausnahmsweise sind aus diesem Anlass sämtliche Instrumentalisten des Orchesters namentlich genannt. Demnach bestand dieses Orchester aus vierzig Musikern. Herr Lewinson, als Heldentenor des Danziger Stadttheaters angekündigt, übernahm den Vokalpart in einem Programm, das vor allem Wagner-Opern vorbehalten war.[71] Zur o. g. Beethoven-Würdigung 1915 sitzen in dem ebenfalls aus vierzig Musikern bestehenden Orchester, das Gleitsmann-Wolf leitet, wiederum ganz andere Musiker. D. h., es gab so viele Musiker im Lager, dass mehrere große Orchester unabhängig voneinander bestehen konnten, ohne dass die Musiker sich gegenseitig vertreten müssen. Dem Kreislauf des Jahres entsprechend boten die Musiker Weihnachtskonzerte, Osterkonzerte, Pfingstkonzerte oder Wohltätigkeitskonzerte, Operettenabende und anderes mehr an. Es gibt auch kurzfristige Besetzungen wie eine Silvesterkapelle, die ein Herr Heber betreute.

Religiöse Feiern mit Musik

Die Christen feierten an Sonntagen deutsch-katholische, deutsch-evangelische und englische Gottesdienste. Etwa alle drei Monate reisten regelmäßig Pfarrer Oskar Goehling oder Pastor A. Scholten eigens aus London an, um vor den Internierten Ansprachen zu halten. Diese wurden von einem festlichen Konzertprogramm umrahmt und haben eher weniger mit einem typischen Gottesdienst-Ritual zu tun. Es scheint, als ob für die gewöhnlichen Gottesdienste keine Programmzettel ausgegeben würden. Möglicherweise gab es ja Gesangbücher, von denen jedoch keines überliefert ist. Die bekannte Abfolge eines christlichen Gottesdienstes erforderte mit großer Gewissheit keinen eigens dafür geschriebenen Programmzettel.

Die Juden bereiteten sich am Freitag Abend um 7.15 Uhr mit einer Feier auf den Sabbat vor. Am Samstag um 10.30 a.m. und 4 p.m. zelebrierten sie ihre Gottesdienste.[72] Die jährlichen Chanukka-Feiern gestaltete die jüdische Gemeinde im Lager ebenfalls mit der Beteiligung von Chor, Solisten und Orchester.[73] Das Programm zu Chanukka am 12. Dezember 1916 enthält achtzehn einzelne Programmpunkte: Von der Weihe der Chanukka-Lichter über Beiträge mit dem Wiener Salonorchester[74], mit Gesangsvorträgen und Rezitationen und bis hin zum abschließenden „Yigdol Marsch". Nach der Quellenlage zu urteilen, konnten mit großer Wahrscheinlichkeit gleichberechtigt nebeneinander Juden und Christen ihre Religionen ausüben. Inwieweit das den relativ wenigen türkischen[75] Internierten zugestanden wurde, ist aus den Quellen nicht ersichtlich.

Theater mit Musik / Musik-Theater

Aus Theaterprogrammzetteln lässt sich rekonstruieren, dass unterschiedliche Ensembles für Zwischenaktmusiken bei klassischen Theaterstücken zur Verfügung standen. Eine besonderes Gewicht hatte dabei offenbar das Deutsche Theater Douglas und das Knockaloe Camp Theater, aber es existierte daneben auch ein Flora-Theater und das Neue Camp Theater.[76] Bühnendekorationen werden im eigenen Atelier des Deutschen Theaters nach Entwürfen von Prof. G. A. Bredow und M. Heckelmann angefertigt. Die Theatermusiken, etwa bei Schnitzlers Schauspiel „Liebelei", bestanden aus kurzen, bekannten Beiträgen. Da es eine Vielzahl von Inszenierungen gab, würde es den Rahmen dieses Artikels sprengen, darauf im einzelnen einzugehen.

Schwänke, Possen, Tragikomödien, Singspiele und Varieté-Vorstellungen bietet das Musik-Theater an. Männer spielten darin die Frauenrollen. So stand Emil Gyoeri in der 150. Vorstellung „Als ich wiederkam" von Oskar Blumenthal und Gustav Kadelburg als Josepha, die Gastwirtsfrau, auf der Bühne. Opern waren hingegen ohne Frauenstimmen unaufführbar. Es findet sich kein Hinweis darüber.

Die „Grosse Lager-Revue in zwei Aufzügen" wurde zum Jahreswechsel 1916/17 im Deutschen Theater Douglas bereits zum 38. Mal gegeben. Die Texte stammen von H. Stettenheimer, J. M. Kadisch, W. Schmieder und H. C. Altmann. Die Musik komponierte Emil Gyoeri. An der Revue wirkten Solisten, Tänzer, Chor und Orchester mit. Friedrich Gleitsmann-Wolf dirigiert die Vorstellungen am Deutschen Theater und besorgte die Instrumentierung. Typisch für Revuen unter Lagerbedingungen[77] erfolgt auch hier die Karikierung des ungewöhnlichen Tagesablaufs, den Interpreten und Publikum miteinander teilen. Der zweite Teil antizipierte die letzte Nacht im Lager mit Akrobaten, Tanz und Pärchen-Walzer sowie einem Schlusschor. Der Kritiker findet das Libretto „eher mittelmäßig", denn es setzte sich „aus mehr oder minder verständlichen, eintönigen oder zweideutigen Anzüglichkeiten zusammen." Und „die darin karikierten Campinsassen" hätten „gute Miene zum bösen Spiel" gemacht. Trotzdem habe sich das Publikum amüsiert.[78] Der „Porridge Marsch" aus der Revue scheint schon lange ein Schlager im Lager gewesen zu sein. Gyoeri hatte diesen bereits zum gemischten Silvesterprogramm von 1915 am Klavier gespielt.

Lagerchor und Lagerkapelle wirkten auch bei einem Turnfest mit, das im Deutschen Theater stattfand. Turnerische Darbietungen, Musik und Marmorgruppen, gestellt von Prof. G. A. Bredow, stehen auf dem Programm.

Instrumente, Noten und Orchestermaterial

Instrumente waren im Lager vorhanden, wie die überlieferten Programmzettel und Photographien belegen. Da Angehörige der Internierten Zugang zum Lager hatten und auch Paketsendungen erlaubt waren, scheint diese Frage offenbar keine größeren Probleme bereitet zu haben. Die Lagerleitung, interessiert an einem disziplinierten und konfliktfreien Lagerleben, stellte sich offenbar nicht dagegen. Noten und Orchestermaterial stellten hingegen ein besonderes Problem dar. Dazu findet sich eine Bemerkung. Danach werden Noten für das Gleitsmann-Orchester den Musikern nur für kurze Zeit von einem Dr. Markel überlassen. Die einzelnen Stimmen daraus müssen von den Instrumentalisten selbst kopiert werden. Offenbar war Markel in der Lage, diese Marktlücke zu füllen und etablierte einen Verleih für Noten, aus dem sich wiederum die Musiker ihr eigenes Orchestermaterial herstellen mussten. Sind von Kompositionen nur Klavierauszüge vorhanden, so besorgt Gleitsmann die Orchestrierung. Wie wichtig die Beschaffung von Noten jedoch ist, lässt sich durch die namentliche Erwähnung von Notenstiftern auf Programmzetteln schlussfolgern.

Zusammenfassend: Die Situation, die sich während des 1. Weltkrieges auf der Isle of Man bot, ist unter musikgeschichtlichem Aspekt einmalig. Nahezu 26.000 Männer unterschiedlicher Religionen leben auf engem Raum zusammen. Sie sind Gefangene, aber ihnen ist erlaubt, sich weiterzubilden, Sport zu treiben, Theater zu spielen, im Chor zu singen bzw. Musik in jeder Form zu machen. Musik hatte verschiedene Funktionen inne: Sie bot den Rahmen für Veranstaltungen aller Art, vom Turnfest über Unterhaltungsabende bis hin zu Gottesdiensten. Ein Konzert-Verein organisierte die Konzerte mit sogenannter U- und E-Musik. Musik diente als verbindendes Element zwischen den aus verschiedenen Zusammenhängen in Großbritannien gerissenen Zivilisten. Mit patriotischen Gesängen, bei Aufführungen von Volksliedern, von Hymnen oder Märschen fanden sich Angehörige verschiedener Nationen zusammen, um ihre eigenen Festtage zu begehen und ihre Solidarität der Heimat gegenüber ungehört und hilflos zu bezeugen.[79] In ihren Heimatländern genossen die Internierten ein schlechtes Ansehen, da sie aus dem Blickwinkel von Kriegsteilnehmern heraus sich keiner wirklichen Gefahr ausgesetzt sahen.[80]

Ursprünglich lebten die meisten Internierten bis zum Kriegsbeginn in Großbritannien, um dort einer Beschäftigung nachzugehen. Die von Internierten bezeugte Absicht, nach Kriegsende weiter in Großbritannien zu bleiben, spricht für deren Offenheit gegenüber den Briten. Mit Sicherheit gab es hier unterschiedliche Auffassungen unter den Internierten. Für die Feindschaft gegenüber den Briten spricht ein überlieferter mehrstrophiger

„Hassgesang an England"[81] von Ernst Lissauer[82], in dessen letzter Strophe es heißt:

> Dich werden wir hassen mit langem Hass
> Wir werden nicht lassen von unserem Hass
> Hass zu Wasser und Hass zu Land
> Hass des Hauptes und Hass der Hand
> Hass der Hämmer und Hass der Kronen
> Drosselnder Hass von siebzig Millionen.
> Sie lieben vereint, sie hassen vereint
> Sie haben alle nur einen Feind:
> E n g l a n d.

Ob dieser Text auch vertont worden war[83] und im Lager gesungen wurde, lässt sich nicht belegen. Dagegen steht möglicherweise der eingangs erwähnte Umgang von Bevölkerung und Internierten, der sich auf einem zivilisierten Niveau bewegte. Die Lagerleitung unterstützte die Internierten z. B. beim Druck eigener Zeitschriften und überließ ihnen die Organisation des Lagerlebens, in dem sie ungehindert ihre Religion und Kultur pflegen konnten. Chöre, Orchester, Musikensembles und Tanzkapellen traten an verschiedenen Orten innerhalb des Lagers auf. Das musikalische Angebot besaß – von Ausnahmen abgesehen – weitgehend unterhaltenden Charakter.

Die Lagerinsassen waren bis auf Briefe, Pakete und Besuche von Verwandten von der Außenwelt abgeschlossen. Die Bewohner der Insel einschließlich der Wachmannschaften bedeuteten weitgehend den einzigen Kontakt für die Männer. Das Radio war noch nicht erfunden.[84] Schallplatten standen den Internierten mit großer Wahrscheinlichkeit nicht zur Verfügung. Von neuen Kompositionen, die inzwischen auf dem Kontinent entstanden sind, waren professionelle Musiker im Lager relativ unberührt. Kein solches Werk findet sich auf einem überlieferten Programmzettel. Die freie Zeit nutzten mit großer Wahrscheinlichkeit die professionellen und Amateurmusiker, um auf ihrem Instrument zu üben und zu musizieren.

Die Situation auf der Isle of Man belegt einen relativ hohen Anteil an Musikdilettanten aus den beiden Kaiserreichen, wie er nach der Erfindung des Radios und der weiteren Verbreitung der Schallplatte[85] sowie des Tonfilms wohl nie wieder anzutreffen sein wird. Unter diesem Aspekt ist die Internierung von fast 26.000 Männern eine einmaliger Fall in der Geschichte, der relativ unbemerkt bis heute geblieben ist. Bisher ist mir noch keine Biographie eines Musikers, der auf der Isle of Man interniert war, und möglicherweise anschließend eine bedeutende Karriere gemacht hätte, bekannt geworden. Auch die Sängerin Elena Gerhardt, die vor dem Ersten Weltkrieg relativ häufig in Großbritannien gastierte und viele Musiker kannte, erwähnt in ihren Memoiren zwar den Dirigenten Karl Muck als

Internierten in den USA, verliert aber kein Wort über die Isle of Man.[86] Eine detaillierte Auswertung der hier betrachteten Konzertprogramme unter dieser ungewöhnlichen Situation steht noch aus.

Internment Camp Magazines Douglas and Knockaloe Camps (Library Ref B115/3f.):

Camp Echo (Douglas) Nos 1-7, Dec 1914 – Jan 1916.

Das Schleierlicht (Douglas) Nos 1-4, May 1916 – July 1916.

Die Lager Laterne (Douglas) Nos 1-14, May 1916 – Mar 1917.

Unter Uns (Douglas) Nos 1-10 incomplete, June – Dec 1917.

Lager Echo (Knockaloe) Nos 1-11, Nov 1916 – Nov 1917.

Nos 1-7, Jan 1918 – Oct 1918.

Lager Zeitung (Knockaloe) Nos 1-19, Oct 1916 – Sep 1918.

Lager Ulk (Knockaloe) Nos 1-3, Sept – Nov 1917.

Werden (Knockaloe) No 1, Autumn 1915.

Quousque Tandem (Knockaloe) Oct – Nov 1915.

„D. H." Zivilgefangenen-Halbmonatsschrift. 15. Mai 1917. Knockaloe-Camp I. Herausgegeben von R. M. Conrad Kirchner; Schriftleitung: L. Freiherr von Reitzenstein. P./W. 4834. Druck und Verlag. R. M. Conrad Kirchner, P./W.957, beide z. Zt. in Knockaloe-Aliens Camp I, I. O. M.

„D. H." Zivilgefangenen-Halbmonatsschrift. 1. Juni 1917. Knockaloe-Camp I. Herausgegeben von R. M. Conrad Kirchner; Schriftleitung: L. Freiherr von Reitzenstein. P./W. 4834. Druck und Verlag. R. M. Conrad Kirchner, P./W.957, beide z. Zt. in Knockaloe-Aliens Camp I, I. O. M.

Notes

[1] Jonathan F. Vance, *Encyclopedia of Prisoners of War*, Santa Barbara u.a., 2000 (Stichwort „Civilian Internees").

[2] E-mail vom 17. Juni 2004 an die Autorin von Matthew Richardson, Curator Social History; Manx National Heritage Library; Isle of Man.

[3] Israel Cohen, *The Ruhleben Prison Camp: A Record of Nineteen Months' Internment by Israel Cohen* (London: Methuen 1917), S. 40.

[4] Diese Anzahl bezieht sich auf Internierte aus den beiden Kaiserreichen und der Türkei, die zu den Kriegsgegnern von Großbritannien gehörten. Wie viele Deutsche es genau waren, geht aus den ausgewerteten Quellen nicht hervor.

[5] Cohen, *Ruhleben*, S. 221.

[6] Margery West, *Island at War: The remarkable role played by the small Manx nation in the Great War 1914-18* (Laxey, Isle of Man: Western Books, 1986), o. S.

[7] B. E. Sargeaunt, *The Isle of Man and the Great War* (Douglas, Isle of Man: Brown & Sons, 1920), S. 11.

[8] Ebenda, S. 9.

[9] West, *Island at War*, S. 81.

[10] Sargeaunt, *Great War*, S. 62.

[11] Ebenda, S. 83.

[12] Ebenda, S. 65.

[13] Nach Matthew Richardson a. a. O.

[14] West, *Island at War*, S. 88.

[15] Nach dem Untergang des von deutschen Torpedos beschossenen Passagierschiffes *Lusitania* in der Irischen See nahmen die ausländerfeindlichen Gefühle in GB zu.

[16] West, *Island at War*, S. 92 und Sargeaunt, *Great War*, S. 65f.

[17] Sargeaunt, *Great War*, S. 65f.

[18] Ebenda, S. 67.

[19] Unterschiedliche Quellen geben unterschiedliche Zahlen über die Insassen an. Matthew Richardson verweist auf eine Anzahl von 23.000 Internierten in diesem Lager; E-mail vom 17.6.2004 an die Autorin.

[20] „The National Orchestral Association, a body of over 2.000 members, has decided to expel all German and Austrian members without exception." In: *The Musical Times*, October 1, 1914 (Volume 55), S. 629.

[21] Sargeaunt, *Great War*, S. 79.

[22] Matthew Richardson, a. a. O.

[23] Sargeaunt, *Great War*, S. 74.

[24] Der Begriff „compound" wird hier verwendet, weil er in dieser Gestalt auf deutschen Programmzetteln des Lagers erscheint. Die Gefangenen benutzten demnach „Camp" als Oberbegriff und „Compound" als Unterbegriff nach dem Gebrauch der Wachmannschaften.

[25] Sargeaunt, *Great War*, S. 78.

[26] Ebenda, S. 69.

[27] Ebenda, S. 58.

[28] Ebenda, S. 72.

[29] Ebenda, S. 74.

[30] Ebenda, S. 80.

[31] West, *Island at War*, S. 97.

[32] Ebenda, S. 87.

[33] Matthew Richardson, a. a. O.

[34] Sargeaunt, *Great War*, S. 64.

[35] West, *Island at War*, S. 91.

[36] Sargeaunt (S. 77) gibt hier eine andere Zahl an als die, die das Archiv, s. o., benennt.

[37] West, *Island at War*, Introduction, o. S.

[38] Sargeaunt, *Great War*, S. 61.

[39] Anonym, Halbmonatsschrift D. H. vom 15. Mai 1917 Nr. 1, Knockaloe-Camp 1, S. 1.

[40] Sargeaunt, *Great War*, S. 8.

[41] Ebenda, S. 81ff.

[42] Vgl. West, *Island at War*, S. 98f.

[43] Ebenda, S. 104.

[44] Sargeaunt, *Great War*, S. 79.

[45] West, *Island at War*, S. 88.

[46] Die Vornamen von Musikern, Schaupielern, Dirigenten, Regisseuren, Bühnenbildnern, Textern und Komponisten werden nur selten auf Programmzetteln und in Musikkritiken von Lagerzeitungen genannt. Auf „Herr" folgte meist der Nachname. Ausnahmen bestätigen die Regel.

[47] Queen's Hall (1893-1941), eine der schönsten Konzerthallen Londons und langjähriger Auftrittsort des London Philharmonic Orchestra. Im Zweiten Weltkrieg fiel diese einem Bombenangriff der Deutschen Luftwaffe zum Opfer.

[48] Alfred Charles Rothschild (1842-1918), Kunstsammler und Musikliebhaber, residierte in Halton nahe Wendover, und in London, Seymour Place. Über die Auswahl seiner Musiker äußert sich Derek Wilson: „Frequently his dinner parties were serenaded by Alfred's personal orchestra, whose members were chosen as much for uniform height as for musical ability." Derek Wilson, *Rothschild: A Story of Wealth and Power* (London: André Deutsch, 1988), S. 259.

[49] West, *Island at War*, S. 98f.

[50] W. Baumfelder, „Musik im Lager", in: „D. H." Zivilgefangenen-Halbmonatsschrift vom 1. Juni 1917, S. 6.

[51] Vgl. Internment Camp Magazines Douglas and Knockaloe Camps; Library Ref B 115/3f; in: Manx National Heritage. Internment during World Wars 1 & 2; Select Bibliography; No. 1 (September 2003), S. 2.

[52] Diese Dokumente tragen folgende Bezeichnungen: Internment Camps 1914-1917; Library Ref B115/2 und Internment Camps; Library Ref B115/1.

[53] Auf einem der Programmzettel taucht z. B. die Bezeichnung auf: Konzert-Verein: Abteilung Grosses Orchester.

[54] Eugen de Baneleur ist gleichzeitig Konzertmeister im Orchester von Gleitsmann-Wolf anlässlich der Beethoven-Ehrung von 1915.

[55] Scheufler übernimmt auch die Leitung des Theater-Orchesters vom Teillager 1. Vgl. *Lager-Echo* Nr. 4/1918, S. 4.

[56] File Prisoners of War – Knockaloe Camps – Exterior; ausdrücklich wird auf der Rückseite der Fotographie der aus Anklam stammende Emil R. A. Priegnitz mit French Horn, der 1903 nach Großbritannien kam und 1914 interniert wurde, erwähnt.

[57] Vgl. dazu Stichwort Orchester, IV. Besetzungen, In: *Die Musik in Geschichte und Gegenwart: Allgemeine Enzyklopädie der Musik begründet von Friedrich Blume.* Zweite, neubearbeitete Ausgabe herausgegeben von Ludwig Finscher. 26 Bde. in zwei Teilen (Kassel, Basel, London, New York, Prag, Stuttgart und Weimar: Bärenreiter u.a. 1994-2005, Sachteil Bd. 7).

[58] Vgl. dazu die Internetseite: www.virtual.finland.fi.

[59] Vgl. *Lager-Zeitung* (Knockaloe) Nr. 16 (1918), S. 4.

[60] Wahrscheinlich sein Bruder C. Mollwo, der oft als Cellist aufgeführt wird.

[61] Vgl. *Lager-Echo* (Knockaloe) Nr. 6 (1918), S. 4.

[62] Knockaloe Teillager 3, 24 Mitglieder, gegründet im August 1915, vgl. *Lager-Echo* (Knockaloe) Nr. 1 (1916), S. 6.

[63] Knockaloe Teillager 1, 25 Mitglieder, gegründet im August 1915, ebenda.

[64] Knockaloe Teillager 2, 22 Mitglieder, gegründet im August 1915, ebenda.

[65] Knockaloe Teillager 5, 16 Mitglieder, gegründet im Dezember 1915, ebenda.

[66] *Die Lagerlaterne* (Douglas), Weihnachten 1916, S. 21f.

[67] Von dem Wiener Johann Schrammel (1850-1893) geprägte kleine Besetzung der Unterhaltungsmusik mit 2 Violinen, Gitarre, Klarinette bzw. chromatische Harmonika. Vgl. Horst Seeger, *Musiklexikon in zwei Bänden* (Leipzig: VEB Deutscher Verlag für Musik, 1966, Bd. 2; Stichwort Schrammel). Vgl. *Die Lagerlaterne* (Douglas), Nr. 1 (1916), S. 3.

[68] Um welches Instrument es sich dabei handelt, kann nicht nachvollzogen werden.

[69] *Unter uns* (Douglas) [Lagerzeitschrift], 9.9.1917, S. 6.

[70] *Lager-Zeitung* (Knockaloe) Nr. 6 (1917), S. 3.

[71] *Die Lagerlaterne* (Douglas) Nr. 3 (1916), S. 4.

[72] *Die Lagerlaterne* (Douglas) Nr. 1 (1916), S. 7.

[73] Siehe das Programm vom 3. Dezember 1918.

[74] Dieses Orchester bekommt in der Lagerzeitung *Die Lagerlaterne* (Douglas) Nr. 10 (1917), S. 3 ausdrücklich eine gute Kritik, weil das Publikum oft Wiederholungen einforderte.

[75] Treaty of Alliance between Germany and Turkey at 2nd of August 1914. Vgl. die Internetseite www.yale.edu/laweb/avalon/20th.htm.

[76] Musikalischer Direktor: O. Lauer; Direktor: A. Gebbing.

[77] Revuen wurden sowohl im Lager Ruhleben bei Berlin, in dem Briten während des 1. Weltkrieges interniert waren, als auch während der Internierung von „enemy aliens" auf der Isle of Man 1940/41 aufgeführt. Vgl. dazu Cohen, *Ruhleben*, S. 87 und Fox-Gál, Eva (Hg.) *Musik hinter Stacheldraht: Tagebuchblätter aus dem Sommer 1940 von Hans Gál. Mit Beiträgen von Eva Fox-Gál und Richard Dove* (Bern und Oxford: Peter Lang, 2003).

[78] Vgl. *Die Lagerlaterne* (Douglas) Nr. 5 (1916), S. 4.

[79] M. Richardson bemerkt dazu a. a. O., dass die Internierten, von ihren Landsleuten in der Heimat als minderwertig angesehen, im Lager Verdienst-Medaillen prägten und diese sich selbst verliehen.

[80] Nach Auskunft von Matthew Richardson, a. a. O.

[81] Ernst Lissauer, *Worte in die Zeit: Flugblätter 1914 von Ernst Lissauer* (Göttingen und Berlin, 1914), o. S.

[82] Der deutsch-jüdische Lyriker und Dramatiker Ernst Lissauer (1882-1937) verfasste das Kriegsgedicht zu Beginn des Ersten Weltkrieges. Lissauer erlangte damit eine tragische Berühmtheit, welche die Rezeption seines vielseitigen späteren Werkes überlagerte. Den Ursachen dazu geht Rainer Brändle in seiner Studie zu Werk und Person Lissauers nach. Vgl. Rainer Brändle, *Am wilden Zeitenpaß: Motive und Themen im Werk des deutsch-jüdischen Dichters Ernst Lissauer* (Frankfurt u. a.: Peter Lang 2002).

[83] In der British Library findet sich kein Beleg über eine gedruckte Fassung (Integrated catalogue, printed music).

[84] Die BBC strahlte ihre erste Sendung am 14. November 1922 aus, vgl. *The New Grove Dictionary of Music and Musicians*, ed. by Stanley Sadie, in twenty volumes (London, Washington und Hong Kong: Macmillan Publishers a. o., Bd. 3) (Stichwort BBC).

[85] Der Schallplattenumsatz lag in Deutschland 1906 bei 1,5 Millionen Stück, 1930 dann bei 30 Mill. Vgl. *Riemann Musik Lexikon*, Sachteil (Mainz: Schott's und Söhne, 1967), (Stichwort „Schallplatte").

[86] Vgl. Elena Gerhardt, *Recital* (London: Methuen, 1953).

Stefan Manz

Civilian Internment in Scotland during the First World War

The article is a regional case study of civilian internment during the First World War. After a brief look at the German migrant community in Scotland prior to the war it explores the mechanics of internment and conditions in the central Scottish internment camp, Stobs near Hawick. In order to avoid the depressive 'barbed wire disease', internees pursued a diverse range of cultural and professional activities. Patterns of repatriation and internal displacement are scrutinized through the example of Fifeshire. These government measures were both a reaction to and a driving-force behind widespread Germanophobia in Scottish society. In this respect, Scotland was representative of Britain as a whole.

The Aliens Restriction Act of 5 August 1914 gave British wartime governments legislative power to deal with 'enemy aliens' as they saw fit in order to protect the home front. Henceforth, the movement of Germans and Austrians who happened to be living or staying in Britain after the outbreak of war was tightly controlled. Two migrants living in Scotland, Friedrich Bernhard Wiegand and Fritz A. Schreiber, are cases in point. Wiegand was born in Naunhof/Saxony in 1878, apprenticed to a wigmaker as a fourteen-year-old and migrated to Glasgow in 1899. He set up shop as a ladies' hairdresser and soon married into a local family. In May 1915, while his wife Rebecca was expecting her third child, he was interned as an 'enemy alien' in Knockaloe internment camp on the Isle of Man. Without the income of the breadwinner, his family was able to escape poverty only through the support of relatives. Wiegand finally returned to his family in November 1918 and managed to rebuild his hairdressing business.[1] Others were less lucky. Lager brewer Fritz A. Schreiber, for example, resigned from his position as Managing Director of the Tennents Brewery in Glasgow in 1916. The Board let him know that

> both internally and externally there has been evinced so very strong a feeling against the re-imposition of the foreign element in the management that the Board have been forced to the conclusion that, in the interests of the business, it will be impossible for them to hold out any hope of your being offered re-instatement.

Schreiber was interned, then repatriated, and died shortly after his return to Germany.[2]

Biographies such as Wiegand's or Schreiber's have received little attention in previous studies of civilian internment in Britain during the First

World War. This is due to methodological and thematic approaches, as well as the sources used. So far, two monographs have tackled the topic. John C. Bird's 1986 study is exclusively based on government sources and describes official measures and the decision-making process.[3] In his *The Enemy in Our Midst*, Panikos Panayi demonstrates that these measures tied in neatly with widespread Germanophobia in British society. Anti-German hysteria and spy-fever turned the German minority into an army of alleged spies and traitors which had to be contained in order to secure the home front.[4] Both studies give a countrywide overview but do not tackle the Scottish context.

This is where the following considerations step in. The regional focus on Scotland allows further scrutiny of the mechanics of internment, the conditions in the central Scottish internment camp, Stobs near Hawick, and the impact of these measures on individuals such as Schreiber and Wiegand. The article therefore presents a regional case study of civilian internment in Scotland during the First World War which can be regarded as largely representative of Britain as a whole. Firstly, however, I shall briefly consider the pre-war German migrant community in Scotland.

According to census records, the German community in Scotland numbered 2,362 in 1911, compared to 53,324 in England and Wales. In the light of recent micro-historical findings, these figures have to be at least doubled.[5] The most numerous and influential professional group were merchants and clerks, mainly trading with their native country. Brewers such as Fritz A. Schreiber introduced the art of lager-brewing to Scotland.[6] Musicians laid the foundations of a professional music scene. Other professional groups were school and university teachers, waiters and hoteliers, hairdressers, bakers and confectioners, glass bottle makers and miners. Women pursued remunerative occupations only as teachers and governesses.

An analysis of membership lists and minute books reveals a high degree of participation in German ethnic activities. The dense network of ethnic organizations was spearheaded by a German evangelical congregation, founded in Edinburgh in 1863. Dundee followed in 1880. Glasgow had two congregations, founded in 1884 and 1898 respectively. Although membership was open to all classes of society, the key positions were held by members of the financial elite and educated middle classes. Segregation along social and gender lines was also apparent in the secular clubs and societies. In Glasgow, for example, the *Deutscher Verein* catered for the middle-classes whereas the *Deutscher Club* attracted mainly artisans and shop-keepers. Towards the end of the century, nationalism became more and more prevalent. A German Navy League was founded in Glasgow in 1899 *(Deutscher Flottenverein Glasgow)*, a second in Edinburgh in 1904.[7]

This ethnic network completely dissolved after the outbreak of war in August 1914. Backed by overwhelming public support – and indeed fuelled by it – the Asquith administration introduced those restrictive measures against 'enemy aliens' that are discussed in detail by Panikos Panayi elsewhere in this volume: registration, internment, repatriation, internal displacement, restrictions in movement, trade restrictions. This pattern also applied to Scotland as the Scottish authorities followed the policies introduced by Whitehall.

The focus on Scotland will now help to illustrate the mechanics and experience of internment. Whilst the War Office was responsible for the running of the internment camps, the police undertook to register and arrest the 'enemy aliens'. The procedure was as follows. Police officers appeared on the doorstep of enemy aliens without any warning and took them to the local police station. After registration of their personal data and possibly one or two nights in a prison cell, the detainees were handed over to the military authorities. They had to pass through two transit camps. First a local one such as the Maryhill Barracks in North Glasgow, then the Redford Barracks in Edinburgh which acted as the central Scottish transit camp. From there the detainees were transported to the internment camps proper.[8]

One detainee was chief chemist Arno Singewald, a colleague of Fritz A. Schreiber's at the Tennents Brewery in Glasgow. He writes about his arrest:

> Ich wurde am 11. September 1914 früh 7 Uhr durch 2 Polizisten meines schottischen Wohnortes Craigendoran nach der Polizeistation beschieden und wie ich ging und stand (ohne Ueberzieher und irgendwelche notwendigen Toilettengegenstände) per Bahn nach Glasgow gebracht. Dort wurde ich zusammen mit einem Oberkellner in den 'Mary Hill' Militärbaracken in eine Arrestzelle gesperrt, in der bereits ein junger Deutscher die ganze Nacht auf einer Holzpritsche ohne Decke zugebracht hatte. Wir [...] wurden 9 Mann hoch mit einem Sergeanten und 6 Mann Bewachung (mit aufgepflanztem Seitengewehr) noch am selben Nachmittag durch einige Straßen Glasgow's, in denen wir mehrfach mit Apfelsinenschalen etc. beworfen wurden, zu einer Station und von da in das Refort [sic] Camp bei Edinburgh gebracht.[9]

The internees usually stayed between one and four weeks in the Redford Barracks transit camp. The compound was surrounded by barbed wire fences and was patrolled by guards on raised platforms. Twelve internees shared one tent in which sleeping accommodation consisted of a sack of straw and two woollen covers. The hygienic conditions were generally unsatisfactory. Johannes Bock, for example, a German traveller who happened to have been in Scotland at the outbreak of war only received his luggage after twenty-one days. Until then he had no soap, or towel, or clean clothes. He did not get changed, even at night,

> weil es gegen Morgen in den Zelten schauerlich kalt wurde. Nur die Schuhe kamen von den Füßen, weil sie als Kopfkissen gebraucht wurden. Des Morgens wusch man sich am Brunnen im Freien, bei etwas Bewegung im Winde wurde man dann trocken. [...] In einer kleinen Leinwandeinzäunung war ein großes Faß – das Bad für 1000 Mann -, für das man warmes Wasser am Nachmittag in der Küche erhalten konnte. [...] An einer Ecke des Platzes waren eine Anzahl Blechkübel aufgestellt, ein Wellblechdach darüber und eine Latte davor, das war die Aborteinrichtung.[10]

The reports by Bock and Singewald do stress, however, that the conditions were not intended as deliberate maltreatment by the military authorities but were due to the difficulties of organising the internment of tens of thousands of 'enemy aliens' and prisoners of war in a short period of time. The guards, as is pointed out in the reports, were not much better off in terms of accommodation and diet.

From Redford, the prisoners were transported to internment camps all over Britain. Arno Singewald, for example, was first sent to the Leeman Road Camp near York, but was soon released, only to be interned again during the wave of germanophobia which followed the sinking of the *Lusitania* in May 1915 – just as hairdresser Friedrich Bernhard Wiegand was. Singewald now came to Lofthouse Park Camp near Wakefield, and finally to Stratford Camp in London before being repatriated in summer 1915.[11] Johannes Bock also passed through Leeman Road Camp before being transported to the *Royal Edward* in Southend-on-Sea, one of several passenger liners converted for internment purposes. Here, he celebrated Christmas 1914:

> [Es verlief] mit einer stimmungsvollen Aufführung, Vorträgen und Musik beim Scheine der Christbaumkerzen weit besser, gar nicht so traurig, wie wir uns vorgestellt hatten. Schöne Weihnachtspakete aus Deutschland, von lieben Verwandten, guten Freunden, getreuen Nachbarn und dergleichen.[12]

In February 1915 permission was finally granted for Bock to leave Britain for the United States.

Unlike Bock and Singewald, many of the former Redford inmates were interned in Stobs, the central Scottish internment camp near Hawick in the Lowlands.[13] As the following table shows the peak number of prisoners which could be traced was 4,592.

	Civilians	POWs	total
February 1915	300	none	300
April 1915	?	?	800
15 June 1915	1098	1278	2376
13 April 1916	2269[14]	2323	4592

Stobs Internment Camp: Number and composition of internees[15]

The camp was used for both 'enemy aliens' and prisoners of war. The two groups were accommodated in separate, but mutually accessible compounds, each consisting of twenty huts measuring 120 feet in length and twenty feet in width and sleeping thirty-three persons on average. The camp was surrounded by barbed wire. One of the inmates was August Blume whose boarding house in Edinburgh went bankrupt in his absence and was finally sequestrated.[16]

Visits by relatives or friends were restricted to Saturdays and were attended by an interpreter. All incoming or outgoing mail had to bear the censor's mark. This ensured that only trivial information – and certainly no criticism – could reach the outside world. As the camp newspaper *Stobsiade* remarks:

> Manchmal fliegt ein Brief über den Stacheldraht. Aus Deutschland oder vom englischen Heim. Das, was wir wissen möchten, steht nicht darin. Natürlich nicht. Auch Pakete kommen an. Wenn etwas sehr Wünschenswertes darin plätschert, behält es der Zensor. Natürlich.[17]

A letter from E. Willinger who had been living in Middlesbrough before the war gives an insight into the nature of outgoing mail. The letter is addressed to the pastor of the German evangelical congregation in Middlesbrough and is quoted verbatim. Its content is almost devoid of any significant information.

> Dear Mr. Abraham,
> this to let you know that we are here in Stops Camp A now. That is to say not all of us from the Ship. there are only about 10 from M´borough and Southbank here. there is quit a young Pastor coming here from Edinbrough (I forgotten his name) but he says he may see you some day, I hope so. It is quit all right here. The Air is splendid. I understand you are going to Lancaster and Lofthouse Park [two other internment camps, S. M.] as well. Please remember me to Paul Schulz, Franz v. Rohn and some of the old M´brough boys. I hope Your Wife and Child are quit well same yourself.

My Adress is E. W. Concentration Camp A. Hut q. a., Stops, Hawick,
Scotland.
Gruß
E. Willinger[18]

The long periods of internment and isolation caused those mental
problems that were aptly described by contemporaries as 'barbed wire
disease'. The inmates had nothing meaningful to do and often felt bored or
depressed. An article in the camp newspaper *Stobsiade* addresses this:

> Mittlerweile werden wir ein wenig simpel, spinnen wohl gar, und geraten
> in den gemütvollen Traumzustand, gemeinhin Dusel genannt. Das Gehirn
> verengt sich. Die Ereignisse des Vorlebens liegen weit zurück. Wie lange
> ist's her, dass wir Mariechen zum Abschied küssten? Gibt es überhaupt ein
> Mariechen, oder gehört auch das zu unsern Hirngespinsten? Gott weiss
> es.[19]

Sexual frustration is expressed through grim humour in the
following 'advert':

> Des Alleinseins müde, sehnt sich Rittmeister A. D. – noch leidlich erhalten
> – nach Ehefesseln (möglichst goldenen). Musikalische Damen ohne
> Anhang mit Klitsche und Kies bevorzugt. Näheres unter 'Hochdruck 80'
> an das Postamt Stobs.[20]

Serious cases of mental illness had to be treated in the camp
hospital. As one of the American inspectors who regularly visited internment
camps all over Britain reported in April 1916:

> Unfortunately there had been three deaths during the last few days before
> my visit, which had told very much upon the nerves of the interned soldiers
> and civilians, as they have so little to think about. [...] Most of the
> prisoners in the hospital were suffering from nerves, colds, wounds, or
> tuberculosis.

During the eighteen months up to April 1916, twelve prisoners died.
Four doctors were in charge of the infirmary, assisted by twenty-eight
German attendants. In cases needing an operation, a surgeon came from
Edinburgh. On the day of the inspector's visit, there were sixty-five patients
in the hospital. The hospital kitchen was staffed by four German cooks.

The healthy prisoners, too, were catered for by their compatriots.
Each of the four compounds had a kitchen with ten to twenty German cooks.
One of them was a chef and the others his assistants. In camp C there was
also a bakehouse which produced bread for the whole camp and employed
fourteen bakers, all soldiers and sailors. The flour issued was made by the
prisoners 'into the sort of rolls and cakes they like.'[21]

There was also a Board of Justice,

which assists in regulating small matters between the prisoners themselves, so that, if there should be any disagreements of slight nature, these may be brought before this Board of Justice, which frequently is enabled to arrange a settlement by apology or otherwise. These committees are all chosen and run by the interned prisoners themselves.[22]

Work, recreation and education were the only ways to escape boredom. Over 500 of the prisoners were engaged in roadbuilding. Others set up workshops where they pursued their professions such as shoemaking, tailoring, or hairdressing. Examples are Otto Watzlaff in Hut 40, 'Haar-Spezialist, Friseur und Huehneraugen-Operateur'; Wilhelm Driesch in Hut 7, 'Feine Herrenschneiderei'; or Gustav Duwe in Hut 27, 'Uhrmacher und Juwelier; Reparaturen aller Art, einschl. Klemmer und Brillen'. The camp school taught a multitude of subjects, for example shorthand, languages or history. An orchestra and various other instrumental groups existed, two military singing societies, one civilian singing society, a library with English and German books, and a theatre society. Gardening, i. e. laying out flower beds was very popular. By April 1916, there were skittle alleys and equipment for gymnastics. Two tennis courts and a recreation ground were in the making. 'Sport-Feste' were organised on a regular basis.

At Christmas 1915, a 'Grosse Weihnachtsrevue mit Musik (Chor u. Orchester), Gesang und Tanz' was staged under the title 'Hallo Stobs!!'. The performers were:

Corps de Ballet: Unter Mitwirkung hervoragender Kuenstler.
Regie: F. Hoffmeyer.
Musik komponiret und arrangiert von E. Beu.
Dramatische Scenen und Text verfasst von H. Beckmann, E. Behrens [...]
Kostueme aus dem Atelier W. Fr. Schulz
Veranstaltet vom Komitee der Civil-Lager mit guetiger Erlaubnis des Commandanten Lieut.-Colonel Bowman.

Christmas 1916, then, saw the staging of 'Der Verschwender. Original-Zaubermaerchen in 3 Aufzuegen von Ferd. Raimund. Musik von Konradin Kreutzer'.[23]

The spiritual needs of both Lutherans and Catholics were catered for. Dr C. van Biesen, a Dutch Catholic priest residing in Hawick during the war, held regular services. The situation for Protestants turned out to be more complicated. Until June 1915, regular services were held by C. Planer, who had been the pastor of the German Evangelical Congregation in Edinburgh and was interned in Stobs after the outbreak of war. When he was released in April 1915, he could not return to Edinburgh as this was a prohibited area cleared of 'enemy aliens'. His congregation had been dispersed. He decided to return to Germany and asked the above-mentioned Gerhard Abraham, the German pastor in Middlesbrough, to continue his work at Stobs. Abraham agreed and came to Stobs probably every two or three weeks. Services were held in the canteen. The organ belonged to the German congregation in Edinburgh and was played by machinist R. Adomat from Hut 63.

More support from outside the camp came from various relief committees: the YMCA, the Society of Friends Emergency Committee for the Assistance of Germans, Austrians and Hungarians in Distress, and the Prisoners of War Relief Agency which was organised by a German chemist living in London, Dr. K. E. Markel. These committees supported internees throughout Britain. The internees in Stobs also received some assistance from those members of the German community in Edinburgh and Glasgow who were not interned because they were female, too old, or naturalized. The German Club in Glasgow provided books from its own library stock for the camp library. Herr Schultzen and Frau Peacock maintained regular contact with the internees and sold some of their handicraft products such as frames or boxes. These items were often purchased by Germans living in Glasgow and Edinburgh who displayed them in their households as memorabilia long after the war.[24]

In the British context, Stobs seems to have been one of the best organised and well attended camps. Albert E. Rosenkranz, who had been the pastor of the German congregation in Liverpool before the war, wrote in 1921 that those of his flock who came to Stobs had no reason to complain about their treatment.[25] Corporal Emil Bahrs, reporting to the German authorities after his release, described his food rations as adequate.[26] The Commandant, Major Bowman, supported the activities of the German pastors as much as he could within the framework set by the war office.[27] During inspection visits, the internees had the chance to talk to the inspectors individually and bring forward any complaints, but:

> Keine der Klagen bezog sich auf die Zustände im Lager oder auf ihre Behandlung oder Beköstigung. Sie betrafen vielmehr in der Hauptsache ihre Gefangensetzung und daß es ihnen unmöglich gewesen sei, ihre Privatangelegenheiten zu ordnen, da man ihnen vor der Internierung nur eine kurze Frist gelassen habe.[28]

Despite these favourable commentaries, however, and despite the range of occupational and recreational facilities, it would be misleading to imagine camp life as being happy. The activities were nothing more than attempts at coming to terms with a difficult situation and trying to avoid insanity in extremely confined circumstances.

From a sociological perspective, no internment camp during the First World War has found as perceptive an analysis as Ruhleben in Berlin. The Canadian sociologist John D. Ketchum was one of about 4,000 mainly British and Commonwealth civilian internees and later published his study *Ruhleben. A Prison Camp Society.*[29] Ketchum's account helps us to explain some of the prisoners' activities in Stobs – and indeed in other British camps, both during the First and the Second World War. The activities were attempts to lend some purpose to a long and otherwise meaningless period of internment. They pursued clear aims, but of modest dimensions, since they had to be realised within the confines of the barbed wire, e.g. a language had to be learned or a competition had to be won. Such activities structured the prisoners' daily routine which otherwise would have lacked any framework. They had a set beginning and an end, and often required preparation and revision. As Ketchum remarks:

> The purposeful activity that followed did more than make camp life interesting, for purpose is the great organizing agent of the personality, establishing priorities among its motives, giving direction and focus to behaviour, and so unifying and stabilizing the self. An aimless life is a disorganized life, and ultimately a demoralized one, for without some goal one way of acting is no better or worse than another. These were of course the chief dangers of a long, meaningless internment, and the series of mental breakdowns showed their reality.

Furthermore, the activities facilitated at least a *mental* escape from imprisonment:

> One cannot be consciously a prisoner while playing centre forward on a football team or translating Goethe in class. In so far as the men immersed themselves in the new roles offered them [...] they ceased to feel themselves prisoners.[30]

I will now turn from internment to general displacement. In the course of the war, the whole of the Scottish East Coast was declared a prohibited area. This meant that 'enemy aliens' were not allowed to reside there and were displaced. The mechanics of displacement can be illustrated by taking Fifeshire as an example. In August 1914 109 enemy aliens were registered. Up to October, all male aliens under forty-five were either interned in Redford or deprived of their permit of residence. Three men in the latter category refused to move away and were imprisoned in Dundee. The policy also applied to women. By October, twenty-one women were left with a permit of residence. Some of them were wives of internees. Eleven were British-born wives of Germans. The others were servants. All seamen landing in the ports of Methil or Burntisland were interned in Redford. By

November, of the original 109 aliens, seventeen were left with a permit of residence, thirteen had been interned, seventy-nine had been removed to non-prohibited areas – and possibly interned at a later stage. Georg Ketterer and his family from Carnoustie, for example, found lodging with 'Mrs McDougal, Govanhill, Glasgow'.[31]

Repatriation was first undertaken on a voluntary basis, but later enforced. In June 1915, the Scottish Advisory Committee on Aliens under Lord Dewar and two Scottish MPs was established. The Committee dealt both with applications for release from internment and exemption from repatriation. Virtually all women, children, and elderly men now applied for exemption. About half of the two thousand applications were granted. Towards the end of the war, however, the rules were tightened again; the Advisory Committee was enlarged and all cases were reconsidered. In August 1918, one hundred and twenty more 'enemy aliens' were either interned or repatriated upon recommendation of the committee.

Amongst those now interned were F. Laurenz from Glasgow, a cabinetmaker, aged sixty-four who had been living in Britain for forty-six years, and Louis Hanway from Lanarkshire, a furrier suffering from a heart disease who had left Germany at the age of nine. Both Laurenz and Hanway had British-born wives. Amongst those now repatriated were Mrs. Leibfried from Edinburgh, a mother of six British-born children and wife of an interned 'enemy alien'; and Martha Mutzke, a domestic servant, aged twenty-eight, whose father and brothers were interned. Leibfried and Mutzke had been resident in Britain for twenty-eight years and fifteen years respectively.[32]

This information enables us to read the following table which gives an overview of the forced movement of people in Scotland during the course of the war.

	Glasgow	Edinburgh	Scotland
registered August 1914	941	624	3170
moved from prohibited areas	247		
registered by 19. 11. 1914 (incl. internees)	1188		
interned by 19. 11. 1914	412	249	1073
resident 19. 11. 1914	617	232	1390
resident 1. 7. 1917	422	41	770 (March)
resident 1. 8. 1918	366		644

Number of 'Enemy Aliens' in Scotland, 1914-1918[33]

Numbers for the immediate post-war period – when further repatriations were carried out – could not be obtained. The number of 556 Germans in Scotland as recorded by the 1921 census cannot be directly correlated with the table due to differing registration methods.

A detailed analysis of Scottish public opinion as reflected through newspaper articles, letters to the editor, speeches, and acts of violence and exclusion in everyday life has shown that the government measures were backed by overwhelming public support.[34] Germanophobia in combination with spy-fever proved to be a fatal mix for the German minority in Scotland. In Glasgow, for example, the self-styled Anti-Alien Movement organised a public meeting in St. Andrew's Hall on 13 June 1916. A crowd of seven thousand cheered enthusiastically when speakers such as former liberal Lord Provost Sir Samuel Chisholm declared:

> The fabric of our industrial, commercial and social life has been honeycombed by the influence of Germans who contribute nothing to our national prosperity, nothing to the promulgation of those ideals of honour and truth on which our glorious Empire rests; Germans, whose secret and often, indeed, very unconscious influence is only to lower, coarsen and degrade (Cheers).

Another speaker demanded: 'I would sweep these alien enemies out of our country root and branch. As a British ratepayer, who has paid taxes for forty years, I maintain that we have fed the lazy Germans long enough' (Cheers).[35] Further examples abound. The Standing Joint Committee of County Elgin alerted Secretary for Scotland McKinnon Wood to

> the danger to the Country in this crisis owing to the number of aliens still at large in our midst. Serious apprehension is being felt all over the Country by the freedom with which these persons – in many cases believed to be paid spies – can move about without interference [...]. My Committee would strongly urge that [...] steps should be taken without delay to have all alien enemies in the Country, both male and female, either deported or interned.[36]

Just as in England, German-owned shops had their windows smashed and anti-German riots occured in towns such as Edinburgh and Dumfries.[37] Establishments such as the Royal Restaurant in West Nile Street, Glasgow, posted a notice in their premises that no German or naturalised Briton of German birth would be served because British customers were unwilling to occupy tables along with them.[38] At the glass bottle works of W. King in Firhill, a trade dispute arose because a number of the workmen 'indicated that working alongside the Germans was distasteful to them.' The two German employees were eventually dismissed.[39] The *Scottish Field* asked

'Do Germans possess souls?', and commented: 'Our childrens' children will still look upon Germans as belonging to an accursed race, a race that stinks in the nostrils of every human being who understands the meaning of honour.'[40] The fact that the Scottish experience more or less mirrored the English one questions an integral aspect of Scottish national identity construction, namely the self-definition as a society historically free from racism and xenophobia. Although recent studies have started to question this notion,[41] none has done so through an investigation of the German minority – which arguably serves best to prove the point.

Germanophobia and spy-fever were a central element of the fears and anxieties of British wartime society. The enemy abroad was projected onto the 'enemy in our midst', i.e. the German minority, which, in the public imagination, was now moulded into an army of spies and traitors. Government measures were both a reaction to and a driving-force behind these public manifestations. Their symbolic significance far exceeds their actual effectiveness and rationality. Internment and repatriation have to be seen as a mere reassurance to the British public that the home front was safe. This appears to be all the more true considering that German espionage during the war was badly organised and a rather marginal phenomenon. Not a single German who had lived in Britain before 1914 was involved. No act of sabotage occurred.[42] The political class had their own agenda, namely political survival during wartime. A *laissez-faire* approach simply would not have been acceptable for the electorate. Prime Minister Asquith, for example, did not support personally the anti-alienist demands and wholesale internment. In May 1915, however, he gave way to public perceptions that Home Secretary McKenna's containment of enemy aliens was too lax and replaced him with Sir John Simon.[43]

It would be misleading, however, to regard the home-front hysteria and its impact on enemy aliens during World War I as a singular historic 'black hole'. It rather has to be seen within a larger historical context. The paradigm of xenophobic terminology did not spring up out of the blue in August 1914 but had developed in the *pre-war* decades.[44] It was now applied to the 'enemy in our midst' in the framework of a socially accepted public discourse. The nationalist right-wing British Empire Union had originally been founded in 1915 as the Anti-German Union and was active up until the mid-1970s.[45] Civilian internment, of course, had its precedent during the Boer War in South Africa and was then repeated during the Second World War, as various contributions to this volume demonstrate. The patterns and policies of internment that had developed during the First World War were able to prove their longevity only two decades later.

Notes

[1] Private papers Frederick McKay.

[2] Scottish Brewing Archive, T 1/6/1, Director's Minute Book, 4 September 1916 (quote); Glasgow University Archives, DC 402/1/2, Protokollbuch Deutscher Verein, p. 135.

[3] John C. Bird, *Control of Enemy Alien Civilians in Great Britain, 1914-1918* (New York/London: Garland, 1986).

[4] Panikos Panayi, *The Enemy in Our Midst. Germans in Britain during the First World War* (New York/Oxford: Berg, 1991).

[5] Stefan Manz, *Migranten und Internierte. Deutsche in Glasgow, 1864-1918* (Stuttgart: Franz Steiner, 2003), chapter II.3, and generally for more details.

[6] Stefan Manz, 'Technologietransfer und Spezialistenwanderung. Eine Augsburger Lagerbrauerei in Glasgow, 1889-1959', *Zeitschrift für Unternehmensgeschichte,* 45 (2/2000), pp. 225-247.

[7] Stefan Manz, '"Wir stehen fest zusammen/Zu Kaiser und zu Reich!". Nationalism among Germans in Britain 1871-1918', *German Life and Letters,* 55/4 (2002), pp. 398-415; idem., *Migranten,* ch. IV.

[8] *Glasgow Herald,* 12 September 1914, 17 September 1914, 23 October 1914, 24 October 1914, 26 October 1914; National Archives [NA] HO 45/10729/255193/45, 20 October 1914, Home Office circular to police authorities; NA HO 45/10729/255193/5, Scottish Office to Chief Constables in Scotland; Johannes Bock, *6 Monate in englischer Gefangenschaft. Erlebnisse eines Bremers* (Bremen: Winter, 1915), 20ff.

[9] Bundesarchiv Militärarchiv Freiburg PH2/588, Arno Singewald an Reichskommissar zur Erörterung von Gewalttätigkeiten gegen deutsche Zivilpersonen in Feindeshand, 8 May 1916, p. 25.

[10] Bock, *6 Monate,* p. 25.

[11] As footnote 9.

[12] Bock, *6 Monate,* p. 35.

[13] Stefan Manz, 'New Evidence on Stobs Internment Camp 1914-1919', *Hawick Archaeological Society Transactions,* 2002, pp. 59-69; Judith E. Murray, 'Stobs Camp 1903-1959', *ibid.,* 1988, pp. 12-25; Julie M. Horne, 'The German Connection. The Stobs Camp Newspaper 1916-1919', *ibid.,* pp. 26-32; Manz, *Migranten,* pp. 278-281.

[14] Includes 178 Austrians and two Turks.

[15] Sources: Bundesarchiv Militärarchiv Freiburg, RM 3/5402, Report John B. Jackson, 27 February 1915, p. 50; RM 3/5579/73f., Report American Embassy/German Division, 26 October 1915; Parliamentary Papers, misc. 30 (1916), Report American Embassy, German Division, p. 15; Tower Hamlets Local Library and Archives (London), TH 8662/52, letter Pastor Planer to Pastor Abraham, 24 April 1915.

[16] *Glasgow Herald,* 2 December 1914.

[17] *Stobsiade* 1, 5 September 1915, Hawick Borders Regional Library, RH 828 R/S.

[18] Tower Hamlets Local Library and Archives, TH 8662/68, 11 May 1915.

[19] *Stobsiade* 1, 5 September 1915.

[20] *ibid.*

[21] Parliamentary Papers, misc. 30 (1916), Report American Embassy/German Division, p. 16.

[22] *ibid.*, p. 15.

[23] Programmes courtesy of Mr. Jake Coltman, Hawick.

[24] *Glasgow Herald*, 19 February 1915; Tower Hamlets Local Library and Archive, TH 8662/52, 59, 60, 64, 77, 80, letters from Pastor Planer to Pastor Abraham between 24 April 1915 and 18 June 1915; Glasgow University Archives, DC 402/1/2, Deutscher Verein Glasgow, Protokollbuch, pp. 133-136.

[25] Albert E. Rosenkranz, *Geschichte der Deutschen Evangelischen Gemeinde zu Liverpool* (Stuttgart: Ausland und Heimat Verlags-Aktiengesellschaft, 1921), p. 211.

[26] Bundesarchiv Militärarchiv Freiburg, PH 2/588, report by Unteroffizier Emil Bahrs.

[27] Tower Hamlets Local Library and Archives, TH 8662/64, Pastor Planer to Pastor Abraham, 7 May 1915.

[28] Bundesarchiv Militärarchiv Freiburg, RM3/5579/74.

[29] John D. Ketchum, *Ruhleben. A Prison Camp Society* (Toronto: University of Toronto Press, 1965).

[30] *ibid.*, pp. 208f.

[31] West Register House Edinburgh, HH 31/10/25478/1107, 24 October 1914, Chief Constable Fifeshire to Scottish Office; HH 37/1/25478/1372c, 19 November 1914, Chief Constable Glasgow to Scottish Office; HH 31/10/15478/1060, Circular Home Office to Chief Constables.

[32] *Glasgow Herald*, 1 March 1917, 16 July 1918, 12 August 1918, 14 August 1918, 24 August 1918.

[33] Sources: West Register House Edinburgh, HH 37/1/1372a, circular Scottish Office to Chief Constables, 12 November 1914; HH 37/1/25478/1372c, Chief Constable Stevenson/Glasgow to Under Secretary for Scotland, 19 November 1914; HH 37/1/25478/895, 2137a, 1444, 2606, 2225; NA, CAB 1/26, Census of Aliens, 1 July 1917, S. 19; *Glasgow Herald*, 1 March 1917, 16 July 1918, 12 August 1918, 14 August 1918, 24 August 1918.

[34] Stefan Manz, '"Our sworn, subtle, savage, implacable and perfidious foe"'. Germanophobia and Spy-fever in Scotland 1914-1918', *Irish-German Studies*, 1/2004, pp. 28-37.

[35] Strathclyde Regional Archives Glasgow, PA 11/II/4, Enemy Alien Danger.

[36] West Register House Edinburgh, HH 31/10/25478/686, Elgin County Clerk to McKinnon Wood, 6 October 1914.

[37] Manz, 'Our sworn...', pp. 33-34.

[38] *Glasgow Herald*, 13 May 1915.

[39] *Glasgow Herald*, 5 June 1915.

[40] *Scottish Field*, April 1915, June 1915, p. 298; also see September 1916, p. 116; November 1916, p. 224; August 1917, p. 63.

[41] e. g. Henry Maitles, 'Attitudes to Jewish Immigration in the West of Scotland to 1905', *Journal of the Economic and Social History Society of Scotland*, 15 (1995), pp. 44-65.

[42] Gerard J. deGroot, *Blighty: British Society in the Era of the Great War* (London/New York: Longman, 1996), pp. 157-60.

[43] Bird, *Control*, p. 92.

[44] Most recently Robert Winder, *Bloody Foreigners. The Story of Immigration to Britain* (London: Little Brown, 2004); for Scotland see Manz, *Migranten*, Einleitung and Chapter V. 1.

[45] Panikos Panayi, 'The British Empire Union in the First World War', *Immigrants and Minorities,* 8 (1989), pp. 113-128.

Internment in the Second World War

Charmian Brinson

'Loyal to the Reich': National Socialists and Others in the Rushen Women's Internment Camp

This article considers the position and activities of a hitherto unresearched group, the 500-600 German and Austrian women who were interned in the Rushen Women's Internment Camp and who acknowledged allegiance to the German government. Although this 'reichstreu' contingent was not made up exclusively of National Socialists, it did include a fair number of them, chief among whom was the self-appointed Nazi organiser in the camp, Wanda Wehrhan. The article examines a range of internee accounts and official and other contemporary documents to ascertain Wehrhan's role and influence, as well as those of other leading members of the group, and, beyond that, the National Socialist presence in Rushen.

The Rushen Women's internment camp was opened on 29 May 1940 on the southern peninsula of the Isle of Man, incorporating the two small seaside resorts of Port Erin and Port St Mary. Almost all of the 4000 German and Austrian female internees had been categorised as 'A' or 'B' since, unlike their male counterparts, category 'C' women remained largely free from internment. Nonetheless, the majority in the camp were refugees from National Socialism, racial and/or political, who in the confusion of the times had been wrongly categorized but who would fairly soon be released. The activities and cultural endeavours of these interned women refugees have already received a certain amount of scholarly attention.[1]

There was, however, a further group of internees in Rushen about whom virtually nothing is known today: these were the 500-600 German and Austrian women who acknowledged allegiance to the German government and who remained in internment throughout the greater part of the war. Collectively termed 'Reichstreue', the women ranged from uneducated domestic servants, with little or no political understanding or conviction; through members of the resident German community in Britain who defined themselves as German rather than British, though not necessarily as National Socialists; to a minority who espoused the beliefs of the National Socialist Party and did their utmost to propagate them within the camp. Chief among this last group was Wanda Wehrhan, wife of the pastor of two of the German Lutheran churches in London and minister to the German Embassy, who took upon herself the role of National Socialist organizer in Rushen.

There had, throughout the 1930s, been a fairly active 'Landesgruppe' of the NSDAP in Britain, for some time under the leadership of Otto Bene, a former hair-tonic salesman, then that of Otto Karlowa. In

London where, in the early 1930s, the German population totalled perhaps 6000, there were deep divisions between supporters and opponents of Nazism though, according to James and Patience Barnes, 'gradually those who were genuinely enthusiastic about Nazism came to dominate the London community, its organizations, schools, exchange programmes and churches'.[2] A leading figure of the party organization in London was Pastor Gustav Schönberger, minister of the Hamburg Lutheran Church in Dalston and a close colleague of Wanda Wehrhan's husband Fritz. In addition, Schönberger ministered to the Deaconesses at the nearby German Hospital, 33 of whom would later find themselves interned in Rushen. As for the size of the NSDAP group, a British Foreign Office memorandum of June 1936 recorded a figure of 288 Nazi Party members in Britain while the London headquarters was 'understood to be in touch with some 1,500 people, some being British subjects of German extraction'.[3] By March 1939, membership of the 'Fascist organizations' (both German and Italian) was calculated at around 1700;[4] and the following month the British authorities decided it was time to circumscribe the activities of the Nazi organization in Britain and expel several of its leading officials, including Herr Karlowa. Pastor Schönberger, too, left Britain for Germany before the outbreak of war.

Those Party members still in Britain in September 1939 (having for one reason or another disregarded the German Embassy's advice of the previous month to return home) were likely to be designated Category 'A' and to be interned immediately. Fritz Wehrhan, for instance, was held initially in a camp at Clacton-on-Sea where, so it is reported by fellow internee Eugen Spier, he concluded a sermon by praying 'for a speedy victory for his great Germanic Führer and warrior Adolf Hitler'.[5] Wanda Wehrhan, surprisingly, was initially designated 'B' – a categorization which was only later changed to 'A' – and was therefore, unlike her husband, not interned until May 1940.

The Commandant of Rushen Camp, Dame Joanna Cruickshank, a former Matron-in-Chief of the British Red Cross Society, was a woman of formidable organizational powers, if little understanding of the situation of most of the women in her charge. Bertha Bracey of the Religious Society of Friends, who was certainly no uncritical admirer of Dame Joanna, set out in an article in the *Manchester Guardian* the difficulties the Commandant faced in May 1940: huge numbers of women, about whom she had received no prior information, to be processed in a very short time and with only minimal help; the presence of 300 expectant mothers and of children as a complicating factor; incidences of serious infectious disease but woefully inadequate medical facilities; and the inappropriate sleeping arrangements – the ubiquitous double beds – in the hotels and boarding houses where the internees were billeted.[6] It was in this last area, in particular, that in the initial chaos serious mistakes were made, as the Socialist refugee Erna Nelki later recalled:

> Die Verteilung war ohne jene Sorgfalt erfolgt. Juden, in Deutschland verleumdet und gehetzt, mussten sich von den siegestrunkenen Naziweibern täglich Beschimpfungen gefallen lassen. Eine teilte das Doppelbett mit einem durch Kindertransporte herübergekommenen Geschöpfchen. 'Geh weg, Jid, du stinkst!' wurde das junge Ding täglich angeschrien. Bis wir anderen ihre Verlegung erwirkten.[7]

A similar case, that of a Jewish girl of 16, 'who for many weeks [...] had to share a bed with a Nazi girl' was even raised by Lord Farringdon in the House of Lords on 6 August 1940.[8]

Such encounters between the Jewish/anti-Nazi majority and the Nazi minority in the camp, both in and beyond the confines of the double bed, caused great distress. Erna Nelki, in a letter to the editors of the camp journal *Rushen Outlook* (a single issue of which appeared in December 1940), described the sheer misery of living cheek by jowl with the National Socialists:

> To me and many other women who have suffered under the Nazi Regime in Germany as Jews or political opponents it is difficult to understand that Nazis who are still in the Camp are able to torture those they choose as their victims. There are houses in this Camp where Jewish women cannot sit in the common room without being insulted and are forced to spend every day and evening in their cold bedrooms. In another house it is not possible to arrange groups to do the housework without insults from the Nazis.[9]

Anti-Semitic remarks were commonplace in the street and even in church. The economist and archivist Erna Simion, a Jewish refugee who played a leading role in the camp, recounted in a later interview that in the local Methodist Church, that was attended by numerous Jewish women because of the kindness of the minister, Rev. J. Benson Harrison, 'there were Nazi women who said, "Oh there is a bad smell, Jewish smell, in this church"'.[10]

Moreover, as Hitler's armies scored one success after another, the Nazi women in Rushen behaved increasingly threateningly towards the refugees in the camp, taunting them with shouts of 'Hitler will be here in July', or similar.[11] The Communist internee Emmy Koenen recalled instances of their exceptionally provocative behaviour at this time:

> Sie rechneten mit einer baldigen Invasion der faschistischen Armee und erwarteten, über das Schweizer Konsulat nach Deutschland gebracht zu werden. So begannen sie sich mit 'Heil Hitler' zu grüßen, legten aus

Steinen Hakenkreuze am Strand aus und beschmierten Hauswände und
Bürgerstiege mit Hakenkreuzen.[12]

Dame Joanna Cruickshank was widely criticised for her failure to
deal adequately with the Nazi elements in her charge, and there were a
number of high-level interventions in the matter from parliamentarians and
other public figures as well as from the refugee organizations. On 23 July
1940 a letter appeared in *The Times* from signatories of the stature of E. M.
Forster, Ralph Vaughan Williams and the Master of the Rolls, Sir Wilfrid
Greene, declaring that 'Jewish and other refugees from Nazi oppression
should not be interned with Nazi sympathisers' in order to 'avoid scenes of
persecution such as have already been alleged'.[13]

In the camp, steps began to be taken to create purely 'Aryan' houses,
though this proved to be a rather more complex matter than anticipated. Erna
Simion recalled the events in a neighbouring hotel where

> there were especially nice, very well educated people, Christians and Jews
> together, they went to the Commandant and asked her not to listen to this
> [demand for segregation] because they were absolutely happy together.
> And our Commandant was flabbergasted, she couldn't understand it.[14]

Another leading internee, the Socialist Ira Rischowski, has spoken of a
similar situation that obtained in the Golf Links Hotel which Wanda
Wehrhan, after moving in there herself, was intent on turning into an
'Aryan' house: 'I remember that some of the non-Jewish refugees declined
very fervently to stay in this German house because they did not want to be
identified with the Nazis.'[15] Eventually two hotels were set aside 'for those
of declared Nazi sympathies', the Windsor House and the Ard Chreg, which
according to Theo Naftel, inspecting the camp on behalf of the International
Cooperative Women's Guild, led to a definite decrease in 'the difficulties
and unpleasantness'.[16] As the refugee population was steadily released
throughout 1940 and 1941, of course, the problem became less severe and
the number of 'reichstreu' houses increased: to three by March 1941, six by
September 1941, eighteen by May 1942 and thirty by early 1944. It is
interesting to note that Dame Joanna, for all that she appears to have gone
along with segregation, reportedly felt it to be mistaken

> because it gave the Nazi women much more opportunity of hatching out
> schemes for and carrying on propaganda, and [because] they would have
> enjoyed less influence if they had remained distributed amongst the other
> internees.[17]

Whatever her own inclinations on the subject, Dame Joanna's career
as Commandant of Rushen Camp undoubtedly foundered on her alleged

failure to control the Nazi women. She was accused both of being afraid of them and of behaving in too friendly a fashion towards them and, specifically, of permitting them to work on the camp staff and thereby gain access to camp records. (Regarding this last allegation, the Home Office privately conceded that Cruickshank had 'found some of the Nazi women her most efficient helpers amongst the internees, and therefore employed a number of them in her office, but always, so far as I could ascertain, under close supervision'.)[18]

The widespread allegations that Dame Joanna had no understanding of the German situation nor of the differences between the categories of women in her care have already been mentioned; and certainly the difficulties the internees encountered in bringing out a camp newspaper – the *Rushen Outlook*, of which they managed to produce one single issue, and the *Frauenruf*, which never saw the light of day – bear these out fully. Intent on preserving 'impartiality', Cruickshank expected the refugees to collaborate with the Nazis in producing their paper, an unrealistic and indeed harmful assumption, as Theo Naftel observed:

> [The anti-Nazi internees] could not understand […] the suggestion that if a Camp newspaper was to appear at all it must not be one-sided and should be run jointly by Nazis and democrats. My personal view is that such a collaboration would be utterly impossible and indeed that any propaganda by democratic groups against Nazi theory and practice should be definitely encouraged and refugees made to feel that efforts on their part to foster democratic ideals in the camp would be welcomed.[19]

Dame Joanna was in effect pressurised by the Home Office to resign from her post at the end of May 1941. She was replaced by the younger and more diplomatic Inspector C. R. Cuthbert from Scotland Yard whose role included overseeing the newly established Married Camp within Rushen. One point, however, should be registered in Dame Joanna's favour in reply to the specific charge that she had failed to control the Nazi protagonist Wanda Wehrhan: for on this, Home Office documents reveal that Cruickshank had indeed kept a very close watch on the troublesome Wehrhan, whom she had requested to be removed from Rushen to Holloway Prison – 'and perhaps we may have to do this' – but that the request for transfer had been turned down for fear of reprisals against the British civilian internees held by the Germans. Clearly there were issues at stake here that went far beyond Wehrhan:

> We have just heard through the International Red Cross that the British women who were interned under very bad conditions at Besançon have now been transferred to Vittel, where conditions are much superior, and

that this change has been due to the favourable reports on Internee camps
in Great Britain which have reached the German authorities.[20]

Wanda Wehrhan was forty-nine years of age in May 1940 when she
was interned in Rushen together with Gisela, the younger of her two
daughters (her older daughter Isolde joined her there later, after numerous
requests for the family to be reunited). Her husband Fritz, who had been
reinterned in March 1940 after a period spent at liberty, would shortly be
deported to Canada; her three sons, however, were back in Germany, the
oldest one on active service. According to the statement he made to the
Home Office Advisory Committee in October 1939, Fritz Wehrhan had
joined the Nazi party 'in or around 1936' since 'he thought it was his duty to
do so' and was a strong supporter of the Nazi regime.[21] It is evident that his
wife fully shared his political views: indeed a Home Office note from 1941
contended that 'this woman is an even more fanatical Nazi than her
husband'.[22]

Unlike many of the Austrian and German maids who formed a
sizeable proportion of the 'reichstreu' contingent, Wanda Wehrhan was an
educated woman who had lived in Britain for years, since 1920 in fact,
assisting her pastor husband in his parish work. She played a major role, for
instance, in running a centre and hostel for German girls in London and it is
likely that many of the contacts made through this work would have been
maintained or renewed in the camp. It is known, moreover, that before
Wehrhan was interned herself, she was active in the local German
community's efforts for internee aid. A report from a former internee, who
succeeded in returning to Germany in April 1940, records:

> Sehr dankenswert waren die mehrfachen Liebesgabensendungen mit
> warmer Unterkleidung, Wollsweatern und dergl. durch Frau Pastor
> Wehrhan in London und Schwester Anna, Oberin des Deutschen [...]
> Hospitals in London. Beide Damen erhielten von wohlhabenden
> Gemeindemitgliedern teilweise recht hohe Geldbeträge zu beliebiger
> Verwendung für die deutschen Internierten.[23]

Indeed the British security services had reason to suspect the parcels
dispatched under this scheme to the Lingfield Internment Camp of
containing rather more than warm clothes. Maps and compasses were found
in the camp whose probable inclusion in the Christmas parcels was attributed
to Fritz Wehrhan[24] – and it is very likely that his wife, too, would have had a
hand in the matter.

In Rushen Camp, Wanda Wehrhan was from the very start a figure
to be reckoned with, acting officially as house representative and unofficially
as self-appointed spokeswoman for the 'reichstreu' contingent. One of the

tasks she took upon herself was the creation of a 'German List', both of internees desiring to live in an 'Aryan' house and, hand in hand with this, of candidates for eventual repatriation. This list she achieved at least in part by intimidation, that is by threatening fellow internees with the fate that would ultimately befall them if they should fail to register their allegiance to the Reich. Yet if this tactic served as her metaphorical 'stick', there was also a 'carrot' she was able to bring into play in the form of the allowances to be paid to 'Reichstreue' by the German Government, through the agency of the neutral Swiss Legation as Protecting Power.[25] As Erna Simion recalled the 'very awkward scene':

> She sat on the beach and was surrounded by the young women who really needed money, who didn't get any money from elsewhere, and they were told by her – and this was a very good propaganda for Nazi things – first of all 'It is your national duty to hold up your national pride', and, secondly, 'I shall give you five shillings per week from the Swiss money which came along'.[26]

In the streets, too, so it was said in April 1941 by a released internee, the women whom Wehrhan was keen to convert to National Socialism

> gathered round her […], where she gave them long lectures on the wonderful life in the Third Reich, and on the attractions of the Hitler regime […] A good many who used to be politically completely uninterested and indifferent [became], through Mrs Wehrhan, ardent Nazis and anti-Semites.[27]

It was reported by the Deputy Commandant Elizabeth Looker, in fact, that by the end of 1940 Wehrhan had no option but to carry out her propaganda activities on the beach and in the street since, as a disruptive influence, she had been barred by decision of the inhabitants from many of the houses.[28] The extent of the agitation caused by the 'German List' is also revealed, interestingly, by a letter from a leading member of the 'reichstreu' group, Bertha Blessing (who, unlike the Jewish and political refugees previously cited, might perhaps have been expected to approve Wehrhan's actions):

> In the last few days there has been a mad excitement over collecting people on to a German list. The already famous Frau Wehrhahn [sic], who thank goodness, had to move out of our house some days ago at the request of the Commandant, has been stirring up trouble through secret intrigues inspired by personal ambition. A horrible and dangerous woman on account of the trust she enjoys amongst the young girls, who are incapable of thinking and who are looking for something to hold onto! […] It is of course a question of money, otherwise she would not have raised so much interest – it is all unpleasant.[29]

During the latter part of Rushen's existence, Bertha Blessing, in her role of Deputy Camp Leader of the 'reichstreu' women, would exert a distinctly moderating influence. Yet it is still instructive to note the question Blessing addressed to the Swiss representatives visiting the camp in September 1941, 'ob sie im Lager und namentlich in ihrem Hotel deutsche Lieder wie das Horst Wessel- und Deutschland-Lied singen dürften'. (She was advised to abstain from this firstly on grounds of tact, and secondly – since 'solche Kundgebungen [...] sehr leicht zu Anständen und Reibereien mit dem englischen Aufsichtspersonal führen könnten' – in order not to endanger her chances of being transferred to the Married Camp.[30]

In view of the pressure Wehrhan was known to be exerting on fellow internees, it is perhaps surprising that she was asked by the Swiss Legation as late as November 1940 to continue to draw up the repatriation list on its behalf. Certainly it is clear from the remarks of Elizabeth Looker on that occasion that the British camp authorities had had more than enough of the ructions Wehrhan was causing. It was, in any case, made clear to Wehrhan by the visiting Swiss, in agreement with Looker, that every woman must be left free to decide for herself on repatriation and segregation, and that the decision had to be registered not just with Wehrhan but also with the camp authorities.[31]

Wehrhan herself, zealot that she was, did all that she could to establish a National Socialist way of life in the camp. To her husband in Canada she would report from the 'Aryan' hotel Mona House where she was living in April 1942:

> On Monday we were allowed to celebrate our beloved Führer's birthday. Sheep in wolves' clothing reproach me a great deal for asking permission for this celebration and it was not refused. It is amazing how few people, nominally so extra devout, have civic courage.[32]

A Manx child from that time (now Mrs Brenda Watterson), who lived in the Mona House, can still recall the Führer's Birthday party which was celebrated by all the internees billeted there with candles, singing and saluting. In pride of place, along the length of the table, the internees positioned a swastika constructed of gorse – full of yellow flowers at that time of year – which they had gathered from the surrounding hillsides. Mrs Watterson also remembers being soundly chastised by her aunt, who ran the hotel, for attempting to join in the celebrations.[33]

As Wehrhan's reputation as a fanatic spread beyond the confines of the camp, it became a factor in all kinds of planning and decision-making related to the Women's Camp. It played a role, for instance, in the deliberations of the Bishop of Chichester, that indefatigable friend to the internees, concerning the provision of German-language church services in Rushen:

> The importance of getting [an] effective Christian representative, who is not a Nazi, is made all the more urgent by what I hear of Miss [*sic*] Wehrhan's activities. She seems to be distributing a lot of poison and to be a very dangerous woman.[34]

It has already been noted that, while Wehrhan undoubtedly exerted a strong hold over some of the women in the camp, she also made numerous enemies there. By 1943, in fact, the Home Office would record with some satisfaction that 'of the 500 or 600 German women in the camp who acknowledge allegiance to the German government, there are only about 5 or 6 who can put up with her'.[35] One of the women with whom Wehrhan appears to have been at odds for much of the internment period was Sister Anna Jochmann, former matron of the German Hospital in Dalston – and, if the story of the internees' parcels is anything to go by, a former ally of hers – who, within a relatively short space of time, had been elected Camp Leader for the 'reichstreu' group (in effect supplanting Wehrhan). The political position of the thirty-three Lutheran Deaconesses, including Sister Anna at their head, who were interned as a group in Rushen, has been termed a conundrum[36] because of the conflicting accounts that exist on the subject. 'There were some awfully nice women,' the Socialist Ira Rischowski would later recall of them;[37] but the Jewish refugee Ernie Braun, on the other hand, who was billeted with the Deaconesses in the Windsor House for a time, remembers their offensively National Socialist behaviour towards her.[38] According to Brigitte Davies, likewise a (half-)Jewish refugee, the Deaconesses' hotel was commonly referred to as 'The Brown House' – 'and everyone kept away from them of course,' she added.[39]

It should also be recalled in this connection that in London the German Hospital had been closely associated with the nearby Lutheran Hamburg Church whose pastor was the very active National Socialist, Gustav Schönberger. Schönberger, as Elizabeth McKeller observes, 'seems to have split the hospital community into pro- and anti-Nazi factions'.[40] Schönberger himself had returned to Germany before the outbreak of war as had 27 of the Deaconesses, with the rest remaining at their posts. They were arrested in May 1940, however, with all but one of them being compelled to leave their hospital in a 'distressed and hurried manner'.[41]

In internment, the Sisters suffered above all from a lack of occupation. 'Elles regrettent que leurs services ne soient requis qu'occasionellement à l'hôpital de Port Erin,' reported the International Red Cross of a visit to the camp in August 1940,[42] and it was a complaint that resurfaced regularly. As time went on, the Deaconesses did manage, however, to involve themselves both in nursing and teaching. They also busied themselves in the religious and musical life of the local Methodist church from which, by early 1941, they appear to have supplanted and excluded the Jewish musicians.[43] It should be noted that the British camp authorities frequently found occasion to acknowledge the assistance of the Deaconesses, and especially of Sister Anna, in the smooth running of Rushen.[44]

The manner in which Wanda Wehrhan had to surrender her leading position in the 'Reichstreu' contingent to the evidently less fanatical Sister Anna and Bertha Blessing was outlined in a Swiss Legation report of May 1942:

> Es darf daran erinnert werden, dass Frau Wehrhan, nach Einrichtung des Frauenlagers in Port Erin, als Wortführerin der reichsdeutschen Frauen auftrat, dabei jedoch ihre Aufgabe vor allem in fortgesetzten Intrigen gegen die Lagerleitung erblickte und sich namentlich durch ihre Sucht, Unruhe und Unfrieden zu stiften, auszeichnete. Nach Aussage des Lagerkommandanten wurde sie jedoch in einer auf die reichsdeutschen Häuser beschränkten geheimen Abstimmung mehrheitlich als Vertrauensperson abgelehnt und an ihrer Stelle wurden Schwester Jochmann und Frau Blessing gewählt.[45]

Wehrhan is known to have complained bitterly about the manner in which the camp election was carried out, also registering intense dissatisfaction with the two elected representatives – with Sister Anna, whom she dismissed as 'nicht geeignet' for the role, and with Blessing who 'als Angehörige einer sehr wohlhabenden Familie, unfähig sei, die verschiedenen Probleme, namentlich der ärmeren Lagerinsassen voll zu verstehen'.[46] Similar complaints, it must be said, emanated from other internees – from Katherina Ackerl, for instance, who likewise complained of Sister Anna's unsuitability on the grounds of unworldliness.[47]

The feud within the 'reichstreu' community seems to have raged on for some considerable time. Certainly, in late 1942, there was still talk of 'Elemente [...] die immer noch versuchten, gegen die Vertrauensleute zu intriguieren [sic] und so Unzufriedenheit zu stiften', with Sister Anna and Bertha Blessing described as being 'von einer sich um Frau Pastor Wehrhan scharenden Minderheit immer noch angefeindet'. Moreover, the contested election issue had still not been laid to rest: so persistent were the rumours that the two representatives had been elected against the wishes of most of the 'reichstreu' internees and, worse, with the help of the British camp authorities that the Swiss, as Protecting Power, had to step in and give Sister Anna a greater degree of support.[48] Despite this, however, in May 1943 there were fresh reports of animosity, of 'neue Verdächtigungen und Verleumdungen', such that Blessing found it necessary to issue a list of the innovations that Sister Anna had recently brought in for the benefit of the 'reichstreu' internees: German language tuition for the schoolchildren, German church services for Protestants, a book club, a reading room and so forth.[49]

On 28 May 1943, Wehrhan was interviewed by the Swiss representatives and given the opportunity to air her grievances. While she claimed to regret the disunity and jealousy amongst the 'reichstreu' women, she laid the blame for these firmly on Sister Anna and Bertha Blessing, 'denen es nicht nur an Initiative und Führerqualitäten fehle, sondern auch am nötigen Verständnis um ihre Aufgaben erfolgreich zu lösen'. Clearly the matter of the camp elections still rankled, moreover:

> Wie aus dem Gespräch mit Frau Wehrhan hervorging, ist ihre feindselige Einstellung offenbar auf einen Vorfall zurückzuführen, der sich bei der Abstimmung über die Wahl des Fürsorgekomitees ereignete, wo sie mit zwei Stimmen unterlag.

Finally Wehrhan was both admonished and exhorted to work for greater harmony, 'da die Vertrauensleute [...] auf die willige Unterstützung der wenigen im Lager anwesenden gebildeten Internierten angewiesen seien' – and she agreed she would try.[50]

Such evidence as there is suggests that Wehrhan did indeed become less disruptive, though probably not in response to the Swiss appeal. A Home Office minute from February 1944 records the observation of J. J. Huber of the Swiss Legation to the effect that Mrs Wehrhan had been taking 'a less active interest in camp affairs' since she had learned of the death of one of her sons on active service and the admission of the second into hospital, suffering from typhus.[51] She must also have been concerned for her youngest son, by then fighting on the Russian front. In addition, her husband had been brought back from Canada in the autumn of 1943, since when she had been concerning herself with promoting his desire for repatriation in order that he 'may spend his last years in the fatherland'.[52]

By late 1943, after three and a half years of internment, the mood in the camp was generally very low. A brief English handwritten summary of the International Red Cross's observations of August 1943 reads: 'Conditions good but morale deteriorating, repatriation recommended.' A further short note in an unknown Foreign Office hand commenting on the first, runs: 'It is good to see that the Germans are cracking.'[53] With the 'reichstreu' element now in the overwhelming majority, the quality of the cultural and educational life in Rushen, both in the Women's and in the

Married Camp, had become greatly inferior to that of the early days of the camp. It was recorded of the Married Camp in August 1943 that 'l'extrême susceptibilité politique du groupe allemand', as manifested in their choice of composers, authors, actors and musicians, often rendered the organization of entertainments difficult,[54] and in a report on the Women's Camp of early 1944 that all attempts to pursue orchestral or dramatic activity had been abandoned.[55]

There is, however, a programme from February 1944 in existence that belies the latter contention since it indicates that five performances were even then being put on of a 'Musical Melange' – in which Schubert, Mozart and Strauss featured prominently – to the accompaniment of the 'W and Y Orchestra' (W being the Women's and Y the Married Camp). The show also included Gertrude Jenning's one-act comedy, *Between the Soup and the Savoury*, in which Isolde Wehrhan played the part of the kitchen maid.[56] Isolde Wehrhan, Wanda's elder daughter, appears to have been something of a theatrical talent, having eighteen months previously also taken the role of a maid in a camp performance of Clare Boothe Luce's 1930s Broadway success, *The Women*.[57] Descriptions of the latter play, which happily boasted a cast of 23 women, point to it as having been an ambitious and successful production, suggesting that it was artistically on a par with performances in the early days of the camp.[58]

Where education was concerned, however, a Swiss Legation report maintained by early 1944 that the intellectual level prevailing in the camp was so low that, despite the existence of books to prepare internees for their Abitur, there were neither the teachers nor the pupils to make use of them.[59] To comply with the German government's wish, as communicated through the Swiss Legation, that civilian internees engage in educational activity, Sister Anna and her Deaconesses provided a course of twenty hours of first aid training which was taken by 212 internees,[60] presumably with an eye to their future participation in the German war effort.

After their visit to the camp of August 1943, the International Red Cross had already concluded that there could by then be no disputing the fact

> que la majorité des occupantes arrivent à la limite de leur résistance nerveuse et psychique et qu'un repatriement en bloc devrait être sérieusement pris en considération par les Autorités responsables.[61]

It is ironic that, despite all the agitation surrounding the 'German List' of would-be repatriates, little had been achieved, even by 1944, in the way of actual repatriation. Some women, children and older men, it is true, had been permitted to return home early on in the war, but since then, except for some exchanges of diplomats and, in 1943, one of a few elderly women internees, almost all initiatives of this kind had foundered. In September 1940, for instance, the German government had proposed repatriating Mary Booth, the 'daughter' [in fact the granddaughter] of the late founder of the Salvation Army, who was interned in Konstanz, in exchange for the group of Deaconesses held in Rushen – but this proposal had been turned down by the British 'in kategorischer Form'.[62] Nevertheless, as the war proceeded and the conditions for British civilian internees in German camps looked likely to deteriorate, the British Foreign Office began to make plans for a large scale exchange of internees on a one-to-one basis.

Certainly the numbers were not in their favour: for while there were calculated to be between 1600 and 2000 British women and children in German hands, fewer than 500 German women and children on the Isle of Man were registered with the Swiss Legation as awaiting repatriation (though these numbers might perhaps be boosted by the inclusion of internees in the Colonies or Dominions).[63] It was not, as things turned out, until the summer of 1944 that the two-part exchange of civilians – the first via Lisbon, the second via Gothenburg – could finally be organised through the agency of the International Red Cross. The group from the Isle of Man, consisting of 470 women, ninety men and twenty-five children, formed part of the Gothenburg exchange of September 1944.[64] Fritz and Wanda Wehrhan, their daughters Isolde and Gisela, Bertha Blessing and the thirty-three Deaconesses were among the party.

In fact, permitting the Wehrhans to leave Britain had not proved a clear-cut decision for the British authorities (with the complicating factor that the daughters, detained under Defence Regulation 18B, were both British subjects). M15, in particular, had expressed the view that internees like Frau Wehrhan who had threatened refugees or gathered information about them were likely to be 'specially energetic and successful in supplying the Gestapo with information' once back in Germany and 'should be refused repatriation'.[65] The Home Office, on the other hand, which eventually overruled M15 on the matter,[66] took the line that 'it would be a great relief to everybody concerned if they could be got rid of'; moreover, in repatriating the four Wehrhans, Britain would be 'rescuing four British subjects from the German inferno'. The minute continued tellingly:

> Perhaps the most salutary treatment for this woman's perverted attitude of mind would be removal from the sheltered life of the Isle of Man to the conditions of present day Germany with defeat looming ahead.[67]

By 1944, the prospective repatriates would of course have been aware that conditions in Germany were bad, even if their inclination was to dismiss British press and radio reports as Allied propaganda. There were some, no doubt, who were too discouraged by then to attempt to return[68] even if Sister Anna, in conversation with the Swiss representatives early in 1944, would maintain staunchly on behalf of her 'reichstreu' constituents,

> dass sie nur den einen Wunsch haben, die Gefahren und Härten, denen – wie ihnen nur zu gut bekannt sei – ein großer Teil der Bevölkerung in Deutschland ausgesetzt ist, mit ihren Volksgenossen teilen zu können.[69]

Nonetheless, life on the Isle of Man, which had remained largely untouched by the hardships of war, would have left internees ill-prepared for the dislocation and devastation – recalled by a Deaconess as 'niederschmetternd'[70] – that they encountered upon their return to Germany; and worse was to follow. Two members of their community died in February 1945 in an Allied bombing raid on Hagen-Eckesey.[71] And Isolde Wehrhan, the young amateur dramatics enthusiast, who returned to Berlin to train as a nurse, was killed in an air raid not long after her arrival there.[72]

Following the departure of the repatriates in September 1944, Rushen Camp, with the Women's and Married Camps now merged into one entity, was no more than a shadow of its former self. Indeed, when the Swiss Legation made its final visit there in February 1945, it found a total population of only 269 adults and seventy children, of whom eighty-five and twenty-six, respectively, were classified as 'Reichstreue'.[73] The group was now led by Bruno Fehle, formerly the director of a London optical company, who as early as August 1939 had been prevented from returning home because of his specialist knowledge of the optical industry.[74] Serious worries were expressed during the February 1945 visit of the Swiss by those Germans who had remained behind: should they now, finally, in the interest of their families, be prepared to take work in non-war industries and thus gain their release in Britain? And how, Fehle wanted to know – 'in bezug auf die Treue zur Heimat' – would the Reich government view such an action, firstly in the case of a German who had been compelled to remain in Britain and, secondly, if he or she had decided voluntarily against repatriation?[75]

With the end of the war in sight, these particular concerns, at least, were to prove short-lived. Bruno Fehle, his wife and three children, the youngest born only three days previously, returned to Germany in May 1945. His home town had been devastated, but the family was fortunate in finding accommodation with Frau Fehle's parents. Fehle established himself in the optical business once more while his son, following the same profession as his father, later returned to the Isle of Man where he had spent several years of his childhood, and settled in Ramsey.[76] In September 1945, the last of the Rushen internees (around 137 adults and children) were transferred to the mainland, to the Canon's Park Aliens' Reception Centre, from where they were repatriated or released.[77] As for Wanda Wehrhan, she and her husband settled in a small village in Upper Bavaria, reported in 1946 by a like-minded former internee to be the place where Goebbels' mother and sister and brother-in-law had been arrested and interviewed a short while before.[78] Yet, the relationship between Wehrhan and the British authorities did not quite end there: curiously, Home Office files contain a letter from the Labour MP Christopher Boyd, from 1956, written on behalf of Wanda Wehrhan, whom he had met on a recent visit to Bavaria. Fritz Wehrhan was by then dead. In his letter, Boyd requested the return of documents of 'sentimental value' still held by the Home Office, such as 'private letters' from Fritz Wehrhan's former parishioners in London, written seventeen years before and testifying to his good character. Somewhat surprisingly perhaps, the Home Office returned the papers (though taking good care to retain copies of them). When, however, the following year, Boyd wrote again, this time applying for the return of newspaper cuttings relating to Fritz Wehrhan's pastoral work in London, the Home Office was unable to oblige.[79] No indications have come to light as to whether Wanda Wehrhan ever revised her political attitudes in the face of personal bereavement and national defeat and dishonour. What does emerge, however, from her last extraordinary exchange with British officialdom is that her capacity for sheer effrontery had remained undiminished.

Notes

Grateful thanks are due to the following for access to archive material as well as for information and advice: Home Office, London; Public Record Office, Kew; Lambeth Palace Library, London; Women's Library, London Metropolitan University; Imperial War Museum, London; Manx National Heritage, Douglas; Politisches Archiv des Auswärtigen Amtes, Berlin; Archiv der Westfälischen Diakonissenanstalt Sarepta, Bielefeld; Ernie Braun; Deborah Cherry; Henry Cregeen; Yvonne Cresswell; Ruth Matthews; Christiane Swinbank; Brenda Watterson; Julia Winckler.

[1] See, for example, Miriam Kochan, 'Womens' Experience of Internment', in *The Internment of Aliens in Twentieth Century Britain*, edited by David Cesarani and Tony Kushner, (London: Frank Cass, 1993), pp. 147-66; Charmian Brinson, '"In the Exile of Internment" or "Von Versuchen, aus einer Not eine Tugend zu machen": German-speaking women interned by the British during the Second World War', in *Politics and Culture in Twentieth Century Germany*, edited by William Niven and James Jordan (Rochester, NY: Camden House 2003), pp. 63-87; and Charmian Brinson, '"Keine verlorene Zeit": Musik im britischen

Fraueninternierungslager Rushen', in *Echolos: Klangwelten verfolgter Musikerinnen in der NS-Zeit*, edited by Anna-Christine Rhode-Jüchtern and Maria Kublitz-Kramer (Bielefeld: Aisthesis Verlag, 2004), pp. 243-63.

[2] James J. Barnes and Patience P. Barnes, 'London's German Community in the early 1930s', in *Germans in Britain since 1500*, edited by Panikos Panayi (London/Rio Grande: Hambledon Press 1996), p. 146.

[3] 'Memorandum on the Question of Proceeding against the Nazi and Fascist Organizations established in the United Kingdom', 9 June 1936, The National Archives [NA], FO 371/19942.

[4] See 'Nazi and Fascist Organizations in the United Kingdom', n. d. [March 1939], NA, FO 371/23035.

[5] Eugen Spier, *The Protecting Power* (London/New York/Melbourne/Sydney/ Capetown: Skeffington, 1951), p. 48.

[6] Bertha Bracey, 'Isle of Man Internment Camps: The Great Improvement Made in Six Months', *Manchester Guardian*, 21 February 1941, p. 4.

[7] Erna Nelki, 'Eingesperrt im englischen Frauenlager', in *Sie flohen vor dem Hakenkreuz: Selbstzeugnisse der Emigranten: Ein Lesebuch für Deutsche*, edited by Walter Zadek (Reinbek bei Hamburg: Rowohlt, 1981), p. 122.

[8] See *Hansard*, House of Lords, 5th Series, vol. CXVII, col. 116.

[9] *Rushen Outlook*, no.1 (December 1940), p. 9.

[10] Erna Simion, 'Civilian Internment in Britain 1939-1945', Imperial War Museum [IWM], Department of Sound Records, 004000, p. 49.

[11] See G. Eric Gordon to Bishop George Bell, 9 June 1940, Bell Papers, Lambeth Palace Library, London, vol. 30.

[12] Emmy Koenen, 'Exil in England: Leben und Kampf im Frauenlager', *Beiträge zur Geschichte der Arbeiterbewegung*, XX (1978), p. 881.

[13] 'Interning Aliens', *The Times*, 23 July 1940, p. 5.

[14] Simion Interview, p. 43.

[15] Ira Rischowski, 'Civilian Internment in Britain 1939-1945', IWM, Department of Sound Records, 004296, p. 44.

[16] Theo Naftel, 'Report on Visit to the Women's Internment Camp in the Isle of Man, January 1941', held in Margery Corbett Ashby Papers, The Women's Library, London Metropolitan University, MICA/A96, Box 486, p. 7.

[17] Home Office minute (Sir John Moylan), 29 May 1941, NA, HO 215/405.

[18] Moylan minute, 21 May 1941, NA, HO 215/405.

[19] Naftel Report, p. 8.

[20] Moylan minute, 29 May 1941, NA, HO 215/405.

[21] See transcript of Fritz Wehrhan's Appeal and Interrogation, 23 October 1939, Home Office [HO], Aliens Department, W13781.

[22] Note appended to Home Office 'B' Advisory Committee document, 24 April 1941, HO, Aliens Department, W13781/4.

[23] Propst Andreas Wackwitz, 'Bericht über die Verhältnisse im Internierungslager Seaton, Devon, England', c. May 1940, Politisches Archiv des Auswärtigen Amtes, Berlin [AA], R41796.

[24] Major-General Sir Vernon Kell (MI5) to Sir Alexander Maxwell (HO), 10 February 1940, HO, Aliens Department, W13781/2.

[25] In fact, during 1940 these payments were still restricted to persons interned before 1 April 1940, though the scheme was later extended.

[26] Simion Interview, p. 33.

[27] See Central Department for Interned Refugees, 'Extract from the report by a woman internee recently released from Port Erin in the Isle of Man', April 1941, HO, Aliens Department, W13781/4.

[28] Report on the visit by representatives of the Swiss Legation to Rushen of 10 November 1940, AA, R41798.

[29] Bertha to Kurt Blessing, 20 June 1941, letter retained by censor and held in HO, Aliens Department, W13781/4.

[30] Report on the visit by representatives of the Swiss Legation to Rushen of 21 and 22 August 1941 (Bericht 803), AA, R42017.

[31] Report on the visit by representatives of the Swiss Legation to Rushen of 10 November 1940, AA, R41798.

[32] Extract from Wanda to Fritz Wehrhan, 24 April 1942, held in HO, Aliens Department, W13781/5.

[33] Interview between the writer and Brenda Watterson, Port Erin, 3 September 2004.

[34] Bell to Rev. W. Paton, 17 May 1941, Bell Papers, Lambeth Palace Library, vol. 31,1.

[35] Moylan to Sir Patrick Duff (Office of the High Commissioner for the UK, Ottawa), 5 February 1943, HO, Aliens Department, W13781/5.

[36] Yvonne Cresswell (Manx National Heritage) in conversation with Julia Winckler, Douglas, 8 July 2002.

[37] Rischowski Interview, p. 57.

[38] Interview between the writer and Ernie Braun, London, 8 April 2002.

[39] Brigitte Davies, 'Civilian Internment in Britain 1939-1945', IWM, Department of Sound Records, 004438, p. 43.

[40] Elizabeth McKeller, The German Hospital Hackney: A Social and Architectural History 1845-1987 (London: Hackney Society Publication, 1991), p. 10.

[41] See Maureen Specht, The German Hospital in London and the Community it Served, 1845 to 1948 (Cookham:Anglo-German Family History Society, 1997), p. 58. The exception was Sister Gertrud Grothaus who, having been designated Category 'C', remained at liberty until July 1940 when she too was arrested.

[42] Report of International Red Cross Visit of 21 August 1940 (Report 24), NA, HO 215/25, p. 4.

[43] See Charmian Brinson, '"Keine verlorene Zeit": Musik im britischen Fraueninternierungslager Rushen', p. 258.

[44] For instance, as recorded in Report on the visit by representatives of the Swiss Legation to Rushen of 10 August 1940, AA, R41798.

[45] Report on the visit by representatives of the Swiss Legation to Rushen of 6 May 1942 (Bericht 813), AA, R42017.

[46] *Ibid.*

[47] Report on the visit by representatives of the Swiss Legation to Rushen of 20 September 1941(Bericht 803), AA, R42017.

[48] Report on the visit by representatives of the Swiss Legation to Rushen of 9 November 1942 (Bericht 822), AA, R42018.

[49] Report on the visit by representatives of the Swiss Legation to Rushen of 28 May 1943 (Bericht 827), AA, R42018.

[50] *Ibid.*

[51] Minute (L. W. Clayton), 8 February 1944, HO, Aliens Department, W13781/5.

[52] Wanda Wehrhan to Swiss Legation, 2 November 1943, HO, Aliens Department, W13781/5.

[53] Appended to International Red Cross to Foreign Office, 30 September 1943, NA, FO, 916/522.

[54] Report of International Red Cross Visit to Camp Y of 13 August 1943, NA, FO 916/522.

[55] Report of International Red Cross Visit to Camp W of 16 February 1944, NA, FO 916/846.

[56] Held IWM, Department of Documents, Folder Misc 35/ Item 648.

[57] *Ibid.*

[58] According to interviews with Kathleen Jones and Mary Kay, 'Civilian Internment in Britain 1939-1945', IWM, Department of Sound Records, 004416 and 004399. See also, 'Rushen', *Isle of Man Examiner*, 9 October 1942, p. 8.

[59] Report on the visit by representatives of the Swiss Legation to Rushen of 29 December 1943 and 6 and 9 January 1944 (Bericht 837), AA, R42018.

[60] For correspondence on this, see AA, Bern 4551.

[61] Report of International Red Cross Visit to Camp W of 13 August 1943, NA, FO 916/522.

[62] See Auswärtiges Amt to Deutsches Rotes Kreuz, 23 September 1940, AA, R41797.

[63] On this, see Foreign Office paper, 'Question of further exchanges of British and German civilians', n. d. [early 1943], and Swiss Legation list, 'German Women and Children interned in the Isle of Man who have expressed their desire to be repatriated', 1 January 1943, NA, FO 916/500.

[64] See Ministry of Health 'Report on the Repatriation of Prisoners of War [*sic*] – S. S. Drottningholm, September, 1944', 18 September 1944, NA, FO 916/813.

[65] MI5 to HO Aliens Department, 19 February 1944, HO, Aliens Department, W13781/5.

[66] See HO to MI5, 3 March 1944, *ibid.*

[67] HO minute (L.W. Clayton), 8 February 1944, *ibid.*

[68] See for example Peter and Leni Gillman, *'Collar the Lot!': How Britain Interned and Expelled its Wartime Refugees* (London: Quartet Books, 1980), p. 289.

[69] Report on the visit by representatives of the Swiss Legation to Rushen of 29 December 1943 and 6 and 9 January 1944 (Bericht 837), AA, R42018.

[70] 'Ankunft aus der englischen Internierung: Erinnerung nach 27 Jahren', Sarepta-Archiv, Bielefeld, Sar 1, 1714.

[71] Information from the archivist of the Sarepta-Archiv, November and December 2004.

[72] Information in letter dated 10 July 1946, author unknown, from material gathered by Deborah Cherry as part of her ongoing work on women detained under Defence Regulation 18B.

[73] Report on the visit by representatives of the Swiss Legation to Rushen of 12 and 13 February 1945 (Bericht 839), AA, R127557.

[74] See Gillman, *op. cit.*, pp. 50-51.

[75] Report on the visit by representatives of the Swiss Legation to Rushen of 12 and 13 February 1945 (Bericht 839), AA, R127557.

[76] Gillman, *op. cit.*, pp. 289 ff.

[77] Memorandum concerning the closing of WY Camp Port Erin, n. d. [August 1945], NA, HO 215/479.

[78] Extract from letter dated 10 July 1946, author unknown (see footnote 72).

[79] Boyd's correspondence with the Home Office is held in HO, Aliens Department, W13781/6 (S).

.

Richard Dove

'Wer sie nicht erlebt hat, der begreift sie nie.' The Internment Camp Revue *What a life!*

The 'bilingual camp revue' *What a Life!*, written and directed by G. M. Höllering, with music by Hans Gál, was conceived and performed in a British internment camp in 1940. While the revue is frequently cited in the literature on internment, its contents have never been discussed or analysed. This article draws on the recently published internment diary of Hans Gál, and other contemporary sources, in order to reconstruct the event and place the performance in the unique context of theatre in internment.

'Das ist die Ballade vom deutschen Refugee/Wer sie nicht erlebt hat, der begreift sie nie.' So ran the refrain of the 'Ballade vom deutschen Refugee', one of the highlights of the bilingual revue *What a Life!*, devised and staged in a British internment camp on the Isle of Man in 1940. While often mentioned in the literature on cultural events in internment, *What a Life!* has never been discussed or analysed. The following is an attempt to reconstruct the content and style of the revue and place it in the context of theatre in internment.

In May 1940, as the prospect of a German invasion grew ever more likely, the British government began the wholesale internment of Germans and Austrians living in Britain, including many thousand refugees. They were interned initially in hastily-devised holding camps and later transferred to more permanent camps on the Isle of Man, a measure resulting in a gradual improvement in the material conditions of internment, as administration slowly caught up with requirements.

Internees were also allowed a considerable degree of autonomy, enabling them to organise various educational and cultural activities, which the authorities encouraged as a means of relieving boredom and maintaining morale. Of course, a high proportion of internees came from academic and artistic professions, including such luminaries as the composers Egon Wellesz and Hans Gál, artists like Kurt Schwitters, John Heartfield and Ludwig Meidner, and innumerable actors, musicians, writers, film makers. Even so, the range and variety of cultural events which took place in internment camps is astonishing, including regular concerts, theatrical performances, art exhibitions and lectures on every conceivable subject.

Despite the retrospective efforts of researchers such as Michael Seyfert,[1] many such cultural events have vanished from historical view, the

ephemeral nature of artistic performance being compounded by the absence
of contemporary records and artefacts in the improvised circumstances of
internment. A few have survived in the accounts of eye-witnesses and
participants. One such account is that of the composer and musicologist
Hans Gál, who kept a detailed diary throughout the four months of his
internment; the entries start on 13 May 1940, the day of his arrest, and end
with his release on 27 September.[2] Gál's diary is a highly personal
document, which was not intended for publication (the title page contains the
note 'Bloss zum Eigenverbrauch!!!'), but was written to help him come to
terms with his own predicament. However, its retrospective significance lies
in its record of his own creative endeavours in internment: the composition
and performance of the *Huyton Suite*, and the music for the 'bilingual camp
revue' *What a Life!*, which has become one of the legendary cultural events
of internment. It was produced by the film and stage director G. M.
Höllering,[3] who had been co-producer of the Brecht-Dudow film *Kuhle
Wampe* in 1931. Gál's text contains a striking portrait of Höllering, at whose
instigation he wrote the music for the revue:

> Höllering ist ein feiner, anziehender Mensch. Er hat mir ein Drehbuch von
> ihm gegeben, das mich überrascht hat; das sieht aus wie echte Filmkunst,
> unter Verzicht auf alle billigen Effektmittel und doch mit Ausnützung
> raffinierter technischer Möglichkeiten. Dass er mehr Regisseur als Dichter
> ist, liegt auf der Hand, aber das mag beim Film kein Fehler sein. Mit
> diesem Manne würde ich gerne arbeiten (11 July 1940, p. 74).

His wish was quickly granted.

Central Promenade Camp, Douglas, in which Gál was interned,
could boast an impressive array of artistic, and above all musical talent.
Among Gál's fellow-internees were such outstanding figures as the music
historian Otto Erich Deutsch, the composer and musician Franz Theodor
Reizenstein, and the young pianist Erwin Weiss, who would later become
Director of the Vienna Conservatory. Gál himself, together with Deutsch and
the Viennese music critic Hermann Ullrich, was a member of the Musical
Commission, which was responsible for arranging a concert programme
within the camp.

Gál had been confined to the camp hospital since the middle of
August with severe eczema. There he was visited daily by his two colleagues
from the 'Musical Commission' and by others involved in the musical and
theatrical programme for the camp, such as Höllering. They were planning a
classical concert and, as a popular counterpart to it, a *bunter Abend*. Both
events were to be held in the Palace Hotel, which housed the camp's
commanding officer. Lying just outside the barbed wire of the camp, the

Hotel also contained a large theatre with an auditorium seating about two thousand.

On 19 August Höllering came to see Gál with the news that he had cancelled the 'bunter Abend', commenting tersely: 'Die eine Hälfte ist schlecht und die andere unmöglich' (p. 110). However, an hour later he returned, bearing an unusual and ambitious proposal.

> Eine Stunde später war Höllering schon wieder da, brennend von einer neuen Idee. Er will eine Revue machen, ein richtiges Theaterstück. Mit Musik. Und natürlich mit meiner Musik. Heute in vierzehn Tagen muss die Aufführung sein, später ginge es nicht [...] Ich habe gelacht. Hier im Spital soll ich Musik machen! Und Musik wozu? Wo ist das Buch? Buch gibt's noch keines. Das muss er erst schreiben. Aber der Titel ist schon fertig: *What a Life!* (p.111).

The last third of Gál's narrative is devoted to a detailed account of his work on the revue and his simultaneous efforts to secure release from internment: two contradictory agendas which were finally reconciled only when he agreed to stay one day longer in order to take part in the second, and final performance of the revue on 26 September 1940.

The publication of Gál's diary and the reconstruction of his delightful musical score have naturally focused attention on his part in *What a Life!* – although this has deflected attention from the work of the actual author and producer, Georg Höllering. Contemporary accounts, including Gál's own, make abundantly clear that Höllering was the driving force behind the revue,[4] initiating, devising, writing and directing it within a remarkably short time. A preview in the camp newspaper *Central Promenade Paper* commented:

> In letzter Minute vor Redaktionsschluss gelang es uns, Interviews mit dem Generalintendanten, dem Chefregisseur und dem Textdichter unserer Revue zu bekommen. Es war verhältnismäßig einfach, denn alle diese Funktionen vereinigen sich in der Hand (oder dem Kopf) unseres Producers Höllering.[5]

Höllering was eager to enlist the talents of others, and he devoted much time and energy to persuading, bullying and cajoling his fellow artists into playing their part. Gál's own manuscript pays rueful tribute to Höllering's persistence and powers of persuasion: 'Aber dieser Höllering ist unabweisbar, und wenn er so arglistig ist, eine gute Idee zu haben, kriegt er mich wieder herum' (p. 127).

From the outset Höllering had a clear concept of the revue: it was to be a montage of scenes from everyday life in the camp, taking the form 'einer rasch ablaufenden, bunten Bilderfolge' (p. 122). Adopting the customary format of the Viennese 'Kleinkunstrevue', the production was to consist of a series of loosely-linked scenes, framed by the commentary of two compères, given alternately in German and English. The bilingual character of the revue was certainly prescribed by the Commandant, since the audience would include both the internees and their captors.

Gál wrote the music for the revue in the most adverse of circumstances. He was still confined to hospital, where the almost complete absence of privacy for composition was matched by the lack of simple necessities such as manuscript paper and, even more seriously, by the absence of musical instruments. Musical composition provided none the less a welcome distraction from his illness: 'Seit die Musik wieder von mir Besitz ergriffen hat, habe ich nicht viel an meinen Gesundheitszustand gedacht' (p. 114). Gál's text also involuntarily confirms how rapidly such creative activities took control, acquiring, amid the daily tedium of internment, almost obsessional importance.

Although Gál initially despaired of completing the task Höllering had so arbitrarily assigned him, his diary entry for 26 August confirms that he actually wrote the music at great speed:

> Das war eine Woche. Arbeit, Arbeit, Arbeit, von früh bis in die Nacht! […]
> Ich habe in sechs Tagen die ganze Musik zur Revue fertiggeschrieben, in fliegender Hast, genau so rasch, als ich eben Noten schreiben konnte. Und da das noch zu langsam ist, habe ich nicht einmal eine Partitur geschrieben, sondern bloss eine Skizze und nach dieser Skizze gleich die nötigen Stimmen (26 August, p. 112).

Höllering had been able to salvage a couple of numbers from the cancelled 'bunter Abend', but most of the lyrics came from Richard Hutter, whose name is among those credited in the theatre programme. Gál described them as short, well-turned epigrammatic verses, which had not originally been written for music (pp. 111-12). As a byproduct of his sleepless nights, Gál was also able, to Höllering's great delight, to translate the lyrics into English.

But Gál's work was far from over. Höllering would visit the hospital at least twice a day, never failing to bring a new idea, which naturally required new music:

> Er fragt teilnehmend nach meiner Gesundheit, […] und dann zieht er aus der Hosentasche ein paar Verse, die ich gerade noch komponieren soll, oder er liest mir eine Szene vor, zu der er da und dort Musik braucht. 'Das machen Sie doch gleich, nicht wahr? Die Leute warten schon darauf.' Genau wie beim Grocer, und ich war immer prompt mit der Lieferung (p. 112).

Figure 1: G. M. Höllering (Courtesy of Andrew Hoellering)

Gál wrote the entire music for the revue while confined to his sick bed, leaving the hospital only to attend the orchestral rehearsals, the first of which took place on 28 August, a mere four days before the first performance. He had already proved his ability to adapt to the constraints of internment. The *Huyton Suite,* named after the transit camp Huyton, near Liverpool, where Gál was held for several weeks before arriving on the Isle of Man, was famously written for flute and two violins, because these were the only instruments and musicians available to him.

On this occasion Gál was more fortunate. The Palace Theatre was equipped with a proper orchestra pit and Gál therefore wrote the music for an orchestra, albeit an improvised one, its make-up reflecting the available musical resources.

> Ich habe natürlich von einer Bilanz der vorhandenen Mittel ausgehen müssen. […] Zwei erste, zwei zweite Violinen kann ich bekommen, eine Viola, ein Violoncell. Es gibt einen ganz fixen Klarinettisten, und natürlich Draber, den brillianten Flötisten (p. 113).

To complete the ensemble he intended to place a piano in the middle of the orchestra and conduct from this vantage point. Most of the songs were to be performed with simple piano accompaniment, a measure designed to help the two singers, neither of whom was a professional artist.[6]

Gál's music for the revue, as well as several of the original lyrics, have survived in his Nachlass.[7] The script is regrettably lost. Given the improvised atmosphere of the revue, and Höllering's habit of making frequent changes and additions, it must be doubtful if there ever was a definitive script, but using Gál's account and other contemporary documents, it is possible partly to reconstruct the style and content of the revue.

> Höllerings Szenarium – es ist eher ein Szenarium als ein Buch, Dialogstellen sind meist nur skizziert – ist wirklich wie eine Photomontage; eine improvisierte Folge knapper Szenen, die für mich etwas ungeheuer Reizvolles haben, weil eigentlich nichts darin erfunden ist (p. 112).

Höllering's conception of the revue undoubtedly owed much to his background in the film industry. Many of the short, loosely connected scenes enacting the daily life of the camp contained little dialogue, conveying their meaning through a succession of simple but typical images. Gál was initially highly sceptical of this technique of montage, referring to the revue rather disparagingly as 'dieses Bündel von Szenen und Musikstücken' (pp. 175-76) but he soon came to recognize the internal logic of the apparently unconnected scenes: 'Aber das eine habe ich gesehen, dass es ein entzückender Abend werden kann und dass der scheinbar bunter Zufall dieser Szenenfolge sehr klar und glücklich gegliedert ist' (p. 121).

In the course of rehearsals it had been decided to make an entry charge of 3*d*. in order to cover the spiralling costs of the production. The price was in fact doubled to 6*d*. for the second performance, the proceeds being donated to the relief of air-raid victims.[8] With its director, its specially commissioned music and stage sets, its rehearsals, theatre programme and theatre tickets, *What a Life!* seemed to bear all the marks of a theatre production outside the barbed wire. There were of course striking differences and *What a Life!* exemplifies many of the intrinsic problems of theatre in internment.

Gál's manuscript constantly emphasizes the improvised nature of the revue and the relative lack of rehearsals, even referring to the first performance as 'diese Bühnenimprovisation':

> [...] alles kam, wie wenn es nicht improvisiert und nun tatsächlich zum ersten Mal im richtigen Zusammenhang erklingen würde, sondern wie wenn es immer so gewesen und allen Beteiligten geläufig wäre. So hatte das Resultat kaum die Mängel, aber alle Frische und Unmittelbarkeit einer Improvisation und es wirkte demgemäß (3 September, p. 123).

In fact, some of Höllering's improvisations were evidently involuntary, simply making a virtue out of a necessity.

Given the lack of available materials, stage sets were sparse and often improvised. The stage designs for *What a Life!* were the work of the Austrian artist Paul Humpoletz, an illustrator and caricaturist who also had some experience of theatre.[9] Höllering relied greatly on him, the camp newspaper reporting that it was difficult to get hold of Humpoletz, 'da er auch in der Revue dringend benötigt und von Höllering als der bekannte Augapfel gehütet wird'.[10] Gál was also impressed by his ability, 'mit einem Minimum an Material erstaunliche Dinge zuwege zu bringen', a judgement which his surviving drawings for the production handsomely confirm.[11]

Rehearsals were a constant problem. Höllering may have felt that he had a captive cast, but he soon found that the ordinary problems of amateur theatre were in fact compounded by the extraordinary vagaries of internment. It frequently proved difficult to get the actors together for rehearsals and there were always absentees, some detained by their jobs within the camp administration, though others perhaps took the production less seriously.

During the weeks of their artistic collaboration, Gál became closely acquainted with Höllering, learning to appreciate both his personal and artistic qualities:

> Ich bin in diesen Wochen [...] mit Höllering sehr vertraut geworden. Er ist
> ein prächtiger Typ, die denkbar glücklichste Vereinigung eines
> Künstlertemperaments voll Phantasie und Unternehmungslust und eines
> ordnungsliebenden, charakterfesten Menschen (p. 102).

He was quick to appreciate the difficulties Höllering faced in marshalling a
small army of amateur actors: 'Wie er die zweihundert Leute, die auf die
Bühne kommen sollen, dirigieren will, ist mir noch ein Rätsel. Und mit
Amateuren, die neugierig sind, was zu sehen und immer anderswo als man
sie gerade braucht!' (p. 120).

In fact, Höllering showed himself to be a masterly director, able to
demonstrate considerable skills in working with actors, not least amateur
actors, skills he had honed during such projects as *Kuhle Wampe*, Brecht's
film of Berlin working-class life, which had featured numerous amateur
actors. He was also an exacting director. Gál portrays him as a perfectionist
who constantly changed and replayed scenes in a manner reminiscent of the
successive 'takes' on a film set.

> Indessen ändert er noch von Probe zu Probe und kaum eine Szene steht
> noch im Dialog fest, dessen es übrigens gar nicht viel gibt. Das Ganze hat
> viel von der Höllering geläufigen Filmtechnik; es ist ein blitzschneller
> Ablauf von Bildern und Szenen, die an sich soviel ausdrücken, dass für
> Worte nicht mehr viel Raum ist (p. 116).

The First Performance

The revue was first performed on 2 September in the Palace Theatre,
Douglas.[12] The internment regulations stipulated that the audience for any
such public performance should not exceed a thousand people but with the
indulgence of the commandant, the audience numbered many more. In
addition, 250 internees were actually taking part in the production.

The theatre programme for *What a Life!* lists eleven scenes, adding
rather archly 'perhaps less, perhaps more, perhaps nothing' – perhaps
alluding to the improvised nature of the revue, or the uncertainties of life in
internment. Gál's comments confirm that Höllering's approach to his
subject-matter was humorous, drawing on the rich comic potential of camp
life. The very title *What a Life!* has an ironical ring. The opening scene of
the revue depicted the internees' arrival at the camp: a long line of men,
moving slowly forward, each with his small suitcase. This silent procession
was followed by the first song, the 'Stacheldrahtballade', the ironical text
belying the sweetness of Gál's melody.

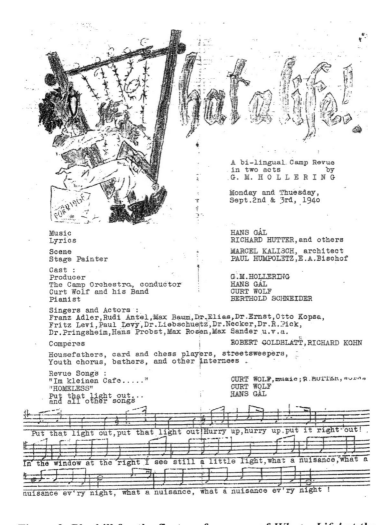

Figure 2: Playbill for the first performance of *What a Life!* at the Palace Theatre, Douglas, Isle of Man, 2 September 1940. (Courtesy of Imperial War Museum)

Die Möwen sehen den Stacheldraht
Den man in Douglas errichtet hat,
Und weil kein Draht hier früher war
Ist ihnen der Zweck des Drahtes nicht klar.
Sie debattieren mit viel Geschrei,
Was wohl der Sinn des Drahtes sei,
Und kommen zu keinem Resultat.
Warum lebt der Mensch hinter Stacheldraht?

Other scenes and songs depicted further aspects of camp life, such as the 'Frauensong', the point of which was that there were no women in the camp. There was also the 'Besensong', which reached the wry conclusion 'Es ist der Mensch, nicht der Besen, der fegt!' as well as the 'Song vom Doppelbett', alluding to the fact that every bed in the camp was occupied by two men.

Central Promenade, like other camps, quickly developed a recognizable social structure, with roles, responsibilities and hierarchies which represented a microcosm of society outside the wire.[13] Höllering portrayed this by means of a big march-past (Gál ironically termed it 'den großen Triumphzug der Campvertreter') which included the various office-holders and activities of the camp.

Central Promenade camp lay directly along the sea front where internees were allowed to walk in the evening. With his eye for amateur actors, Höllering discovered there two middle-aged Jews from Berlin, Herr Levi und Herr Meyer, who seemed to personify the characters of a scene he had already envisaged. They were to portray two refugees from Berlin who meet each other again as internees in the camp and recount their respective experiences. They had never acted before in their lives, but Höllering insisted they were not required to act, simply to play themselves: Herr Meyer and Herr Levi. Gál noted: 'Die beiden sind zum Brüllen. So habe ich gelegentlich bei Reinhardt in der Josefstadt spielen sehen. Diese Szene wird ein Clou, da sitzt jedes Wort' (28 August, pp. 116-17).

The scene 'The Camp Conservatory' illustrated the opinion of many internees that music was a 'major nuisance' in the camp. A group of musicians assemble and 'blasen, fiedeln, spielen und singen wild durcheinander, bis ein in der Mitte sitzender Zeitungsleser mit allen Zeichen der Verzweiflung den Schauplatz verlässt' (p.130). Gál scored the scene as a 'quod libet', an extended musical parody, consisting of a series of familiar quotations from well-known classical works, juxtaposed so as to emphasize their discord. He was uncertain of the effect, wondering if the joke was really only apparent to the musically educated (p. 147).

The subject of the revue was the daily life of the camp; its appeal therefore lay in its direct relevance to both actors and audience. However,

Gál was apprehensive as to how the audience would react to the intrinsic comedy of the events on stage, since the successive episodes enacted precisely their own tragicomic situation.

> Der Vorhang geht hoch. Man sieht einen Stacheldrahtzaun, <u>unseren</u> Stacheldraht, unseren Käfig.Und <u>wir selbst.</u> Unseresgleichen treten auf, arme, jammervolle Internierte mit ihren Handköfferchen [...] Das Ganze war schließlich nichts als ein wahrhafter Bilderbogen unseres eigenen Lebens (3 September, p. 123).

His fears proved unfounded; the audience at the first performance enjoyed themselves unreservedly. When Herr Levi und Herr Meyer swapped stories of their successive escapes from Berlin to Vienna, from Vienna to Prague, Warsaw, Amsterdam, Paris, London, ending with the slogan: 'Join the refugees and you will see the world', the audience could hardly stop laughing.

The scene to which the audience responded most enthusiastically was the Finale. Whereas the outline of every other scene had been furnished for him to write the music, the Finale was based on an idea Gál himself had actually proposed. In fact, it had needed great persistence to get his proposal accepted, since Höllering had originally had a different idea for the final scene.

Wartime blackout measures were also in force on the Isle of Man, and the camp guards were particularly vigilant. 'Put that light out' was an injunction frequently heard in the camp, although on several occasions it had turned out that the supposed light was not a light at all, but the reflection of the moon in one of the windows. The satirical thrust of the scene is unmistakeable. Gál noted:

> Wir hören den Ruf 'Put that light out' dutzendemale jeden Abend, gebrüllt, geheult, gezetert, gebellt [...] Er soll nun in Form eines Songrefrains in die Revue kommen und ich hoffe ihn in dieser Form im Lager so populär zu machen, dass die Wachen nicht umhin können, sich über sich selber lustig zu machen, wenn sie ihn künftig noch einmal ausstossen (26 August, p. 113).

In the actual performance, the point was not lost. The audience hesitated a moment, then burst into loud laughter. At the final curtain there was prolonged applause.[14]

The content and approach confirm that while Höllering wished to put camp life on stage, he also wished to convey its inherent absurdity. While it was certainly possible to poke gentle fun at camp rules and regulations (i. e. at the authorities) there were obvious limits to such criticism. Like all theatrical performances in internment camps, *What a Life!*

was subject to censorship – and inevitably also self-censorship. Höllering's primary intention was to amuse and instruct his fellow-internees, not to indulge in satirical *Zeitkritik*. Satire is essentially critical and corrective, seeking to change the situation it portrays, and for this very reason, satire in the context of internment was possible only to a limited extent. After all, the only major change which was possible was release from internment — and internees were all too aware that release depended on the concurrence of the authorities.

The Second Performance

The second performance of *What a Life!*, originally planned for 3 September, had had to be postponed indefinitely, which left ample time for rewriting, but also cast doubt on the availability of many of the performers. The revue exemplifies the intrinsic difficulties of theatre in internment, above all the ever-shifting population of the camp, as new internees arrived — and others began to be released.

For the second performance, Höllering had to recruit a new complement of extras, since many of the original cast had already left the camp.[15] Richard Hutter, author of most of the lyrics for the original revue, had been released even before the first performance, and thus never even saw his work on stage. Others might leave at any time. The 'English' tenor, Hans Karg-Bebenburg, had volunteered for the Pioneer Corps while Gál himself had applied for release on grounds of 'medical hardship', namely the severity of his eczema. (In fact, they would leave the camp together on the morning after the second performance of the revue.)

Höllering, however, was delighted at the postponement which gave him the chance to make sweeping changes and improvements. Gál observed ironically: 'Die Möglichkeit, noch einmal zu experimentieren, hat ihm neue Arbeitslust gegeben. Wo hat man sonst die Chance einer solchen Versuchsbühne?' (6 September, pp. 125-26). After several years working in the film industry, Höllering was once more under the spell of live theatre. He hoped to create a definitive version of the revue, representing something of lasting documentary value 'als kunstlerischen Niederschlag unseres Lebens im Internment'.

The revue was to be completely restructured. For the first performance, Paul Humpoletz had designed a poster depicting a caricature of a ballad-singer, seated on a porridge chest, playing a harp with strings of barbed wire (p. 127). For the second performance, Höllering proposed to put the *Balladensänger* on stage. (In the first version, the intervals during the scene changes were filled by the two compères and the songs.) The *Balladensänger* would perform in front of the curtain, reciting successive verses of a ballad which recounted the trials and tribulations of the German refugees, a device intended both to bridge the scene changes and to provide a narrative link between otherwise unconnected scenes.

The ballad was to be performed – in the style of a *Moritat* – by a little-known provincial actor called Max Baum, whom Höllering had first discovered in the original ill-fated *bunter Abend*.[16] Gál was dubious of Baum's suitability for the role, considering him something of a ham actor: 'er war mir, wenn ich ihn gelegentlich rezitieren hörte, mit seinen übertriebenen Akzenten und wilden Gestikulationen immer unerträglich' (p. 127). However, Höllering, always a shrewd judge, had perceived qualities in Baum, such as his good diction and his confident stage manner, which he was sure he could mould into an outstanding performance. While Baum was to *perform* the Moritat, there still remained the question of who was to write it.

With Richard Hutter's release, there apparently remained no one able to write light song lyrics. Höllering refused to be defeated and conscripted the musical historian and Schubert scholar, Otto Erich Deutsch, to carry out this task. Deutsch was therefore a somewhat unwilling author of what became the highlight of the revue, the 'Ballade vom deutschen Refugee'.

Deutsch did not find it easy to write lyrics in the required style. His first attempt was rejected as 'unusable', both in style and content. Gál was therefore forced to write the music first, leaving the unfortunate Deutsch to write the lyrics to fit the music – rather than vice versa. Despite this initial rejection, he refused to be discouraged and made heroic efforts to write the lyrics in the required style: 'Deutsch arbeitet mit Hochdruck an seiner Stacheldrahtballade. Wenn er vier Strophen bringt, werden drei verworfen und die vierte umgeformt. […] Die erste Gruppe von vier Strophen steht nun fest und ist ungemein stark' (p. 134).

The first verses contained gentle criticism of the policy of the British government in interning the bitterest opponents of its enemy. However, criticism of internment was muted; by contrast, the fourth verse consisted of a satirical reference to the Third Reich. To give the scene greater impact, Höllering commissioned a series of caricatures, larger-than-life portraits portraying the leading Nazis as bloodthirsty monsters, which were carried across the stage behind the *Balladensänger*. Gál commented somewhat primly: 'Das ist gerade an der Grenze des guten Geschmacks, aber die Umstände entschuldigen dergleichen' (15 September, p. 134). The 'Ballade vom deutschen Refugee' became a great favourite in the camp, its popularity spreading to the neighbouring Onchan Camp, where a version of the text appeared in the camp newspaper, the *Onchan Pioneer*.[17]

Unique in this revue — and almost certainly in the entire history of revue – is the 'Ballade vom armen Jakob', written by the sociologist Norbert Elias. As *Rektor* of the 'Camp University', Elias had played a leading role in organizing the lecture programme and himself gave lectures in Sociology. Much to Gál's surprise, he also had literary ambitions:

> Professor Elias, der Soziologe, der – wie sich nun herausstellt – auch eine literarische Seite hat, kam mit einer eigentümlichen, ausgesprochen interessanten Dichtung, halb in Prosa, halb in Versen, die mit Musik und einer Art lebender Bilder illustriert vorgetragen werden soll, 'Die Ballade vom armen Jakob' (p. 135).

Gál clearly felt that he was dealing with a work of poetic depth and resonance – he refers to it throughout as a 'Dichtung' or 'Gedicht'. It was certainly an ambitious piece, written for performance by speaker, choir and piano.[18] On stage, it ran for some fifteen minutes, telling the story of 'der ewige Jude von heute' who is persistently caught up in the disputes of others and always becomes a convenient scapegoat, a fate reiterated in the choral refrain at the end of each episode: 'Und dann schlugen alle im Verein/Auf den armen kleinen Jakob ein.'
Poor Jacob is forced to wander through life, driven from one country to another, finding no home, until he finally realizes that his home is humanity.

> Aber am Morgen machte er sich wieder auf seinen Weg
> Und wenn sie ihn nicht totgeschlagen haben,
> wandert er noch immer ohne Geld
> ein Stück weiter um die weite Welt (*Die Ballade des armen Jakob*, p. 34).

Though almost blinded by his worsening eczema, Gál completed the music for 'Der arme Jakob' within a few days. For a long time he was uncertain if Elias would even finish the ballad on time: 'Prof. Elias hat uns lange damit aufgehalten, dass keine endgültige Reinschrift von ihm zu bekommen war. Auch ihn hat die Faszination des Theaters ereilt, er ist voller Enthusiasmus' (p. 142). 'Die Ballade vom armen Jakob' is far removed from comedy, let alone satire. It is eminently serious in conception and tone, indeed Gál feared that it would be out of place in the revue, but Höllering was unperturbed – and was proved right.

The second performance of *What a Life!* finally took place on 26 September 1940. The audience of more than a thousand included the Camp Commandant and his entire staff, together with officers from other camps. Hermann Ullrich's review of *What a Life!* (the only one ever published) noted that the second production bore little resemblance to the first, and apart from the opening scene and the final scene, had been entirely reworked. In his opinion, the twin highlights of the show were the two ballads, which he considered equally successful.[19] Reflecting on the evening, Gál had some reservations about 'der arme Jakob' – finding it 'szenisch unfertig', though conceding its strong emotional impact. However, the highlight of the performance was, in his opinion, the 'Ballade vom deutschen Refugee':

> Der Höhepunkt war – ich hatte nicht daran gezweifelt – die Moritat an der Stacheldrahtharfe. Und ein Mensch hat damit gestern sicherlich ein Erlebnis gehabt wie nie zuvor: der arme Baum, der noch nie in seinem Leben so gefeiert worden ist. Seine Leistung war tatsächlich außerordentlich, er ist in einer Weise über sich hinausgewachsen, wie es der größte Optimist nicht erwartet hätte (27 September, pp. 148-49).

The last word on the production belongs to Hermann Ullrich, who ended his review by thanking

> unserem unvergesslichen Gál, den Dichtern, Künstlern, Musikern und allen, die an dieser Revue opferbereit und unverdrossen mitgearbeitet haben […] für einen Abend, von dem wir noch lange zehren und an den wir denken werden, wenn wir diese Insel schon lange verlassen haben.[20]

The revue had undoubtedly come to represent something much greater than itself – a community born of adversity, of mutual aid and support which few had expected but virtually all had experienced.

Once released from internment, Gál and Höllering went their separate ways. Gál went back to Edinburgh, eventually obtaining a post at the University and becoming one of the founders of the Edinburgh Festival. Höllering returned to his first love, the cinema; during the war he made documentary films for the Ministry of Information, thereafter becoming the owner and manager of London's Academy Cinema. Although the two men did meet again towards the end of the war,[21] the unique collaboration between director and composer was never repeated.

Notes

I should like to thank the staff at the Imperial War Museum for help in accessing appropriate material as well as Eva Fox-Gál and Andrew Hoellering for their comments. Above all, I am grateful to Ian Menzies and the late Professor Erwin Weiss for sharing their memories of the performance of *What a Life!*

[1] Michael Seyfert, *Im Niemandsland. Deutsche Exilliteratur in britischer Internierung* (Berlin: Das Arsenal, 1984).

[2] Hans Gál, *Musik hinter Stacheldraht. Tagebuchblätter aus dem Sommer 1940*, hrsg. von Eva Fox-Gál (Berne: Peter Lang 2003); page numbers cited in the text refer to this edition. Gál (b. Vienna 1890, d. Edinburgh 1987) was Director of the Städtische Musikhochschule, Mainz 1929-33. He became an early casualty of Nazism, being dismissed early in 1933. He arrived in Britain in 1938, coming to Edinburgh at the invitation of the pianist and musicologist Donald Tovey.

[3] Georg Höllering (b. 1897 Baden bei Wien, d. London 1980). Co-producer *Kuhle Wampe* 1931-2; returned to Austria in 1933, thence to Hungary and finally to Britain 1937. He was interned in 1940, and after his release made several short documentary films for the Ministry of Information 1942-44. See *London Calling. Deutsche im britischen Film der dreißiger Jahre* hrsg. von Jörg Schöning, (Munich: Edition Text + Kritik 1993).

[4] In an interview given many years after the event, Höllering disarmingly insisted that the idea for the revue had come from the Camp Commandant, which, if true, would be a unique case of intercultural collaboration. See Seyfert, *Im Niemandsland*, p. 218, note 18.

[5] 'Hoellering über seine Revue', *Central Promenade Paper*, no. 1, 16 September 1940, p. 12.

[6] In the first performance, the English songs were sung by Dr. R. Pick, the German songs by Max Rosen. For the second performance, Pick was replaced by Hans Karg-Bebenburg. See the respective theatre programmes, held in the Imperial War Museum and the Akademie der Künste, Berlin.

[7] The volume *Musik hinter Stacheldraht* includes an accompanying CD with Gál's *Huyton Suite* and a reconstruction of the music for *What a Life!* Gál's music for the camp revue was found in a bundle of discarded papers in his 'Nachlass'. His grandson Simon Fox has written a full score from the original manuscript.

[8] An initial donation of £10 was made to the Lord Mayor's Air Raid Distress Fund, with further donations to follow. See *Central Promenade Paper*, no. 3, 30 September 1940, p. 12.

[9] Paul Humpoletz (1889-1972) illustrator, cartoonist and caricaturist.

[10] *Central Promenade Paper*, no. 2, 22 September 1940, p. 8.

[11] Humpoletz's original drawings for the stage sets for *What a Life!* are held in the Museum of Jewish Heritage in New York.

[12] See pp. 123-25.

[13] This is the premiss of Richard Friedenthal's autobiographical novel of internment *Die Welt in der Nussschale* (Munich: Piper, 1956). Cf. also 'Die Ballade vom deutschen Refugee'.

[14] 'Zum Schluss gab es Beifall ohne Ende' (p. 124). Gál's memory of the occasion was confirmed by Erwin Weiss – one of the last surviving participants of the revue – in an interview with the author in 2003.

[15] Among the extras were the historian Julius Carlebach and Michael Kerr, son of the famous theatre critic Alfred Kerr and later to become a High Court judge.

[16] Max Baum played a series of parts with provincial theatres during the 1920s; from 1932 to 1936 he performed at the Stadttheater Memel, but, as a Jew, was dismissed and expelled from the Reichstheaterkammer in 1936. He subsequently emigrated to Britain, where he joined the Freier Deutscher Kulturbund, acting in productions of the 'Kleine Bühne' from 1944 to 1946.

[17] *The Onchan Pioneer*, no. 29, 16 March 1941, p. 4. A complete run of the paper, comprising forty-seven issues (27 July 1940 to 21 July 1941) is held by the Manx National Heritage

Museum, Douglas and also by the Wiener Library, London. There is also an incomplete run in the Imperial War Museum.

[18] The text was published over fifty years later in an edition by the Insel-Verlag: Norbert Elias, *Die Ballade vom armen Jakob*. Mit Illustrationen von Karl-Georg Hirsch und mit einem Nachwort von Hermann Korte (Frankfurt am Main /Leipzig: Insel 1996).

[19] Ullrich, 'Rückschau auf die Camp-Revue "What a Life"', *Central Promenade Paper*, no. 3, 30 September 1940, p. 3.

[20] *Ibid.*, p. 8.

[21] Communication from Andrew Hoellering, July 2005.

Jennifer Taylor

'Something to make people laugh'? Political content in Isle of Man Internment Camp Journals July-October 1940

This article explores the extent to which internees on the Isle of Man were permitted to comment on the Government's internment policy in the various journals published in the camps. It seeks to establish the type and extent of censorship and to explain why some journals were banned while others were not. Detailed textual examination indicates that tone and emphasis were significant factors in composing acceptable material, while external evidence suggests that both the character of the camp Commander and the internal politics of the camp had an impact on the success or otherwise of publications.

On 16 August 1940 an extraordinary scene took place in the Mooragh internment camp in Ramsey on the Isle of Man. A middle-aged Austrian novelist was solemnly called into the Commander's office and reprimanded. His offence: to have collaborated in the production of a camp journal which had expressed too graphically the detainees' fears, had railed too eloquently at the injustice of interning Hitler's opponents and had articulated too plangently their longing for release. The current circumstances, Robert Neumann was told, demanded writing which would boost morale and provide something 'to make people laugh'.[1] Since the editorial team under the Austrian journalist Josef Kalmus[2] had evidently failed to provide such material, permission to publish was summarily withdrawn. Thus the issue of the *Mooragh Times* which had appeared four days earlier was the first and only issue of that journal. Over on the south-west coast of the island, the women of the Port Erin and Port St. Mary camps had fared even worse, for their formidable Commander, the First-World-War veteran Dame Joanna Cruikshank, exerted an iron discipline over every aspect of camp life, including the clothing her charges should wear when meeting their husbands (trousers were banned). Two projected journals, *The Awful Times and Daily Rumour* and *Der Frauenruf* had their publication prevented by Cruikshank's censorship procedures, while similar considerations ensured that *Rushen Outlook* appeared only once, on 4 December 1940, and that *Der Pfingstbote* was circulated illegally.[3] There were, however, two editorial teams who were more successful, achieving relatively long print runs of internment journals. The *Onchan Pioneer,* the first journal to appear on the Island, commenced publication on 27 July 1940 and ceased only on the closure of Onchan Camp to German detainees July 1941. 47 issues were produced, the last dated 20

July 1941. Similarly *The Camp*, published in Hutchinson Camp in central Douglas, achieved 44 issues between 21 September 1940 and 1 November 1941. Additionally, the *Central Promenade Paper* was issued from the Central Promenade Camp in Douglas from 16 September 1940 to March 1941[4], when the camp was closed and the prisoners moved to Onchan. Although relatively few issues are extant, these provide enough evidence to indicate that the editor, the German Communist economist Wilhelm Necker, was extremely skilful in analysing and circumventing censorship procedures. The only other camp housing German-speaking internees to produce a journal was Sefton, also located on the promenade in Douglas. As this camp was not opened until October and publication did not start until November, the *Sefton Review*[5] falls outside the time scale of this article, which concentrates on the period before release procedures were formalised in October 1940.[6]

These internment journals owe their existence to the charitable impulses of those who supported the internees. The exile press reported regularly on the collection and distribution of funds for this purpose.[7] Among such support was the provision of spirit duplicators, and it was on these machines that the camp journals were produced once the initial ban on receiving radio broadcasts and newspapers had been lifted in mid-July.

In the field of exile literature these journals occupy a special place since they were produced under extraordinary conditions,[8] not the least of which was the high turnover of editorial teams and contributors, a reflection of the relatively short periods of internment in any one location. *The Camp*, for example, had five editors in its fourteen-month publication history: Michael Corvin, a survivor of the *Arandora Star* who had formerly worked as an editor for Ullstein in Berlin,[9] Carlo Pietzner, Henry Gustav Dittmar, Freimut Schwarz and Hans Schulze, who had formerly edited the *Onchan Pioneer*.[10] Clearly, too, these publications were subject to censorship: 'We are not a free newspaper in the sense of the law', wrote Michael Corvin in the second issue of *The Camp*.[11] Editors who wished to continue to publish had to develop an acceptable house style, and it is this aspect of self-censorship which this article seeks to explore more fully. Consideration will also be given to formal censorship arrangements, and the question of whether there were other factors – such as the personality of the camp commanders or issues specific to the situation of each camp – which could account for the success or otherwise of the camp journals.

Mid-July 1940 is a key date in the history of internment journals, for after that time internees were permitted access to selected print and broadcast media. This meant that the internees were in contact with the outside world and no longer forced to rely solely on rumour, a factor as important as the provision of the duplicating machines in the genesis of these publications. Once the information flow had improved and the machines been provided, publications could be planned. The success of the *Onchan Pioneer* is all the more remarkable since the camp, which opened in early June, had barely been in existence for six weeks when the journal first appeared. As its readers were advised in the first issue, the journal was appearing merely one week after the British press (in the form of the *Daily Telegraph)* had been allowed in the camp.[12] Central Promenade Camp, on the other hand, which opened at roughly the same time, did not publish until mid-September. The extent to which the long time-span between the opening of the camp and the first issue was indicative of difficulties with the authorities has been definitively documented in the case of Rushen, where the delay in publication was attributed to Dame Joanna's reservations about the wisdom of publishing anything at all. Where Central Promenade Camp was concerned, the delay can probably be explained by the inept way in which the Deputy, a certain Lt. Johnson[13] ran the camp in the Commander's absence. Johnson's regime resulted in a complaint to the Commander of all the Isle of Man camps, Lt. Col. S. W. Slatter, and the resignation of the Camp Speakers (the internees' representatives) at the beginning of September. Oblique reference to these difficulties is made in the remarks of one of the newly-elected Speakers published in the first issue of the *Central Promenade Paper*:

> Internees are reminded that the issue of the CPP does not indicate any change of camp policy. It is however suggested to consider for further co-operation with the editors such categories of internees as can prove before a special tribunal their unswerving loyalty to the former Camp Government.[14]

A further indication of internal disagreements is provided by the resignation of J. F. Reinholz from the *Onchan Pioneer* 'for private reasons', announced as early as the sixth issue of the journal, on 7 September 1940. Reinholz's place as co-editor with Walter Sachs was taken by Leopold Lehmann, formerly editor of the *Berliner Tageblatt* and the *8 Uhr Abend-Blatt*, whose previous experience no doubt stood him in good stead for the task of producing a successful newssheet under the difficult conditions of internment.

The potential for tension can be deduced from the first page of the first issue of each journal. It became the common practice for the Commander to write a few lines welcoming the enterprise, and for the editor or another representative of the internees to reply. These formalised exchanges highlight the discrepancies between the way in which the authorities envisioned the role of the journals, and the objectives of the internees themselves. The Commanders tended to see it as their task to improve morale by providing their charges – who were not permitted to work and therefore debarred from participating in the war effort – with meaningful activity. As we shall see, the preoccupations of the internees were very different. Major C. R. C. Marsh greeted the first issue of the *Onchan Pioneer* with remarkable empathy:

> The occasion of the first issue of a camp paper may cause some doubt in the minds of the editorial staff, somewhat akin to that of a theatrical producer awaiting the result of a first night performance: how will the audience accept it? Here with so much talent in camp doubt should not arise and I feel that Onchan will produce a paper which will meet with universal approval.[15]

His hint at divisions of opinion within the camp was answered by the Camp Supervisor, G. W. Schiller, with the morale boosting slogan, 'Die Aufgabe des *Onchan Pioneer*: Pionierarbeit im Sinne aufbauender Kameradschaft!'. However, in the unsigned editorial which follows, entertainment ('Zerstreuung') is the last, and therefore presumably the least important, of the listed aims of the journal, while reporting events internal to the camp comes second. Significantly, priority is given to overcoming the sense of isolation and helplessness, 'Die quälende Absperrung von dem dramatischen Ablauf einer zukunftsentscheidenden Zeit' occasioned by detention on this off-shore island, a condition inadequately remedied by access to the national press and the opportunity to produce a camp journal. In its turn, the first edition of *The Camp* was welcomed by Captain H. O. Daniel, who placed the publication in the context of cultural and intellectual enterprise of his camp, which he himself is credited with doing much to foster[16]: 'The publication of a Camp Journal comes in the natural sequence of new enterprises which, I am glad to say, happen with great regularity in Hutchinson Camp'. He continued by praising the initiative of the internees: 'It is a matter of congratulation that men of all classes, brought together under present conditions, have been able as quickly to acclimatise and organise themselves'.[17]

The Campfather's response, lacking the Commander's optimism, was measured: 'Taking in account existing circumstances, a journal like this must of necessity be limited in it scope but in spite of this, we confidently hope, it will be worth while having.'[18]

As might be expected, the greatest discrepancy between the vision of the Commander and perception of the editorial team is to be found in the statements of Major P. Alexander, the Commander of Mooragh Camp, and Robert Neumann, editorial spokesman. Alexander was extremely prescriptive in his description of the journal's function: 'I should like to commend the enterprise of those who have made this Camp Journal possible and hope that it will do much to make camp life brighter and happier, for that is its purpose'. He concluded in the bracing tones of a Sunday School teacher: 'Nothing useful is accomplished by grumbling or self-pity, but self-help and help to others can work miracles'.[19] For his part Neumann began by shooting himself and his colleagues in the foot: 'Wir wünschen dieser Zeitschrift ein kurzes Leben. Sie sterbe bald mit ihrem Anlass' and continued in Churchillian cadences, which nevertheless constituted an insult to his captors:

> Uns den Gefangenen soll sie lebendig bleiben als ein Dokument der Schande. Und unseren Gefängniswärten als ein Zeugnis dessen, wie eine grosse Nation im Sommer 1940 zum erstenmal in den Jahrhunderten ihrer heroischen Geschichte es für richtig befunden hat, den Feldzug zur Befreiung der abendländischen Kultur zu beginnen damit, daß sie ihre treuesten Freunde, die erbittertsten Feinde ihrer Feinde gefangengesetzt.[20]

As we have seen, the two parties clashed over this first issue, and the journal was not continued. The key to the first stage of successful publication, it would seem, was to accentuate the positive. This was the approach taken by the editors of the *Central Promenade Paper,* whose opening statement, which used identical imagery, offered a positive counterpoint to Neumann's negativity: 'Zur Geburt dieses unseres jüngsten Lagerkindes wünsche ich nichts sehnlicher, als daß es wachse und gedeihe.'[21] However, this upbeat attitude did not prevent Necker from publishing extremely disturbing material on the aftermath of the fall of France, as will be demonstrated later.

By September, when the *Central Promenade Paper* came to be published, a clear censorship policy had been established. 'What the editors say' gives a clear summary of the conditions under which camp journals could be produced. These rules seem to have been formulated with specific reference to the *Mooragh Times* experience. Camp journals had to be 'properly' censored by the Camp Intelligence Officer (the first time this official had been explicitly mentioned). 'Such journals should be purely for the purpose of brightening Camp Life and are not permitted as vehicles for complaints and political propaganda of any sort', it is stated[22], virtually echoing Major Alexander's position. The editorial comment on these restrictions is one of almost weary resignation:

> Das ist der Rahmen, in dem sich unser Geist bewegt, Stacheldraht und beschränkende Mittel bilden weitere Begrenzungen objektiver Art, während wir nach der subjektiven Seite nicht zuletzt mit unserem vielzeitig zusammengestellten Leserpublikum zu rechnen haben.[23]

To emphasize the point, each edition of the paper carried the following imprint on the final page: 'Published by CPP, edited by Necker and Barazetti, censored by the Commander.'

A further censorship requirement was that the journals should not be sent out of the camp without the express permission of the Home Office, which had to be informed of the identity of the recipient. This was possibly a reaction to the events of the previous August when Robert Neumann had sent copies of the first issue of the *Mooragh Times* to several national newspapers, including *The Times,* the *Daily Herald* and the *News Chronicle,* together with information about the contributors which emphasised their history of opposition to National Socialism, an approach which had infuriated Alexander.[24] How much the reaction to this contact with the outside world stemmed from that officer's own sense of insecurity (he was a newly-promoted member of the Territorial Army, whereas his counterpart at Onchan, although not outranking him, was an experienced member of the Regular Army who had seen active service as early as 1923) is a matter for speculation. However, the editors of the *Onchan Pioneer* had experienced no such negative repercussions when they sent an early issue of their journal to the Bishop of Chichester, George Bell, a well known supporter of the refugees, who had visited the Island in July and in August advocated their release in the House of Lords. His letter, dated 27 September 1940, acknowledging receipt of the magazine, appeared on the first page of the 13 October issue.[25] Similarly, publication of *The Camp* was allowed to continue although a letter from sixteen artists interned in Hutchinson Camp deploring the harmful effect of incarceration on their art had appeared in the *New Statesman and Nation* 28 August 1940:

> Art cannot live behind barbed wire […] the tensions under which we exist here, the sense of grievous injustice done to us, the restlessness caused by living in close proximity with thousands of other men […] prevent all work and creativity.[26]

The choice of language also offers evidence of censorship and self-censorship. The decision to write in English was not solely a sign of cultural assimilation.[27] The Isle of Man was the second or indeed third internment location for the majority of internees. By the time they arrived on the island familiarity with the censorship system had taught them that letters that were written in English were more likely to reach the recipient than those written in German.[28] We shall see that while contributions in German were by no means unacceptable, a crucial part of the editors' strategy to get their points across successfully was to quote from British political sources and to frame their arguments in the language of the host country. In the case of *The Camp* this prudent political tactic became editorial policy – 'But, my friend, tell the story in English! Otherwise those who have to decide about your release and about your future life will not be able to understand' [29] – resulting in the unusual phenomenon of a predominantly monolingual journal.

A close examination of the *Mooragh Times* and a comparison with the approach of those editors who successfully steered their newssheets past the censor gives some indication of the extent to which the content of the first and only issue of this journal elicited the ban. The first thing that strikes the reader is the sheer confidence and ambition of the production: sixteen quarto pages inclusive of graphics. In contrast the early issues of the *Onchan Pioneer*, although produced in the larger foolscap format, never exceeded eight pages, while the eight-page first issue of *The Camp* was printed on one side only, with an editorial apology for 'some deficiencies'. Paper shortages, always an issue in wartime, are mentioned in the first two issues of the *Onchan Pioneer*. In both cases this tactic of a tentative, gradual start proved a politic course. The dull format, smudged print, blank pages and lack of illustrations in the earlier issues of these two journals may have been primarily due to technical difficulties, but these very deficiencies had the unintended consequence of making these publications appear unthreatening to the censor.

The self-confident stance of the editors of the *Mooragh Times* is even more evident in their approach to the material. There are many examples of irony and scepticism. Friedrich Steiner's 'Eine epochale Entdeckung' offers a mock anthropological approach to a puzzling new race discovered on an island in the Irish Sea – the refugees, who eat a strange mixture called porridge and spend their days in the peculiar communal pastime of writing release applications. Two anecdotes of camp life, written in English, 'The Onion' and 'Organizing a Stove', demonstrate the theft and cunning that were needed to feed and warm the detainees. Finally, Bruno Heilig's 'K. Z. und I. C.' was printed on the back page. This ironic juxtaposition of the two systems penned by a former inmate of Dachau and Buchenwald whose concentration camp novel, *Men Crucified*, was to appear the following year, depicts a British camp in which there are no long days of hard labour, where the internees are permitted to lounge in the sun and the nice Tommies apologise if the roll-call lasts too long. Yet as the piece concludes with the assertion: 'In Deutschland hatte uns einer interniert, dessen Todfeinde wir sind, und der das von uns wußte',[30] it was hardly surprising that this emphatic approach did not commend itself to the British authorities. Much more acceptable was the sycophantic, almost childlike gratitude expressed in the second issue of the *Onchan Pioneer,* where an account of a tragic sea bathing accident, in which two men drowned, began with the observation: 'Wir müssen anerkennen, daß die Offiziere bemüht sind, uns das Seebad zu ermöglichen' and continued in the tone of a school prefect:

> Ist dieses Hinausschwimmen auf große Entfernungen wirklich nötig? Es gefährdet die Kameraden selbst, vergrössert die Verantwortung des begleitenden Offiziers und hat nun zu einer Einschränkung der Badenden auf 100 am Tage geführt.[31]

The irony and scepticism of the *Mooragh Times* offered a subversive critique of the internment policy which proved unacceptable to the authorities intent on boosting morale. But since release was the burning political issue that concerned all internees, it was inconceivable that any camp journal could exist without dealing with this argument. On 9 August 1940, three days before the appearance of the *Mooragh Times*, the *Onchan Pioneer* had carried a strap on its front page which, with reference to a recent Churchill speech screamed: 'What is our station, Mr. Churchill? It can't be the idleness of an internment camp!'. How was it that such a *cri de coeur* was permitted in one case but not in the other?

The editors of the successful journals based this success on finding acceptable ways of criticising the policy and arguing for release. The solution they found was a very simple one: not to formulate their arguments themselves but to quote British supporters of their cause, a task facilitated by the availability of the British newspapers in the camps. This tactic was adopted from the outset by the *Onchan Pioneer* which, in the very first issue, quoted from the Commons debate on 10 July in which the Under Secretary of State for the Home Office, Mr. Osbert Peake, had stated: 'The feeling towards the refugees [...] has changed many times [...] now it is swinging back'.[32] By the next issue the editors were able to outline their approach explicitly. Concentrating on the positive, despite expectations disappointed by the July White Paper,[33] which had confined release proposals to category C detainees, they declared 'We are not without friends':

> It is not the task and the intention of the *Onchan Pioneer* to start a polemic discussion about the policy which had led to our internment. We therefore will refrain from defining our own attitude and from giving our own opinion in this paper. Other, however, will speak for us. [...] Major Cazalet, Viscount Wolmer, Mr. Peake [...] Miss Rathbone, Colonel Wedgewood [*sic*]. [34]

Similarly the 3 November issue of *The Camp* remarked that the recent visit of Lord Lytton had boosted morale and shown the internees they were not forgotten. The same issue refers to Lord Cecil's programme on the BBC Home Service which had appealed for the release of those who had been 'improperly interned'. The virtue of such selective quotation and reference was that it could be argued the editors were reporting rather than commenting, an approach to which no censor could raise objection. The *Mooragh Times* dealt with the issue in a way which was much less politically astute. 'Zur Rechtslage der "B" Fälle'[35], a long critique of the White Paper, outlined the anomalies in the categorisation system, criticised the ways in which those running the tribunals had approached their task and suggested better means of addressing the problem. This confident criticism of the institutions of the host country ignored the sources of support within those institutions, and failed entirely to appreciate the effect which could be achieved by judicious quotation from such sources. Such citation is confined to a short paragraph reprinted from the *Manchester Guardian* of 9 August, outlining methods of release for refugee farm workers. Michael Corvin, the editor of *The Camp,* was more perspicacious, commenting: 'We are not a free newspaper in the sense of the law, but thanks to the Commander we are free in the moral sense and thus able to give constructive criticism of whatever disturbs us',[36] thereby acknowledging that this loss of freedom meant that communication had to be mediated through the authorities.

Those editors who recognised this fact used British supporters as a framework for the internees to plead their own cause. But such argument had to be properly formulated. The authorities had to be petitioned with due decorum, and the emphasis had to be on the positive, that is, the future, not on past official intransigence. Churchillian rhetoric might certainly be adopted. The earliest example of such a text is a telegram to Churchill printed in the first issue of the *Onchan Pioneer:*

> The overwhelming majority of the internees of the Onchan Internment Camp assure H. M. Government of their complete and unreserved loyalty and wish to express their earnest desire to serve in H. M. Forces in any capacity which may be assigned to them. As Refugees from Nazi Oppression we respectfully urge H. M. Government to give us opportunity of taking a share of Great Britain's finest hour and we solemnly express our eagerness to do everything in our power to help Great Britain in her momentous struggle.

Having got this past the censor, the internees then felt confident enough to frame similar arguments directly, that is, without a prominent British addressee, as in the following example, which appeared when the Battle of Britain was at its height:

> In the days through which we live we witness the most momentous struggle of modern times. [...] Yet, it is Britain alone which makes her historic stand undaunted and brave, fighting the decisive battle for her future and the future of the whole world.

> We, who are at present not allowed to work and fight for the struggle for
> common ideas [...] greet in admiration the men of the RAF who defend
> this island with their lives, their skills and their courage. The memory of
> their deeds will be 'like a beacon on a hill for all men to wonder at'. [...]
> For the happiness of future generations is defended today.[37]

Similarly, with reference to the proposed technical school in Hutchinson
Camp, representatives of the internees wrote:

> We [...] are waiting [...] for our release, and we are waiting for the victory
> of this country in its struggle against Nazidom. But there are two ways of
> waiting; the one, just to wait for things to happen, aimlessly, listlessly, in a
> tiring and tiresome inactivity, the other one to pass the time with work, to
> learn, to train one's mind, to live with a purpose.[38]

Under the cover of such patriotic rhetoric, more open and explicit
criticism could gradually be introduced, as in the following example which
appeared in mid-October:

> We believe that the internees should obtain a chance to make full use of
> their time, which is now being wasted. We do not want Red Cross or any
> other Prisoner of War Work. We want to prove our loyalty to Great Britain
> and our hatred of Nazidom and it is our aim to participate to the best of our
> ability in the industrial War Effort of this country.[39]

Indeed Wilhelm Necker, the redoubtable editor of the *Central Promenade
Paper*, was particularly adroit in introducing material which contravened his
editorial mission of 'brightening camp life'. For example, lamenting the
death of Rudolf Olden, drowned in the Atlantic en route to the USA when
the *City of Benares* was torpedoed, Hans Marguiles wrote: 'This death
illustrates the senselessness of Olden's fate during the last months. He left
England because he was prevented from helping in this war, what [*sic*] we
are all prevented from doing, though it is his and our war'.[40] In the same
issue Necker recounts the fate of German refugees after the fall of France:
'Ganze Lager wurden den Nazis übergeben'. The reports of those who
reached safety, including the Mann brothers and Franz Werfel, are
outweighed by the bad news that Walter Hasenclever, Irmgard Keun, Otto
Pol and his wife had committed suicide.[41] Necker, a financial journalist, had
had a particularly turbulent career in exile, having been dismissed from his
post in Czechoslovakia as a result of German diplomatic intervention.
Compared with his former task of serving as propaganda adviser to the
Czechoslovak General Staff, running a camp newspaper could hardly have
taxed his political acumen.

   The women's camps provide the exception to this rule of the gradual
relaxation of scrutiny and the establishment of a *modus operandi*. Dame

Joanna, in her desire to appear even-handed, remained extremely nervous of permitting any opinions to appear in writing. Her responsibility differed from that of the Commanders of the men's camps in that she had in her charge a large number of expatriates (as distinct from refugees) many of whom had Nazi sympathies, including a group of nurses, deaconesses from the German hospital, and German economic migrants working as maids in England. In particular, the activities of the notorious Wanda Wehrhan, wife of the former pastor of the German Embassy, who engaged in political propaganda within the camp, caused Cruikshank endless trouble with London, leading to imputations of lack of control. While the journals in the men's camps refer obliquely to similar problems – Major Marsh of Onchan had posed the question 'how will the audience accept [the paper]'[42] and the editors of the *Central Promenade Paper* refer equally coyly to their 'vielseitig zusammengestellte Leserpublikum'[43] – such matters were less acute, since the composition of the population was different. There were fewer Nazi sympathisers, primarily because males in this category were subject to deportation, a procedure not applied to women.

Finally, the question must be asked, what was lost as a result of the bans? The successful journals developed into much more than vehicles for political debate or pleas for release. These journals chronicled and commented on the activities in the camps, thus encouraging such activities, particularly in the intellectual and cultural sphere. For example, the group of prominent visual artists in Hutchinson Camp published an ambitious Christmas and New Year Almanach 1940-1941, which was issued with *The Camp,* and from December 1940 the *Onchan Pioneer* published a series entitled 'Our Camp in Pictures' which, it was suggested, could be kept as a souvenir of the Island once the subscriber had been released.[44] Moreover, the aspirations of the refugees themselves – to restore and maintain communication with the outside world – were fulfilled. Although issued with a cover price of 2*d*, the *Onchan Pioneer* was sold on a subscription basis, the idea being that subscribers would continue to receive their journal after they had been released, thus ensuring distribution on the mainland. Finally, these publications form part of the network of exile publications which supported the refugees. The press of the Austrian Centre, *Zeitspiegel* and *Young Austria,* carried extensive reports on initiatives to help the internees and many letters from the internees themselves: for example, in August 1940 the Young Austria youth leader, Hans Probst, reported extensively on the activities of the young men in Central Promenade Camp and requested donations of books, money and clothing.[45] Some idea of what has been lost by prohibiting the publication of the *Mooragh Times* can be formed. Bruno Heilig's prose meditation on camp life had to appear elsewhere[46] and as far as I am aware no internment camp novel was to issue from his pen. Additionally, Robert Neumann's plan to encourage prose descriptions of daily life in the camp was frustrated by the ban. Neumann's novel, *The Inquest,* published in 1944, clearly reflects his experience in the camp, but the absence of publication opportunities in the camp itself no doubt discouraged younger writers.

Nevertheless, in considering internment camp journals as a whole, we can say that the aspirations and achievements of their editors and contributors transcended the limited brief envisioned by their military captors who had so misguidedly sought to mould and limit the product of insecure and vulnerable refugees by instructing them to provide the camp with 'something to make people laugh'.

Notes

[1] See Richard Dove, '"KZ auf Englisch": Robert Neumann's internment diary', in *England? Aber wo liegt es?*, ed. by Charmian Brinson and others (Munich: iudicium, 1996), pp. 157-167 (p.157).

[2] For Josef Kalmus, later known as Joseph Kalmer, see Tanja Gausterer and Volker Kaukoreit, 'Der Journalist Joseph Kalmer – eine Spurensicherung', *Zwischenwelt*, April 2005, pp. 30-33.

[3] For this and subsequent references to Rushen, I am indebted to Charmian Brinson, in particular '"In the Exile of Internment" or "Von Versuchen, aus einer Not eine Tugend zu machen": German-Speaking Women Interned by the British during the Second World War' in *Politics and Culture in Twentieth-Century Germany*, ed. by William Niven and James Jordan (New York/Woodbridge: Camden House, 2003) pp. 63-87; Brinson is able to authenticate all of these titles with the exception of *The Awful Times and Daily Rumour,* the existence of which is attested solely by two references in the *Onchan Pioneer,* 'Bath Regulations in the Hotel Majestic', 29 September 1940, p. 4 and 'The Awful Times and Daily Rumour', 27 April 1941, pp. 1-2, raising the possibility that references to this title may be a hoax.

[4] The first four issues have survived, but internal evidence suggests that no.4 was not the final issue; the entry in Liselotte Maas, *Handbuch der deutschen Exilpresse 1933-1945* (Munich: Hanser, 1976), Vol.1, p. 129 mistakenly states that only one number was issued.

[5] Seven issues of the *Sefton Review,* published between November 1940 and February 1941, are extant.

[6] See 'Advisory Committee sitting on the island', *Onchan Pioneer*, 13 October 1940, p. 1.

[7] See, for example, W. Scholz. 'Solidarität', *Zeitspiegel,* 14 September 1940, pp. 2-4; 'Charlie Chaplin hilft den Internierten', *Young Austria,* Beginning of November 1940, pp. 2-3, 'Weihnachtshilfswoche für die Internierten', *ibid.,* p. 4, 'Weihnachtshilfe', *Zeitspiegel,* 21 November 1940, p. 8; 'Ostern für die Internierten', *Zeitspiegel,* 23 March 1941, p. 1.

[8] See Jörg Thunecke, 'Die Isle of Man-Lagerzeitungen *The Camp* und *The Onchan Pioneer*: Kultur im Ausnahmezustand', in *German-speaking Exiles in Great Britain*, ed. by J. M. Ritchie (Amsterdam/New York: Rodopi, 2001), pp. 41-58 (p. 50).

[9] Michael Corvin was one of the pseudonyms used by Leo Freund, novelist, dramatist and writer on science and political economy who lived in Berlin in the early 1930s; it has not, however, been definitively established that the editor of *The Camp* was Leo Freund. I am indebted to William Abbey for this information.

[10] See Klaus Hinrichsen, 'The Camp', one page typescript, Imperial War Museum, E. 88/292.

[11] Michael Corvin, 'Review', *The Camp*, 29 September 1940; since this journal was not paginated, no page numbers will be cited.

[12] See unsigned editorial, 'Was wir wollen', *Onchan Pioneer*, 27 July 1940, p. 1.

[13] See Hans Gál, *Musik hinter Stacheldraht: Tagebuchblätter aus dem Sommer 1940*, Hrsg. Eva Fox-Gál (Bern/Berlin/Brussels/Frankfurt am Main/New York/Oxford/ Vienna: Lang, 2003), pp. 117-8, 121-2; the Lt. Johnson referred to here may possibly be W. H. Johnson of the TA Reserve who had been on special employment since November 1938, most probably as an Intelligence Officer.

[14] 'What the Speakers say', *Central Promenade Paper*, 16 September 1941, p. 1.

[15] *Onchan Pioneer*, 27 July 1940, p. 1.

[16] See Klaus Hinrichsen, 'Visual Art Behind the Wire', in *The Internment of Aliens in Twentieth Century Britain*, ed. by David Cesarani and Tony Kushner (London: Cass, 1993), pp.188-207 (pp.194-5). Hinrichsen mistakenly reverses the officer's initials.

[17] 'Commander's Introduction', *The Camp*, 21 September 1940.

[18] *Ibid.*

[19] *Mooragh Times*, 12 August 1940, p. 1.

[20] *Ibid.*

[21] 'What the Speakers say', *Central Promenade Paper*, 16 September 1940, p. 1.

[22] 'What the Editors say', *Central Promenade Paper*, 16 September 1940, p. 2.

[23] *Ibid.*

[24] Quoted in Dove, *op. cit.*, p. 164.

[25] Major Marsh had ceased to be Camp Commander by that time – his promotion was announced by the *Onchan Pioneer* on 9 August 1940.

[26] Quoted in Hinrichsen, 'Visual Art Behind the Wire', p. 188.

[27] See Thunecke, *op. cit.*, p. 43.

[28] See editorial note to 'Unsere Freunde schreiben', *Young Austria*, Beginning of January 1940, pp. 4-5 (p.4).

[29] 'These lines concern you, YOU PERSONALLY!', *The Camp*, 15 September 1940, (unsigned editorial).

[30] Bruno Heilig, 'KZ und IC', *Mooragh Times*, 12 August 1940, p. 16.

[31] 'Kameraden schreiben', *Onchan Pioneer*, 9 August 1940, p. 5.

[32] 'Die Regierungserklärung über unsere Zukunft!', *Onchan Pioneer*, 27 July 1940, p. 5.

[33] Two White Papers on release were issued in quick succession, the first on 31 July 1940, the second, containing several amendments in response to negative criticism of the first, in early August; cf. 'Das "White Paper" und wir' *Onchan Pioneer*, 9 August 1940, p. 1.

[34] I. e. Col. Josiah Wedgwood, MP; 'We are not without friends', *Onchan Pioneer*, 9 August 1940, p. 3. For further details of Parliamentary interventions in support of the internees see Yvonne Kapp & Margaret Mynatt, *British Policy and the Refugees 1933-1941* (London/Portland Oregon: Cass 1997), pp. 131-134.

[35] Dr. B., 'Zur Rechtslage der "B-Fälle", *Mooragh Times*, 12 August 1940, pp. 10-11.

[36] Michael Corvin, 'Review', *The Camp*, 29 September 1940.

[37] 'The Battle for our Future', *Onchan Pioneer*, 31 August 1940, p. 1; cf. also 'Ready to Fight and Work', *Onchan Pioneer*, 29 September 1940, p. 1, quoted by Michael Seyfert, *In Niemandsland. Deutsche Exilliteratur in britischer Internierung* (Berlin: Das Arsenal, 1984), p. 107.

[38] *The Camp*, 29 September 1940.

[39] 'Open Letter to the Commander', *The Camp*, 15 October 1940.

[40] Hans Marguiles, 'Obituary for Rudolf Olden', *Central Promenade Paper*, 30 September 1940, p. 2.

[41] Wilhelm Necker, 'Deutsche Refugees in Frankreich', *Central Promenade Paper*, 30 September 1940, p. 2. In the case of Irmgard Keun, Necker was mistaken; she had returned to Germany where she was working illegally.

[42] *Onchan Pioneer*, 27 July 1940, p. 1.

[43] 'What the Editors say', *Central Promenade Paper*, 16 September 1940, p. 2.

[44] 'Our Camp in Pictures', *Onchan Pioneer*, Christmas issue, December 1940, p. 5.

[45] Hans Probst, 'The Camp Youth', *Young Austria*, Beginning of August 1940, pp. 1-2; extracts from this letter quoted in *Österreicher im Exil. Großbritannien 1938-1945. Eine Dokumentation*, ed. by Wolfgang Muchitsch (Vienna: Österreichischer Bundesverlag 1992), p. 105.

[46] Bruno Heilig, 'Das Meer', *Young Austria*, Mid-October 1940, p. 3.

Lucio Sponza

The Internment of Italians 1940-1945[1]

After a survey of the hurried and muddled policies pursued by the British government immediately following Italy's entry into the war, this article outlines the basic facts about the internment of Italians and then focuses on the internees themselves: their life in the camps, their various activities and their efforts to maintain contacts with their families. The conclusion argues that although the internment must be seen in the context of the grave situation of the spring of 1940, the vicissitudes of internees also had to do with the prejudice against immigrants.

When, on 10 June 1940, Mussolini declared war on Britain and France – 'fearful of being too late for the spoils'[2] – some 18,000 Italians living in Britain became at a stroke 'enemy aliens'. Many of them were promptly arrested to be interned, as Mussolini's move was expected and policies for action had been laid down.

The question of general internment had been raised four weeks earlier, on 11 May, at the first War Cabinet chaired by Winston Churchill, as the new Prime Minister. Until then a selective policy had been implemented, which distinguished the 'enemy aliens' according to the level of danger to security they supposedly represented. The 'phoney war' had been suddenly terminated with the German armies' thrust in April and May. When the Germans broke through at Sedan, 'the road to Paris was open', as Churchill reported to the War Cabinet on 15 May. At the same War Cabinet meeting, one of the topics for discussion was the possible invasion of Britain and the danger from 'parachutists and Fifth Column elements'. The list of the 'various bodies and groups of persons in this country against whom action would need to be taken' was headed by 'Italians and British subjects of Italian origin'.[3]

During the dramatic days of the evacuation of the British Expeditionary Force, following the debacle of Dunkirk, the British ambassador in Rome, Sir Percy Loraine, cabled the Foreign Office informing them that Italy's entry into the war was now a certainty. Yet, at the end of May it was still not clear what should be done about the majority of Italians in Britain, except that some 1,500 'desperate characters', in addition to 'the 300 British subjects connected with Italian institutions in this country', should be seized and the 'desperate characters' should be deported as soon as practicable.[4] On the day Italy entered the war Churchill instructed the Home Secretary, Sir John Anderson, to arrange for the general internment of male Italians aged 16–70 (later 16–60), with less than twenty years' residence in Britain. It was also decided, however, to deport as many as possible – males and females, of all ages – to Italy. As for the 1,500 'desperate characters', they should be either kept in internment in Britain, or sent for internment to Canada. There was no mention of the 300 British subjects of Italian origin, who were mostly the British-born children of Italians, whose detention was to be enacted on the basis of Defence Regulation 18B.[5]

Who were the Italians in Britain? Unlike the Germans and Austrians who were also rounded up, only a few Italians were refugees from Fascist Italy. The vast majority were economic immigrants – to use a current expression of our own time – who had been living in Britain for a long time, had raised families and had generally become integrated into British society. Most of them were engaged in catering and food dealing, as managers, directors, cooks and waiters in hotels and restaurants, but also as shopkeepers, café owners and ubiquitous ice-cream street vendors throughout the country. During the tense months of the 'phoney war' they had hoped that Mussolini would not plunge Italy into war, but they took a rather fatalistic view of their immediate future: only a few returned to Italy, as their Consular authorities strongly advised them to do. They were not prepared to throw away what had been achieved in a life-time of hard work and sacrifice. They had faced all sort of difficulties in the past and, they believed, the new ordeal would probably soon be over.

Around 4,500 Italians were arrested and interned, including 400 merchant seamen (regarded as military prisoners of war), 300 British-born sons of Italian immigrants and, of course, the often quoted 1,500 'desperate characters'. The last category consisted, in the words of the Aliens Advisory Committee of the Home Office, of 'Italians who are known to the authorities to be professing *Fascisti*'.[6] The lists of these 1,500 dangerous men had been supplied by MI5 (the branch of Military Intelligence responsible for counter-espionage), apparently on the basis of mere membership of the Fascist Party, a principle soon judged as inadequate and misleading by government departments – notably the Foreign Office.

Criticism of the indiscriminate policy of general internment came into the open after the sinking of the *Arandora Star*, early in July 1940. The former luxury liner was carrying around a thousand deportees to Canada, including 717 Italian and 138 German/Austrian 'enemy aliens', as well as 240 German merchant seamen. Of the 621 who lost their lives in the disaster, 446 were Italian, and it emerged that some of the victims were not 'desperate characters', but well-known anti-Fascists and Jewish refugees. The ensuing inquiry, led by Lord Snell, revealed that a number of errors had been committed, but its conclusion was that no serious criticism of the programme of deportation was justified. Yet, the tragedy of the *Arandora Star* led to important policy changes. Firstly, any further deportation overseas of internees was abandoned; secondly, the administration of internment camps was transferred from the War Office to the Home Office, thus drawing a clearer distinction between military prisoners of war and civilian internees; thirdly, two advisory committees were established, one to keep internment policy under review and the other to monitor the welfare of internees; fourthly, the procedures for the release of internees were laid down in various White Papers.

As far as the Italians were concerned, a Home Office Advisory Committee was set up to examine the applications for release, under the chairmanship of Sir Percy Loraine (the last British ambassador in Rome, already mentioned). Whether membership of the Fascist Party should in itself imply an unfriendly – if not hostile and dangerous – attitude to Britain, resurfaced now, as Sir Percy (and the Foreign Office) disagreed with the view of MI5 (shared to some extent by the Home Office). A document was at that time circulated to support Sir Percy's opinion. The author was an Italian Jewish refugee, Bruno Foa, who had luckily escaped arrest and internment and had left for the United States. Foa maintained that membership of the Fascist Party did not necessarily imply pro-Fascist sentiments: 'The possession of a membership card – he wrote – is in everyday life as much a necessity as, say, a birth or citizenship certificate in a democratic country'.[7] Although the rift between Sir Percy and MI5 remained, and the Security Services' meddling in the working of the 'Loraine Tribunal' represented a cause of great frustration for the former ambassador, the release of internees began in the autumn of 1940 and proceeded with regularity, though very slowly at first. The main category for release involved Italians who had been living in Britain for at least twenty years and were judged to be friendly towards their adopted country; then came the category including the 'invalid and infirm', affecting mainly the elderly of the interned community; and then the category of Italians who agreed to join the Auxiliary Military Pioneer Corps and were prepared to take up any employment designated by the authorities. By the end of 1941 the total number of Italian internees had halved to around 2,000.[8] The pace slowed down throughout 1942 and for most of 1943. At the time of Italy's surrender and consequent armistice (8 September 1943) around 1,500 Italians were still behind barbed wire, but thereafter the number of releases accelerated and by the end of the war in Europe, in May 1945, only 573 Italians were still interned. These were mainly merchant seamen, who did tend to have genuine Fascist sympathies and were separated from the bulk of other Italian internees who were housed in other camps, as will be mentioned later.

Virtually all 'enemy aliens' kept in Britain were interned on the Isle of Man, in the Irish Sea, which had the advantage of isolation and available accommodation, with its abundance of hotels and boarding-houses, normally opened in the summer for holidaymakers from the mainland and from Ireland. Eleven camps were eventually established, six in Douglas, the capital town, on the eastern coast of the island; two in the south of the island: one to house women and their children, the other to accommodate married couples, with or without their children. Each camp, consisting of a number of hotels/boarding-houses, was given an official name (often derived from the name of the main hotel it included) and normally contained 'enemy aliens' of the same nationality.

The Italians were initially sent to two Douglas camps: Douglas and Metropole; later in 1940 some of them were moved to Granville Camp, also in Douglas. As the number of internees decreased, due to releases, some camps were closed down and the remaining inmates were moved elsewhere. In November 1941, for instance, Granville Camp was closed and its internees were either moved into a newly cleared camp at Onchan, near Douglas, or joined Germans, Austrians and Finns at Mooragh Camp, at Ramsey, in the north of the island. Metropole became the camp of Italian merchant seamen. By the end of the war Metropole Camp had also been closed and its internees moved to the one remaining compound: Peveril Camp, at Peel, on the western coast. The last Italian internees were released in July 1945.

Living conditions, accommodation and general welfare in internment camps were regularly monitored by the International Red Cross (IRC), while occasional visits were made by government officials, members of the Advisory Council on Aliens, and by various representatives of religious and humanitarian organisations – notably the Young Men's Christian Association (YMCA) and the Quakers' Society of Friends.

In one of the earliest reports by an IRC visitor at the Palace and Metropole camps, a list of requests was submitted, to be passed for consideration to the relevant authorities. First of all, the internees whose families resided either in Italy or in other countries asked for their relatives to be informed as soon as possible about their internment address and that a correspondence service be established. Incidentally, the question of mail from relatives – infrequent and delayed – was to remain a constant concern of the Italians throughout their internment, emphasising the importance they attached to family connections (see below). Most of the issues raised in the early IRC report indirectly pointed to the main dangers of internment life:

boredom and consequent depression.[9] Through their elected 'camp leaders', therefore, the internees expressed the desire to be allowed to work voluntarily both inside and outside the camps. Other requests to sustain various activities concerned books to be added to the existing libraries in the camps and sports equipment.[10] In subsequent reports a common request was also for musical instruments.

Let us now expand on the issues raised by the internees of Palace and Metropole camps, by taking them in reverse order: sports and games; education, cultural and spiritual activities; work and enterprise; and family links.

During the rainy days and long winter nights, such indoor games as cards, billiards, draughts and chess were common, although the most popular was a game which required no equipment whatsoever. This was the age-old Italian game of 'morra', in which two players try to guess the sum-number of the fingers of the one hand that each of them quickly and simultaneously displays. As the game progresses and increases in tempo, the numbers are shouted louder and louder, as excitement seizes the players. At weekends, if there was adequate open space (Onchan was the best camp in this respect), the most popular outdoor pursuit was – of course – football. The game of bowls was also a favourite pursuit, as it only required a limited space. 'For that purpose' – was written in a report – 'they are using wooden balls of all shapes and sizes'.[11] On fine summer days sea-bathing, within a circumscribed precinct of the camps, was a much relished recreation. Visits to local cinemas and country walks were sometimes organised, in limited numbers and under escort.

As for education, cultural and spiritual activities, the list of books attached to the mentioned IRC report consisted of thirty-five items which ranged from language grammars and dictionaries (Italian, Latin, Greek, Spanish and especially English), literature (Italian, English and Latin), history (Roman, Italian and English), philosophy (in particular, Plato), mathematics ('Infinitesimal calculus'), sciences (physics, chemistry and biology) and – last but not least – religion (including: '3 dozen penny Catechism' and '3 dozen penny prayers (sic) books. Catholic Truth Soc.'). It is likely that only the last noted devotional items were widely read. All the preceding topics were probably suggested by a small number of internees. Unlike the German and Austrian internees, the great majority of Italians had a modest level of formal education. It was rumoured, in this respect, that the distinguished scholar, Arnaldo Momigliano, unsuccessfully asked to be sent to a German/Austrian camp, as he dreaded the prospect of sharing his day-to-day life with uneducated shopkeepers, cooks and waiters. Also in terms of musical talent the Italian camps could not match the German/Austrian camps (as is well known, in one of the latter the original nucleus of the Amadeus Quartet took shape). Still, a YMCA report commented favourably on the band of an Italian camp.[12]

Educational provisions varied from camp to camp and were mainly focused on the young internees, aged 16 to 18. It seems that only towards the end of 1941 was a general scheme adopted, in which, apart from regular English classes, the emphasis was on various scientific and technical subjects: mathematics, physics, chemistry, technical drawing, tools, electricity and 'Practical Installations' – whatever that entailed.

Spiritual and religious assistance was provided to young people and adults by the several Italian missionary priests who had to follow their countrymen into internment. Sunday mass was held in each camp in one of the largest rooms available, which was transformed into a chapel for the occasion. In the summer, weather permitting, religious functions were officiated in the open. One pious internee wrote in his memoirs: 'In dangerous times, not only the faithful but also the so-called incredulous (sic) would approach the Church for protection and consolation'.[13]

A different source of consolation was sought through work and enterprise. All internees were assigned some task to enable their common life to function. A few were elected by their own fellow-countrymen as 'house' and 'camp' leaders; some became co-ordinators of the various voluntary activities pursued in the camps. Certain routine operations, such as house cleanliness and keeping the open spaces clean and tidy, had to be performed in turn by 'fatigue parties'. Specific individuals were permanently assigned semi-skilled or skilled tasks, such as managing food provisions, cooking, canteen service, clerical work and medical support (British doctors regularly visited camps and if necessary internees were taken to one of two hospitals in the island, so designed). Yet, there was still plenty of time to kill for the majority of internees and they could choose to direct their energies and enterprise in practical work both inside and outside the camp.

Practical and imaginative activities within the compounds involved, for instance, the making of nets, baskets, artificial flowers and other decorative objects, out of twigs or any scrap of metal and timber that could be found. In a few instances inventiveness went too far, as in the case of Luigi Trombetti, the sometime owner of a 'fish restaurant' in South Wales. This is how the story was reported in the *Isle of Man Examiner*, without identifying the internee:

> Deemster [Judge] Farrant on Monday found himself with no alternative but to order an Italian internee to forfeit £200 for breach of the Distillation of Spirits Act, which was passed in 1867. [...] Evidence was given that by the use of an ingeniously made still, which was produced in Court, he had

distilled from fermented potatoes, beetroot, fruit and sugar, a liquid which on analysis was found to contain 43.8 per cent by volume of proof spirit. [...] The still consisted of a metal container for the 'mash' with a copper pipe leading to another container in which two copper balls, as used on the ball-tap of a cistern, were soldered together to act as condensers. Cold water was allowed to circulate around the condensers, from the bottom of which a pipe led to a porcelain gravy-bowl in which the distillate was collected.

The £200 fine – enormous, at the time – was subsequently reduced to a still hefty £10. Trombetti was also accused of making souvenir rings, in great demand by internees who were about to be released, out of 'silver' coins (two-shilling and half-crown pieces): he was given a month's imprisonment for 'defacing coins of the Realm'. No discount to the penalty was applied here, as it was a second offence.[14]

Voluntary and paid work outside the camps was allowed as early as August 1940. The terms and conditions of this mainly rural occupation were laid down by the island's Government Office.[15] On average, up to the end of 1943, about 60 per cent of all Italian internees had some regular employment outside their camps. In the last two years of the war that proportion increased, to reach monthly peaks of 90 per cent. This was due partly to the stronger demand for work and partly to the fact that those who were still interned were younger and more energetic. Such willingness to do productive work must have surprised many pundits, who regarded the Italians as a lazy lot. Here is one example, offered to the Home Office: 'Many of these Italians are quite content to be kept at the expense of the State doing nothing in internment camps'.[16] The Italians' indolence was also associated with the fact that most of them were considered to have 'no political convictions, but were desperately anxious to be on the winning side at the end of the war [...]. They will then go and sell ice-cream to the winners'.[17]

Even if the Italians had no strong political motivation, they could not be said to have a strong economic motivation either. The monies paid by the employers to the Camp Commanders, on the basis of 'a shilling per day per man', were divided into three equal parts: one third was credited to the cash accounts of the internee-workers concerned;[18] one third was destined to the Camp Welfare Fund, administered by a Home Office Welfare Officer resident in the camp; and one third was assigned to the Treasury of the Isle of Man government, to be used for the purchase of material and machinery in support of the employment of internees. This last third was in effect a tax levied by the island's authorities for the benefit of local employers.

The national government queried the fairness of this arrangement, which enabled 'Manx farmers [to get] sweated labour',[19] but the Isle of Man authorities ignored the criticism and the London government dropped the matter. Perhaps Westminster did not want to upset a deal which was highly advantageous both locally and nationally, as became clear in the autumn of 1942, when the Foreign Office suggested that Italian internees should be deprived of certain privileges (such as the visits to local cinemas) so as to put pressure on the Italian government to improve the allegedly unsatisfactory conditions in which British internees were kept in Italy. The Home Office rejected the suggestion with the following argument:

> The proposal to withdraw certain privileges now allowed to Italian internees would not effect its object [because the Italian government had shown disregard for the fate of Italian internees], while it might impede our war effort, as most of the Italians interned in the Isle of Man have volunteered for labour outside the camps and are doing valuable work in aid of the Air Ministry, or as agricultural workers who are assisting in gathering the biggest harvest in the Island for many years.[20]

The 'valuable work' in question consisted in the construction of a reservoir as a water-supply to an airfield in the north of the island. It was a task entrusted to internees from Metropole Camp, which accommodated the merchant seamen and others, equally regarded as fanatical Fascists but also – perhaps because of this – highly disciplined.[21] Internees from Metropole Camp did cause concern for activities outside the camp, but not on political and ideological grounds. At about the time of the disagreement between the Foreign Office and the Home Office, three Italians escaped in two separate incidents. They were all soon discovered in nearby boarding-houses, where they went to meet relatives who had come to the island to visit them. In one case, 'the internee was found in the lodgings of his wife outside the camp [...]. He had spent every night with her during the previous week'.[22]

The internees were allowed to send two letters per week, with no limits on the number they could receive. Still, they were eager to see their relatives as often as possible – which really meant that such visits would take place as often as the family could afford: in addition to travelling costs, boarding-house bills had to be paid. Those visits were very important for both the internees and their relatives, as they all strove to maintain the unity of the family in such dramatic circumstances. In a report on the internee-patients in one of the Island's hospitals it was noted that:

> A large number of the [Italians admitted] had their relations left in Italy and they became more depressed as news of their families became less frequent. There seems to be more neurasthenia amongst those with families in Italy than those living in this country.[23]

Visitors with any spare money would take advantage of the relative abundance of food and other necessities available in the island, compared to the mainland's more austere rationing. Others, especially if involved in catering and food dealing, would bring an excessive amount of items for the internees sometimes in breach of the strict regulations on what was allowed into the camps. The most glamorous attempt at such smuggling concerned Signora Maria Pacitti, who tried to make Christmas (of 1942) less miserable for her husband, Guglielmo, at Onchan Camp. Here is the list of contents, as drawn by a camp officer, with his comments and queries:

> 1 pair trousers; 1 cheese grater; 1 piece Parmesan cheese, about 2 lbs. (not rationed); 2 large packets Co-op processed cheese, probably about 10 lbs. total (rationed – ordinarily unobtainable now); 200 Churchman's No1 cigarettes; 2 bottles salad oil, unlabelled (rationed?); ½ lb. Rowntree's Cocoa (rationed?); 1 tin drinking chocolate – found to be mixed with sugar [which was rationed]; 1 packet of coffee (size about 4 ½ lbs.) – found to contain a 4 lb. package of sugar inside; 2 tins red peppers; 1 lb. bottle of Bovril; 1 turkey with 2 tins of condensed milk secreted in its inside; 1 paper bag containing garlic.[24]

Since her husband's internment, Signora Pacitti managed the family confectionery and tobacconist shop in Glasgow single-handedly. In normal times, many Italian women assisted in the running of family cafés and shops, although their main responsibilities were in their homes. Now that many men were forced away, women had to take charge of all aspects of family life – and they usually did it with success. In this they might be helped by the all-important kinship network.

Some general observations can be made in conclusion. Once the experience of internment was behind them, Italians tried to re-establish their family life, so central to their existence and identity. All in all, they succeeded in restoring the old values and bonds, while maintaining a distinct separateness from British society at large. To some extent, a persistent anti-Italian attitude by much of the British public was a contributory factor. Certainly, the story of the internment of 'enemy aliens' raises several broader questions, which can only be hinted at here: the difficult balance to be struck between individual freedom and national security, the prejudiced suspicion often nurtured towards minorities, the issue of mixed loyalties in immigrant communities, the process of social control exercised by the authorities and various agencies at times of political crisis, the role and function of the state in the extreme circumstances of war and 'international terrorism'.

To return, in a few final words, to the topic of the internment of 'enemy aliens', here is a quotation from a distinguished historian on immigration into Britain:

> In its pursuit of aliens as part of [its internment] policy the government could draw upon a strong strains of anti-alienism and anti-Semitism that existed within British society. Indeed, the internment episode can be regarded as the culmination of the hostility which had been directed towards the alien refugees before the war.[25]

Notes

[1] For this article I have drawn from some of my published work on the subject, in particular: 'The British government and the internment of Italians', in *The Internment of Aliens in Twentieth Century Britain*, ed. by D. Cesarani and T. Kushner (London: Frank Cass, 1993), pp. 125–44; 'The internment of Italians in Britain' in *Enemies Within. Italian and Other Internees in Canada and Abroad*, ed. by F. Iacovetta, R. Perin and A. Principe (Toronto/ Buffalo/London: University of Toronto Press, 2000), pp. 256–79; *Divided Loyalties. Italians in Britain during the Second World War* (Bern: Peter Lang, 2000), pp. 95–181.

[2] A. J. P. Taylor, *English History, 1914–1945* (Oxford: Oxford University Press, 1985 [1965]), p. 488.

[3] The National Archives (formerly Public Record Office; hereafter indicated with NA), CAB [Cabinet Papers]: 65/7, 123 (40), 15 May 1940, p. 139; Churchill's reference to Sedan is on p. 131. On the 'Fifth Column panic', see F. H. Hinsley and C. A. G. Simkins, *British Intelligence in the Second World War* (London: HMSO, 1990), pp. 47–64.

[4] NA, CAB 65/7, 148 (40), 30 May 1940, p. 313.

[5] NA, CAB 65/7, 161 (40), 11 June 1940, p. 419.

[6] NA, HO [Home Office] 213/492, 'Disposal of Italians in this country. Report by the Aliens Advisory Committee', 15 June 1940, p. 1.

[7] NA, FO [Foreign Office] 371/25210, 209, 'Foa Memorandum', p.2. It was humorously said in Italy, *sotto voce*, that the acronym PNF (Partito Nazionale Fascista) actually stood for 'Per Necessità Familiare' – For Family's Sake.

[8] Detailed figures of all interned 'enemy aliens' were provided by the Home Secretary, Herbert Morrison (who had replaced John Anderson in October 1940), in a written answer to the House of Commons in November 1941. Here is an extract from that comprehensive table, with the numbers of internees in Britain alone. Germans and Austrians: 1,792, of whom the majority were women (1,198); Italians: 1,903, including only 10 women. See *Hansard* (Commons), Fifth Series, vol.374, col. 2073 (11 November 1941).

[9] From the outline of the 'fixed routine' attached to the report under consideration and indicated in the next note, it is obvious that boredom was a high risk: '7.30 a. m.: Roll Call; 10.30 a. m.: Walk or Bathe; 2.30 p. m.: Draw rations (two men per house); 3.30 p. m.: Walk or Bathe; 6.30 p. m.: Roll Call; 10.45 p. m.: Lights out'.

[10] NA, HO 215/25, 'Conditions in internment camps. Visits to the Isle of Man by members of the International Red Cross. Report by R. Haccius', 20 August 1940.

[11] NA, HO 215/53, Report by J. W. Barwick, of the YMCA, 'August 1940'.

[12] NA, HO 215/48, YMCA Report on Metropole Camp, 10 August 1943.

[13] Calisto Cavalli, *Ricordi di un emigrato* (n. p. [London]: Edizione 'La Voce degli Italiani', n.d. [1973]), p. 85.

[14] *Isle of Man Examiner*, 'Italian internee to forfeit £200', 31 March 1944, p. 1. See also: NA, HO 214/42, 'Trombetti Luigi'.

[15] See *Isle of Man Daily Times*, 'Alien labour on farms', 22 August 1940, p. 2. The Isle of Man enjoyed – and still enjoys – a degree of independence from London. The islanders elect their own legislature (House of Keys) and their own government. The national legislation only applies to the Isle of Man if explicitly required; on the other hand, the laws passed by the House of Keys must be approved by the British Crown.

[16] NA, HO 213/47, 'Departmental Advisory Committee on Italians'. The quotation is contained in a draft reply to a letter Sir Percy Loraine wrote to the HO on 13 March 1941. The draft is attributable to one Prof. R. S. Chorley.

[17] NA, HO 215/30, 'Conditions in [internment] camps. Report by Alexander Paterson, July 1941', p. 28.

[18] Internees were allowed to be in possession of at most 5 shillings at any one time, without special written permission of the Commandant. They could also draw a credit up to £1 per week on their accounts, to be spent at the camp canteen.

[19] NA, HO 215/325, 42B, 'Employment-Pay (1940–41)'. The comment was minuted by Sir John Moylan (Head of the Aliens Dept., HO), on 2 June 1941.

[20] NA, HO 215/175 [11A], 'Discipline in Camps for Italian internees (1942–43)'. Letter of H. A. N. Bluett (HO) to Sir Harold Satow (FO), 5 October 1942.

[21] At first Italians were not separated according to their political views and on a few occasions anti-Fascists were harassed by pro-Mussolini characters. By late 1941, the real (or assumed) Fascists were moved to Metropole Camp, while Granville Camp contained those with opposite views. The Italians in Palace Camp, on the other hand, were regarded as 'Fascist or of doubtful sympathies'. As camps were closed and the remaining internees moved to other sites, distinctions were further blurred, but Metropole Camp maintained the reputation of housing the 'rabid Fascists'.

[22] *Isle of Man Daily Times*, 'Three escape: one visits his wife in Douglas boarding-house', 14 December 1942, p. 2.

[23] NA, HO 215/47, 'Ballaquane Hospital, Isle of Man (1942–43)'. From the Annual Report (1943) by Lt.Gen. R. E. Flowerdew. Altogether, twenty-seven Italians died while in internment camps because of illness or accident. The only case of suicide occurred when the extremely depressed Lionello Togneri jumped from a top-storey window; see *Isle of Man Daily Times*, 'Tragedy at a Manx internment camp', 18 December 1941, p. 4.

[24] NA, HO 214/66 [3C], 'Personal files: Pacitti Guglielmo', 16 December 1942.

[25] Colin Holmes, *John Bull's Island: Immigration and British Society*, 1871–1971 (London: Macmillan, 1988), p. 192.

Nicole M. T. Brunnhuber

After the Prison Ships: Internment Narratives in Canada

Deportation to Canada has generally been treated as another awkward chapter in the history of Britain's internment policy of the Second World War. An examination of contemporary internment texts provides insight into the authentic reactions of those subjected to months, even years, of exclusion and acute uncertainty. This paper seeks to complement existing research by identifying the characteristics of the Canadian internment experience, and to establish Canada's (inadvertent) role as a country of exile for German-speaking refugees. In so doing, it is also intended to promote awareness of neglected exiled writers and internment texts within the field of exile studies.

By the end of July 1940, approximately 4400[1] German and Austrian internees had survived hazardous and unpleasant Atlantic crossings only to find themselves imprisoned in specially allocated camps in Canada's eastern provinces. For the vast numbers who had hoped that deportation would bring adventure or lead to emigration to the USA, the following months, in some cases, the next two years, could only have been a frustrating disappointment. Deportees were branded class 2 Prisoners of War and were denied refugee status until 1 July 1941. Nevertheless, retrospective accounts, particularly by those amongst the roughly 1000 who chose to stay in Canada,[2] tend to emphasize the experience as ultimately positive, extolling Canada as a generous nation of freedom and opportunity. A letter by H. F. Reichenfeld to the editor of *To-Day Magazine*, which had published an extract from Eric Koch's seminal *Deemed Suspect: A Wartime Blunder*,[3] illustrates the depth of feelings of gratitude to Canada, and the reluctance to criticize the Canadian role in the treatment of deported internees. Reichenfeld, psychiatrist in charge at the Royal Ottawa Hospital, insists that he 'was not exposed to the humiliating experiences described by Eric Koch', and condemns the book as a biased contribution to the 'kick Canada cult'.[4]

Reichenfeld's sentiments are not singular and become still more understandable with the benefit of hindsight. However, since, as the conflicting representations of Koch and Reichenfeld illustrate, memory clearly diverges from individual to individual, *ex post facto* accounts are not necessarily entirely reliable in ascertaining authentic responses to historical events. As early as May 1941, H. M. Prison Officer, Alexander Paterson, after months of visiting camps and conducting interviews with internees and authorities alike, recognized the gaps and ambiguities of the Canadian deportation experience, and commented in his official report: 'After a whole year of self-pity and exchange of grievances, it is impossible to reconstruct the true story of what happened in all its unhappy details.'[5] An examination of internment accounts, including texts not originally intended for the public eye or the relevant authorities, sheds some light on the actual responses to internment in Canada.

Insecurity and uncertainty are key features of the collective textual production by internees in Canadian camps, and the entire Canadian experience is commonly depicted as an endless journey into the unknown. This is not surprising, since deportees only learnt of their destination during the final stages of the crossings. Even if dressed up in a jovial tone, a common feature of internment verse, a poem by an anonymous author in camp B, New Brunswick, emphasizes this point:

> One day the order comes to go
> to an unknown destination.
> We had to go, we could not know
> Of our deportation.[6]

This sense of the unknown was not, however, assuaged once the deportees found themselves on solid, Quebec ground. By all accounts, Canada was not an option for those fleeing the Nazi regime. During the inter-war years, Canada had pursued a strict immigration policy, and, with a few exceptions, the roughly four thousand Jewish refugees who were admitted had demonstrated that they had access to capital or could be employed in agriculture.[7] Thoughts of North America as the home of freedom and opportunity remained strictly associated with the USA even months after arrival in Canada. In 'Internee Julius Caesar', one of several short stories written by Carl Weiselberger during his Canadian internment, the path to freedom lies not in Canada, or even in release back to England, but 'nach Amerika hinüber, geradewegs bis an den Fuß der Freiheitsstatue von New York'.[8]

Besides being perceived as merely a transit venue by the thousand or so deportees who hoped to emigrate to the USA,[9] Canada appears to have featured only marginally in the European consciousness, and was, in the words of Henry Kreisel, 'a country that I barely knew by name and that was only a large red stretch on the school maps we had used in Vienna in our geography lessons.'[10] Several deportees support Kreisel's admitted ignorance of Canada, such as the concert pianist, John Newmark, who explains, 'Geography lessons in Bremen, Lower Saxonia, Germany did not deal too much with such a faraway British colony.'[11] Even if Koch's claim that the summer uniforms of the Canadian guards led some of the new arrivals to believe that they had landed in India seems somewhat exaggerated,[12] the lack of knowledge of Canada could only have fuelled the sense of disorientation on the part of the European newcomers.

Feelings of isolation and abandonment, exacerbated by acute unfamiliarity with the country to which they had been deported, are often articulated in terms of an alienating vastness of the Canadian landscape. Noting his first impressions in his diary in camp L, Quebec City, Heinz Warschauer describes the St. Lawrence river and the summer scenery with the desultory conclusion: 'Es gibt keine Beziehung zwischen Mensch und die Natur um ihn. Das ist Traum, Romantik, Einbildung.'[13] Even after months in the camps, primary texts indicate that the deportees had not found any closer connection with the 'host' country. 'Herbst Neunzehnhundertvierzig', a poem by Robert Lamprecht, written in camp Q in Monteith, is suggestive of a profound sense of displacement couched in a deadly despondency:

> Es rinnt der Regen ins herbstgraue Land,
> der Himmel ist fahl wie Totenhand
> und die Erde ist kahl und leer.
> Meine Seele ist stumpf und grau ist ihr Pfad
> Und naht sich dem Ende.[14]

The overwhelming and enduring sense of alienation seems not to have been simply a result of the 'doppelte Heimatlosigkeit'[15] of the deportees, who had already suffered the humiliations and confines of internment in Britain, and often German concentration camps prior to their flight into exile. In Canada, the uncertainty and repeated upheavals forced upon the internees, as hopes for release or emigration dissipated amidst numerous relocations to camps elsewhere, augmented feelings of helplessness and a lack of autonomy. Ernest Pollak recorded his anxieties upon learning that Jews and gentiles were to be separated, and that he was to be moved from Monteith to camp L in October 1940:

> What will tomorrow bring? Will the new camp be better? Will there be work or is it a step towards the final release? In any event, tomorrow we shall be sitting in the train again travelling ten, twenty or thirty hours towards the unknown.[16]

Ernest Borneman's response to the decision to separate Jews and gentiles is considerably more acerbic and draws a clear distinction between the internment experience in Britain and Canada: 'The racial principle was one which would never have been accepted in England.'[17]

In spite of strict censorship rules, such concerns were not limited to private expression, but occasionally emerged as collective public protest in camp newspapers. 'Good Bye Camp L', an article in the *Camp L Chronicle*, articulates the concerns of Pollak and his voiceless peers, arguing: 'We know each other by now, we have lived, suffered, laughed and worked together. We have built up a sound and efficient community.'[18] More vehement is the front page article, which clearly seeks to make a public appeal against the perceived insensitivity of the Canadian authorities: 'Let us say: it is a most unfortunate thing we are suffering from. This disease is called: lack of organization and lack of psychology.'[19] Such complaints are corroborated by Paterson's report, which sympathizes with the deportees, and alludes further to a fundamental conflict between Canadian and European psyches: 'The Canadian tends to be a man of rigid and unimaginative mind, and therefore not well-suited to taking care of sensitive and temperamental human beings.'[20]

Even if such reasoning appears grossly unjust and suggestive of a cultural European elitism vis-à-vis the Canadians, several accounts describe thick barbed wire, armed machine gun turrets and extremely strict discipline in the camps. The fact that such harsh treatment had its origins in Britain's original declaration that the deportees were individuals 'whose removal from this country it is desired to secure on the ground that their continued presence in this country is bound to be a source of the most serious risk,'[21] seems to have been overlooked or simply not known by some deportees. Instead, texts often focus on the injustice of their situation at the hands of the Canadians, and indicate the profound sense of victimization of the authors. Borneman's internment diary illustrates a preoccupation with unjust treatment and his report, 'Transport on M. S. Ettrick and Internment in Canada', records a litany of offences by camp authorities, even claiming that articles of the Geneva Convention were deliberately ignored in the treatment of internees.[22] He describes robberies by guards on arrival in camp L, and states that a mentally disturbed man, isolated in a separate hut was shot as he tore at the barbed wire on his window.[23] Writing in his diary in Sherbrooke, camp N, Borneman even claims that guards would come in and pull away blankets in the night '"to see if internees are undressed". (Homosexuality running high among soldiers. New Years' Eve drunk guards coming into dormitory to rape internees)' [sic].[24] Borneman's latter claim is not corroborated in other primary documentation researched for this paper, but is cited in Koch's Deemed Suspect.[25] (Interestingly enough, Koch dedicates an entire section to the 'Gay Life' amongst the internees.)[26]

It should be stated that even Borneman was eventually appeased as conditions and treatment improved,[27] but the predominant grimness of his accounts constitutes a remarkable concentration on the negative aspects of the Canadian treatment of deportees. Nevertheless, the extent of universal outrage at being labelled Prisoners of War is evident in numerous letters and diaries, which often dwell on the POW uniforms as symbolic of the unjust humiliation of their mistaken identity. According to Henry Kreisel, the arrival of such attire at camp B caused an 'internal crisis'.[28] The significance of their POW status as an insult and a further hindrance to contact with the Canadian world outside the camps also manifests itself in Weiselberger's internment fiction. In 'Die Geschichte von der Geige', a young internee longs for nothing other than the arrival of his much beloved violin. At night, he dreams of giving a concert before a Canadian audience, but on realizing that he is clad in POW uniform, the dream quickly becomes a nightmare: 'Schweiß stand auf seiner Stirn, er schämte sich furchtbar vor den Damen und Herren im Parterre.'[29]

Represented as a deep source of shame in Weiselberger's story, for Ernest Pollak, the issue of POW status is the ultimate paradigm of the Canadian, as opposed to British, internment experience. As he recorded in his diary, his reply to the question of what was the greatest difference between internment in Britain and Canada in an interview with the authorities, emphasizes their POW status as central to the internees' resentment of the Canadian administration: 'How can we trust you when you treat us here like prisoners-of-war?'[30] Clearly in the case of Pollak, Canada was to remain associated with harsh treatment and the ignominy of the POW label. Returning to England in February 1941, he sardonically remarks: 'The journey home to England proves to be the only enjoyable part of the Canadian adventure. There are no more guards on board the ship.'[31]

Even documents testifying to a less virulent and more objective attitude to the Canadian authorities indicate dismay at the camp regimes, and are suggestive of a nostalgia for Britain. Undoubtedly, letters such as Andreas Göritz's report from Douglas on the Isle of Man to Eric Koch could not have helped: 'I do not know whether it is cruel if I write you that this camp is so comfortable that I would not mind to spend the summer here providing we had access to the weaker sex. The treatment is infinitely better than what we have been used to.'[32]

Nostalgia for Britain could only have been intensified by the deportee's initial ignorance of Canadian culture, which, in turn, had little chance of dissipating within the strict confinement in the camps. Such exclusion from the outside world, compounded by the mislabelling of internees as POWs, seems to have lead to a profound identity crisis, which finds clearest expression in Weiselberger's internment fiction. Particularly for those who strove to abandon their German-speaking origins, but found no commonality with their North American environment, assuming a British cultural identity may have provided one means of asserting their ideological beliefs and maintaining a sense of personal stability. This response is articulated in Weiselberger's 'Der Mann mit den tausend Gesichtern', which begins by describing rehearsals for a camp cabaret. One of the performers, a former Cambridge student, is singled out for his manifest 'Englishness'. Not only is he to sing English songs, 'englischer natürlich als der englischste Engländer', but his entire survival mechanism and the means of preserving his dignity depend on his acquired British identity:

> Alles konnte man diesem Jungen nehmen: die Freiheit, die alte Heimat, die
> Eltern und Geschwister, nur an seinem englischen Akzent durfte man nicht

rütteln und an der Pfeife, die er bald in den rechten, bald in den linken
Mundwinkel schob.[33]

The narrative itself thematizes a loss of individual identity in the
face of a seemingly inaccessible Canadian culture. The central protagonist,
Hoffmann-Chameleoni, formerly a successful impressionist, now 'ein leeres
Gefäß' (p. 87), succeeds in escaping to the outside world in his costume as
the camp's Canadian carpenter. However, his adventure into freedom is far
from liberating, as he quickly realizes that the Canadian world is 'nicht
meine Welt', and even cars, houses and people seem alien and threatening
(p. 94). The narrative makes it clear that the protagonist's unease in the
outside world is not a result of a fear of being caught, since each individual
encountered amicably greets the disguised escapee without a second glance.
Rather, it is the successful assumption of a Canadian identity which terrifies
Hoffmann, as he interacts with each passer-by: 'Vielleicht bin ich es bereits,
der Kanadier, und weiß es nicht, erschrak er einen Augenblick' (p. 96). Only
once he has voluntarily identified himself to the camp guards driving by, and
is sitting on the floor of the truck 'war er wieder ganz zu sich selbst geraten!'
(p. 98). For Weiselberger's 'Chameleoni', physical liberation entails utter
self-alienation; a German-speaking internee simply has no place in Canadian
life, which, as the story concludes, remains 'sehr fern und unwirklich'
(p. 100).

In the midst of the 'unreal' Canadian world, some deportees seem to
have developed a tendency to withdraw into idealizations of pre-exile
existences and memories of pre-Nazi European culture. In Weiselberger's
unpublished 'Die Pantoffeln des Generals', such retreat from reality is
precarious, even self-effacing, and reduces life in the camps to a
'Gespensterdasein'.[34] As the narrator shows a new arrival around the camp,
he points out the 'Sonderfälle' (p. 3) of the camp. For the most part, these
eccentrics are fixated with features of European culture. One elderly
gentleman spends his time lying on the ground, drawing masterpieces in the
air with his hands, 'naturalistisch, klassizistisch, impressionistisch,
expressionistisch, surrealistisch, wie du nur willst' (p. 4). Even if the
'painter' succeeds in warding off the disenchantment of his fellow internees
by means of his bizarre antics, his behaviour is to be seen as 'unheimlich',
even 'gespenstisch' (p. 5). Similarly, the 'Typologe', a former academic
psychologist, obsessed with the desire to discover 'etwas Epochemachendes'
(p. 5), and the 'Geigenmacher' submerge themselves into constructs of a
bygone cultural reality in an effort to escape the anonymity and futility of
their actual existence. Their acute rejection of contemporary truth is made
manifest in the violin-maker's refusal to let anyone in the camp play his
meticulously crafted instruments simply because 'Menschen von heute
dürfen nicht darauf spielen' (p. 8).

The moral of the story, however, is crystallized in the fate of the 'General', who parades around the camp in a Napoleonic pose. On one occasion, during roll call, he demands to be recognized as an officer, only to stumble ignominiously and lose his slippers, much to the hilarity of guards and prisoners alike. His modus vivendi at the end of the story drives home two perceptions of the Canadian internment experience: as a grotesque absurdity on the one hand, as symbolized by the whirling merry-go-round on the other side of the barbed wire (p. 21), and as a challenge to accept the situation and maintain contact with the real world, no matter how unpleasant in the midst of war, on the other. When the 'General' re-emerges from his humiliating performance during roll call, his voice sounds different: 'Irgendwie wahrer [...] als ob man einen Vorhang von ihr [der Stimme] gezogen' [sic] (p. 21). For the first time, he recognizes reality, and admits the preposterousness of his former posturings (p. 21). Weiselberger's tale illustrates, albeit to an extreme, some of the responses to the Canadian dilemma. As much as clinging to the past or some constructed identity seems understandable, particularly given the degradation and irony of the identity imposed upon them, Weiselberger urges his peers to acknowledge the true situation, no matter how grim, injurious or even absurd it may be.

The difficulty of accepting one's lot in Canadian internment was, however, not merely a question of tolerating personal degradation or material discomfort, but aggravated by the physical distance from war-torn Europe. Whilst family members, especially of younger deportees, may have found solace in the fact that at least those interned in Canada were safe from German bombs,[35] for the deportees themselves the distance from the war exacerbated anxieties and feelings of futility. Such sentiments were, of course, shared by internees in Britain. However, internees on the Isle of Man enjoyed comparatively prompt correspondence with the outside world, and could reassure themselves of the safety of friends and family. Moreover, internees in Britain who had volunteered for the Pioneer Corps were released in October 1940,[36] whereas even those who had also volunteered in Canada had to wait longer, and returns proceeded at a much lower rate.[37] The pragmatism of Pollak's comment on being excluded from the war is charged with a collective sense of inutility:

> In the meantime the first bombs have been dropped on London and the Battle of Britain has begun in earnest. And we are here in Canada behind barbed wire. Perhaps we should be pleased to be safe and not complain? We find that hard to swallow.[38]

Such concerns also made their way into more literary endeavours, such as 'Nach Heinrich Heine' by an anonymous author:

> Ich weiß nicht was soll es bedeuten,
> Dass ich in Kanada bin.

Es kommt auch anderen Leuten
So vor, als hätts keinen Sinn.
Man sollte doch tatsächlich meinen,
Man könnte was für England tun.
Stattdessen zwingen sie einen
Auf Staatskosten auszuruhen [sic].[39]

At first glance, this text seems to be a nostalgic recourse to Germany's cultural legacies, as already discussed. However, the poem is not merely a parody of the German lyrical classic, but assumes anti-Fascist dimensions as homage to a poem whose authorship the Nazis categorically denied. The political framework reinforces the political statement of the content and strives for association with a prominent German, who had literally experienced exile himself, and been ousted from his rightful place in the German literary canon by the National Socialists.

Recourse to the lyrical form, as opposed to simply recording personal grievances in a diary, further suggests a public political motive in exposing the internees' plight and their anti-Fascist position, even if, for the time being, the public was restricted to the camp audience. This helps explain the proportionally high number of poems dealing with exclusion from the war, as correspondence from Britain increasingly detailed the horrors of the Blitz and the sacrifices of life on the home front. In response, a number of poems indicate a desire to bridge the geographical and circumstantial barriers between the Canadian internment experience and life in wartime Britain. The untitled poem already referred to above (p. 166) concludes its comedic account of deportation with an explicit declaration of universality:

You are with us
And we with you.
We are today and tomorrow too
All of us – we and you [sic].[40]

Alfred Becker's 'Song vom verwischten Unterschied', written in 1940, and addressed to a partner in England is more specific. As the title indicates, Becker's text is a lyrical attempt to equate the restrictions and censorship of the Canadian camp experience with the constraints of wartime Britain:

So lebst Du. In Freiheit, sollte man denken,
und bist genau betrachtet nicht freier als ich,
denn alles, womit sie mich hier bedenken,
serviert zu Hause der Krieg für Dich.[41]

Such expressions of association with those directly confronted with the war are indicative of more than a desire to declare solidarity with the anti-Fascist cause, but betray a personal sense of shame for seemingly sitting out the war in far-off Canada. Furthermore, it is highly likely that such texts were also a means of avoiding succumbing entirely to the banalities of life in internment and adopting a 'camp mentality', as the months passed by with no clear end in sight. Kreisel's description of the poor conditions found on arrival at camp I, Isle aux Noix, implies that by June 1941, seemingly endless imprisonment in Canada had reduced the psychological horizons of the majority of internees: 'It is remarkable that most of us don't say: I wish I were free again but most say: O, were we back in camp B.'[42]

The importance of finding some meaning in the Canadian camps is the central theme of Weiselberger's 'Kain und Abel in Kanada'. The camp itself is introduced as a static, even deadly environment, where the posts supporting the barbed wire are '483 Galgen', each bearing an invisible corpse.[43] The two title figures are both writers who have lost their life's work, for each, 'der Sinn seines Lebens' (p. 65). The ensuing juxtaposition between the two men clearly outlines two contrasting responses to internment in Canada. Whilst Kain, characterized by 'Unrast' (p. 65), is devoured by resentment, Abel succeeds in finding inspiration even amidst the stasis of a Canadian camp and, after having lost everything, sees confinement in North America as an opportunity 'sein Leben wieder anzufangen' (p. 65).

Admittedly, the spirited attitude of Weiselberger's Abel seems somewhat heroic, even implausible, particularly in the context of the predominantly despondent accounts and the conditions endured. Consequently, in spite of its documentary value, this narrative by Weiselberger betrays the author's own struggle to attribute some sense of purpose to the languor of the Canadian experience and motivate his fellow internees. Whether Weiselberger's peers actually adopted Abel's positive attitude remains unlikely, for even the more encouraging aspects of Canadian internment frequently receive ambivalent treatment in primary accounts, and, on close analysis, often in Weiselberger's own fiction.

One positive feature of Canadian camp life was the opportunity to work, mostly in the forests cutting wood for 20 cents a day, and, occasionally unaccompanied by guards. The crucial factor of this development, was not, however, the financial remuneration, but release from confinement within the camp, which as Henry Kreisel declared, meant that 'one almost feels free.'[44] For Weiselberger's 'Rabbi mit der Axt',[45] the opportunity of physical labour prompts a theological dilemma, which is, however, typically resolved as a positive opportunity provided by the Canadian experience. However, in 'Die Pantoffeln des Generals', there is markedly less emphatic endorsement of such work, which rendered existence in the camps only 'ein wenig besser, ein wenig lebendiger' (p. 1).

A close analysis of Weiselberger's internment narratives exposes further elements of ambiguity on the part of the author. Although food in the Canadian camps was ample and nourishing, the narrator of 'Die Pantoffeln des Generals' betrays a distinctly cynical response: 'Manchmal hat man das Gefühl, sie füttern uns, sie füttern uns fett, damit wir nur ruhiger bleiben' (p. 1). Such discontent, however, is not an indication of Weiselberger's personal ingratitude, but finds a degree of corroboration in Paterson's report. Nutritional excess had a distinctly detrimental effect on the younger internees, whom Paterson declared 'grossly over-fed and under-exercised'.[46]

Paterson's concern for the well-being of the boys and young men amongst the internees is not merely a manifestation of philanthropic concern for juveniles, but refers to another fundamental feature of the Canadian internment experience: namely, the high proportion of young men and boys. Aside from the fact that young, unmarried men had been encouraged to 'volunteer' for deportation, according to Paterson, 'hundreds' of schoolboys, who had barely turned sixteen, found themselves onboard the ships headed for Canada.[47] According to a report by Canada's Central Committee for Interned Refugees, an analysis of camp N, the largest camp for 'B' and 'C' internees, and deemed demographically 'typical', concludes that 45% were under the age of 25.[48]

Retrospective accounts by those who had been deported to Canada at a young age tend to emphasize the educational opportunities Canada provided once McGill University opened its doors to allow internees to matriculate in the summer of 1941. Conversely, at the time, Paterson was convinced that 'the general effect on all of them [boys and students] after a year in Canada is bad'.[49] The written testimonies by younger internees themselves betray a growing melancholy, occasionally fulminating in wrathful frustration or an abject loss of faith. Concluding his account of the heavily armed transfer to camp I in the early summer of 1941, Henry Kreisel, who had just turned eighteen, is reduced to an expression of utter disillusionment: 'It is enough to make anybody lose faith in the world and in mankind.'[50]

In spite of such acute despondency, Kreisel's Canadian internment was triumphantly resolved. In November 1941, he was released to prepare for the senior matriculation exam, and went on to win a four-year scholarship to read English at the University of Toronto, and become a Lecturer of English and Comparative Literature at the University of Alberta and successful English-language novelist. Whilst Kreisel's academic achievements and the realization of his decision during internment to become an English-language writer would seem to promote the educational possibilities of the camp schools and the wealth of time available for intellectual pursuits as a distinct bonus of internment in Canada, a closer consideration of these aspects paints a less unilateral picture.

Undeniably, the facility to study in Canada was an outstanding gesture, offering a fresh start and an invaluable education to the young men who had frequently been forced to abandon their schooling in Europe. However, the uncertainty and conditions of their situation in the camps cast a dark shadow on intellectual endeavours in preparing for matriculation. The diary of Heinz Warschauer, who had been writing his doctoral thesis in history before fleeing to Britain, illustrates the psychological burden of camp life. In August 1940, Warschauer recorded that he had begun reading part two of Goethe's *Faust* for the first time, only to comment 'dabei gemerkt wie nun Nervosität und mangelnde Konzentrationsfähigkeit eine Dauererscheinung geworden sind in mir'.[51]

In addition to intense anxiety provoked by the external factors of Canadian internment, younger internees seem to have suffered, as much as benefited, from the demographic diversity of the camps. In fact, the cramped living conditions seem to have launched a generation conflict to the extent that Weiselberger took up the issue as a theme for his story, 'Die Wette'.[52]

The two young protagonists of the narrative challenge each other to throw a bowl of vegetables at the pompous camp cook. Besides boredom, they are motivated by a profound disillusionment with the older generation. As Heinz prepares for lunch, he strikes a pose which represents

> eine ihm unbewusste Kampfansage gegen die Würde des Alters, gegen Titel, gegen diese alte Generation, die ihre Sache so schlecht gemacht und das Leben in den Dreck geführt hatte [...] Wer waren sie denn, diese Alten, die genau so interniert waren und auf demselben Scheißhaus, Arsch an Arsch, neben einem saßen? (p. 3).

Although somewhat less graphic than Weiselberger, Kreisel provides the same reasons for conflict between the generations. In his diary, he recorded a complaint by an older gentleman regarding the disrespect of the younger internees. Kreisel does not deny the accusation, but explains that in the close confinement of the camps, the human fallibilities of the elderly, normally concealed beneath a 'mantle of dignity', are exposed.[53]

With the rupture of such social norms, the conditions and duration of internment in Canada entailed both exposure to and exclusion from an entirely new way of life. Certainly, primary documentation paints a grim picture of Canadian internment, characterized by isolation, mistaken identity and uncertainty. Whilst on the whole, internees had no choice but to adapt to camp life, the original cultural cleft between Europe and Canada could only be overcome by those who chose to stay, and only once they were released. For the majority, it appears that deportation to Canada only strengthened their European identities. The high proportion of academics and successful entrepreneurs amongst those released into Canada, and the success stories of Kreisel and Weiselberger as Canadian writers would suggest that Canada was a generous country of exile. Nevertheless, Canada's overall role in the history of refugees fleeing Nazi terror hardly suggests a positive assessment. Perhaps a ray of light can be gleaned from the fate of those amongst the initially undesirable deportees who chose to stay, and for whom Canada finally emerged as a unique venue for re-birth, opportunity and reconciliation between Canadian and European cultures.

Notes

[1] Largely due to the haste with which the British government implemented its deportation policy, there is considerable conflict in the statistics provided by British and Canadian records and subsequent publications on the subject. In his 1941 'Report on Civilian Internees sent from the United Kingdom to Canada during the Unusually Fine Summer of 1940', Alexander Paterson states that a 'total of 4799 men and boys were within a fortnight transported across the Atlantic', (The National Archives, PO35 996 HP00147; National Archives of Canada, Eric Koch fonds, MG30-C192, vol.2), p. 2. The figure of 4400 is an estimate based on the statistics provided for each of the three deportation ships which reached Canada provided in Peter and Leni Gillman, *Collar the Lot! How Britain Interned and Expelled its Wartime Refugees* (London: Quartet, 1980), pp. 169, 182, 204, 244, and Ronald Stent, *A Bespattered Page: The Internment of His Majesty's Most Loyal Enemy Aliens* (London: Deutsch, 1980), p.96. On p. 205, Peter and Leni Gillman state that 1700 merchant seamen and other category 'A' internees and 2700 category 'B' and 'C' internees were transported to Canada. It should be kept in mind that several individuals had been falsely classified as category 'A': Although all Germans on board the ill-fated *Arandora Star* were 'A' class, Judex argues that approximately 150 had been wrongly classified, since included were those who had entered illegally, overstayed their original permit or been falsely judged at their tribunals. See Judex [Herbert Delauney Hughes], *Anderson's Prisoners* (London: Victor Gollancz, 1940) p. 83. Stent also talks of a 'number of mislabelled refugees' aboard the *Arandora Star* (p. 101). For example, two German trade union leaders, Valentin Witte and Louis Weber, were drowned, as was Karl Olbrysch, former KPD Reichstag member, who had already endured three years imprisonment and one year in a concentration camp in Germany.

[2] Peter and Leni Gillman state (p. 276) that 972 deportees chose to remain in Canada.

[3] Eric Koch, *Deemed Suspect: A Wartime Blunder* (Halifax: Goodread Biographies, 1985). (Originally published New York: Methuen, 1980).

[4] Letter from H. F. Reichenfeld to the editor of *To-Day Magazine* (Toronto), 31 October 1980, in the National Archives of Canada, Eric Koch fonds, MG30-C192, vol. 1, pp. 1-4, p. 4.

[5] Paterson report, p. 2.

[6] The poem is in the National Archives of Canada, Eric Koch fonds, MG30-C192, vol. 1, 'Correspondence between Eric Koch and other internees, A-F', p. 2.

[7] Koch, *Deemed Suspect*, p. ix.

[8] Carl Weiselberger, 'Internee Julius Caesar', in *Carl Weiselberger: Eine Auswahl seiner Schriften*, ed. by Peter Liddell and Walter Riedel (Toronto: German-Canadian Historical Association, 1981), pp. 74-83, p. 74.

[9] In his report, Paterson stated (p. 9) that over a thousand deportees had registered for emigration to the USA. These hopes were ultimately dashed when after several attempts by Paterson, including plans to send internees to the USA via Newfoundland or Cuba, he was

informed on 15 April 1941 that the American authorities would not accept former internees. The subsequent US Immigration Act of June 1941, authorizing 'the refusal of visas to aliens whose admission into the United States would endanger the public safety', made it definitively clear that internees in Canada would not be able to realize their dream of freedom in the United States. Quoted in Gillman, *Collar the Lot*, p. 274.

[10] Henry Kreisel, Introduction, 'Diary of an Internment', in *Another Country: Writings by and about Henry Kreisel*, ed. by Shirley Neumann (Edmonton: NeWest Press, 1981), pp. 18-44, p. 20.

[11] Account by John Newmark in the National Archives of Canada, Eric Koch fonds, MG30-C192, vol. 1, 'Correspondence, report & other material re. his internment, 1939-1941', p. 102.

[12] Eric Koch, 'The Reunion of Internees 1980 in Montreal' in the National Archives of Canada, Eric Koch fonds, MG30-C192 vol. 2, 'To the Spies who Never Were' by Harry Rasky', pp. 1-36, p. 27.

[13] Heinz Warschauer, entry for 29 July 1940 in his 'Diary, July–September 1940' in the National Archives of Canada, Warschauer fonds, MG30-D129, pp. 1-29, p. 2.

[14] Robert Lamprecht, 'Herbst Neunzehnhundertvierzig' in the National Archives of Canada, Eric Koch fonds, MG30-C192, vol. 1, 'Lamprecht, Robert. Poetry 1938-1940'.

[15] Walter Riedel, 'Im großen Menschenkäfig: Zu Carl Weiselberger's Erzählungen aus der kanadischen Internierung', *Seminar*, XIX 2 (1998), pp. 136-49, p. 139.

[16] Ernest Pollak, *Departure to Freedom Curtailed* (Lewes: Ernest Pollak, [n. d.]), p. 43.

[17] Ernest Borneman, 'Transport on M. S. *Ettrick* and Internment in Canada' in the National Archives of Canada, Eric Koch fonds, MG30-C192, vol. 1, pp. 1-7, p. 3.

[18] 'Good Bye Camp L', *Camp L Chronicle*, 2 October 1940, p. 4.

[19] *Ibid.*, p. 1.

[20] Paterson report, p. 6.

[21] Viscount Caldecott, Secretary of State for the Dominions, to Vincent Massey, High Commissioner for the Canadian government in London. Ottawa, PAC Dept. of National Defence, RG 24 c4, quoted in Gillman, *Collar the Lot*, p. 164.

[22] Borneman, 'Transport', p. 4.

[23] *Ibid.*, p. 4.

[24] Ernest Borneman, Internment Diary, National Archives of Canada, Eric Koch fonds, MG30-C192, vol.1, pp. 1-39, p. 13.

[25] Koch, *Deemed Suspect*, p. 139.

[26] *Ibid.*, pp. 157-59.

[27] Borneman, 'Transport', p. 6.

[28] Kreisel, 'Diary', p. 26.

[29] Carl Weiselberger, 'Die Geschichte von der Geige', in *Weiselberger, Auswahl*, p. 105.

[30] Pollak, *Departure*, p. 53.

[31] *Ibid.*, p. 56.

[32] Andreas Göritz to Eric Koch, 24 March 1941, in the National Archives of Canada, MG30-C192, vol. 1, 'Correspondence to Otto Koch May 1941'.

[33] Carl Weiselberger, 'Der Mann mit den tausend Gesichtern', in *Weiselberger, Auswahl*, p. 84. Further page references appear in the text.

[34] Carl Weiselberger, 'Die Pantoffeln des Generals', dated 25 July 1941, National Archives of Ottawa, Weiselberger fonds, MG30-D191, vol. 1, pp. 1-21, p. 1. Further page references appear in the text.

[35] Margaret Mayer, for example, repeatedly expressed relief at the deportation of her younger brother, Eric (Otto) Koch in their correspondence during the summer of 1940, held at the National Archives of Canada, Eric Koch fonds, MG30-C192, vol.1, 'Correspondence to Otto Koch, June 1940'.

[36] Stent, *Bespattered*, p. 243.

[37] In his report, Paterson states (p. 12) that 287 men returned to England on 26 December 1940, followed by 274 men on 24 February 1941 and 330 on 26 June 1941. By the time the last Canadian internment camp was closed in September 1943, 1537 internees had been returned to Great Britain, see Michael Seyfert, *Deutsche Exilliteratur in Britischer Internierung: Ein unbekanntes Kapitel der Kulturgeschichte des Zweiten Weltkriegs* (Berlin: Arsenal, 1984), p. 35.

[38] Pollak, *Departure*, p. 37.

[39] The poem is held in the National Archives of Canada, Eric Koch fonds, MG30-C192, vol.2, 'Behind Barbed Wire: Poetry, Sketches etc. 1940-1941'.

[40] See Note 6 above, p. 4.

[41] Alfred Becker, 'Song vom verwichsten Unterschied' in the National Archives of Canada, Eric Koch fonds, MG30-C192, vol. 2, 'Behind Barbed Wire: Poetry, sketches, etc. 1940-1941', p. 2.

[42] Kreisel, 'Diary', p. 37, entry for 24 June 1941.

[43] Carl Weiselberger, 'Kain und Abel in Kanada', in *Weiselberger, Auswahl*. Further page references appear in the text.

[44] Kreisel, 'Diary', p. 28, entry for 2 January 1941.

[45] Carl Weiselberger, *Der Rabbi mit der Axt. Dreißig Geschichten*, ed. by Herta Hartmanshenn and Frederick Kriegel (Victoria B. C.: University of Victoria 1973). Translated into English for publication in Koch (see Note 3 above), pp. 104-10.

[46] Paterson report, p. 16.

[47] *Ibid.*, p. 16.

[48] 'Central Committee for Interned Refugees Report on Emigration of Interned Refugees' of 24 June 1941 by C. Raphael in the National Archives of Canada, Eric Koch fonds, MG30-C192, vol. 2, p.1

[49] Paterson report, p. 15.

[50] Kreisel, 'Diary', p. 36, entry for 21 June 1941.

[51] Warschauer, 'Diary', p.13, entry for 4 August 1940.

[52] Carl Weiselberger, 'Die Wette', dated 22 June 1941, National Archives of Ottawa, Weiselberger fonds, MG30-D191, vol. 1, pp. 1-8, p. 1. Further page references appear in the text.

[53] Kreisel, 'Diary', p. 30, entry for 3 January 1941.

Birgit Lang

The Dunera Boys: Dramatizing History from a Jewish Perspective

In 1940 nearly 3000 internees were deported from Great Britain to Australia, most of them refugees from National Socialism. The deportees were boarded on the *HMT Dunera* and upon arrival interned for about a year in different camps in the Australian outback. Director Ben Lewin was the first to make this extraordinary voyage into a film. This article will investigate how Lewin's TV mini-series *The Dunera Boys* (1985) represents and dramatizes the historical events and how reference to a Jewish comic tradition allows him to represent aspects of homosexuality and gender issues neglected in documentaries on the same topic, while at the same time limiting his view on the complexity of the Jewish experience.

In July 1940 2,732 male internees were deported from Great Britain to Australia. The *HMT Dunera* mostly transported refugees from National Socialism, among them 444 survivors of the previously torpedoed and sunk *Arandora Star*, but also some German National Socialists and Italian fascists.[1] The internment and deportation of enemy aliens formed part of the British reaction towards the German invasion of the Low Countries and Italy's entry into the war.[2] Like Canada, where the *Arandora Star* had originally headed, Australia had agreed to take in a certain number of internees and prisoners of war on the condition that the British government paid for all costs and granted the return of the internees.[3] However, in contrast with the Canadian case, in which several boats reached their destination, the *HMT Dunera* was the only boat to reach the Australian shore.

Three features distinguish the Australian situation. Firstly the mistreatment of the deportees on board the *HMT Dunera*, which eventually led to the trial by court-martial of three members of the crew, amongst them the commander W. P. Scott, who was subsequently dismissed.[4] Secondly, the German-speaking refugees suffered prolonged internment in two partly self-governed camps in Hay and later in Tatura. While those internees who remained in the UK left internment within a few months, most 'Australians' were stranded in different camps in an Australian 'no man's land' for more than a year, some until 1944.[5] The Australian government did not want to set the internees free and, owing to the war, transport to the UK was scarce (and dangerous). Thirdly, most internees joined the Eighth Employment Company of the Australian Army to support the Australian war effort, and in the end about half of the men decided to stay in Australia, the others returning to the UK or other parts of the world. Within the Australian émigré community the '*Dunera* Boys' always formed a distinctive and highly successful group.

Forty-five years after the arrival of the *HMT Dunera*, Ben Lewin became the first director to make a film of this extraordinary voyage. His highly acclaimed TV mini-series won four Australian Film Awards in its year of production and even today rates in the top thirty-six of all Australian mini-series produced.[6] In 1989 the re-edited series was published as a feature film. The fact that producer Bob Weis and director and writer Ben Lewin decided on a dramatization is unusual considering that all subsequent film productions devoted to the '*Dunera* experience' have been documentaries.[7] This article will argue that situating the mini-series playfully and deliberately at the border between documentary and film blurred the boundaries between fact and fiction from the very outset and was crucial for its success. By using documentary-like features in his series, Lewin created a notion of authenticity that made his work appealing and partly controversial to his audience. At the same time the fictitiousness of his characters and of the plot created a framework allowing him to investigate aspects of the *Dunera* incident which are not represented in documentaries, as the comparison with Judy Menczel's *When Friends were Enemies* (1991) will show. The representation of women, for example, allows Lewin to portray the loneliness and the sexual deprivation of a group of imprisoned men. While being able to portray new aspects of the *Dunera* experience, the depiction of Jewishness signifies an actual shift in the historical narrative, situating the film firmly in its own historical time frame. The latter also implies new cinematic and aesthetic strategies, namely an aesthetic of ironic inversion, which forms an integral part of the interplay between fact and fiction in the series. The ultimate success of *The Dunera Boys*, it can be argued, emanates not only from the close-knit network of meaning constructed through the amalgamation of fact and fiction, but also through the realization of what Lewin thought of as the European Jewish comic tradition.

'Is this documentary or is this fiction?'[8] was how Lewin identified the key dilemma of his TV drama. At this point the question arises why the '*Dunera* experience' should suggest itself as a documentary. The answer is threefold: first of all, in the mid-1980s the story had novelty value, in that it highlighted a hitherto unknown aspect of Australian and British history, secondly the overall dramatic storyline (expulsion, internment and, in retrospect, a happy end) promised a fluent narrative, and thirdly the multitude of eloquent survivors and autobiographical sources (written testimonials, short stories etc.) available must have been attractive to potential filmmakers. These reasons also held true for Ben Lewin, whose first impulse had been factual rather than fictional: 'When I first came across this material I was really a documentary film-maker and I saw it as a documentary.'[9] Lewin had first stumbled upon the topic in Melbourne, when he befriended the photographer Henry Talbot, a former '*Dunera* boy'. In the course of his subsequent research Lewin conducted interviews, accessed the newly available official documents in the National Archives in London[10] and familiarized himself with the two monographs available at the time: Benzion Patkin's *The Dunera Internees* and Cyril Pearl's *The Dunera Scandal*.[11] The official documents and Pearl's account provided Lewin with a historical narrative, and Patkin's book and the interviews allowed him to access written and oral autobiographical accounts. Whereas later filmmakers decided that telling the history of the *Dunera* and giving some of the survivors a voice seemed a worthy cause for a documentary, Lewin decided to fictionalize the story, partly because a more experienced writer had advised him to do so.[12] More importantly, after distilling the most interesting aspects from his original material Lewin found his first script 'monumentally boring to read, [it] had no dramatic structure and really no dramatic characters'.[13] The material did not provide enough creative tension, being either too abstract (the overall historical narrative) or too specific (autobiographical accounts). Fictionalising the story allowed Lewin to gain control over the structure of the film and over his characters, which he could invent.

    The Dunera Boys consists of four parts, which follow a chronological time line. The first part starts off with the flight of the young violin soloist Alexander Engelhardt from Austria and his arrival in London. Engelhardt, an acculturated Viennese Jew soon plays the violin in the 'Little Vienna', an émigré café. He starts a secret affair with Naomi Mendellsohn, a working-class Jewish girl he meets at the movies. Naomi's father and brother own a fish stall in an East End market in London. Naomi and her brother Morrie have grown up in London, but their father's strange accent gives them away as second-generation immigrants. When 'enemy aliens' begin to be interned, Engelhardt and Morrie are among them.

    The second episode begins with a shot of the *Dunera* on open water. The audience is soon introduced to the degrading and inhumane conditions on the boat, as the internees are robbed of their belongings and beaten up by soldiers. The focus shifts from acculturated to orthodox Jews, who despite the atrocious conditions manage to maintain a strong sense of group identity and pride. Their leader Rabbi Aronfeld at one point hits a soldier without being punished and upon arrival in Sydney he walks down the gangway with an upright Torah, welcomed by an angry Australian mob. The subsequent journey ends with the arrival of the refugees at the train station in Hay.

The third part is mostly set in the camp and describes the gradual improvement in the relationship between the refugees and the Australian soldiers guarding them. Morrie and Friedkin, the disobedient and effeminate pupil of Rabbi Aronfeld, go for occasional strolls to the city, while in London the British government decides to release the refugees, and Naomi Mendellsohn, whose father recently died, tries to find them.

The fourth episode portrays how the Australian government slows down the release process. Within the camp the Australian authorities are challenged, this time by the revue performer Lippe. This initiates a phase of transition and disruption within the internment community, when Morrie is shot while taking off for a rendezvous in Hay, and Friedkin runs away and will only return as an Australian soldier, leaving his orthodox background behind. When Captain Webber, the representative of the British government, belatedly arrives at Passover, he comes to resolve the matter and proclaims the exodus from the camp, an event of symbolic significance since Passover celebrates the Jewish exodus from Egypt. Finally, as Naomi arrives in Australia, she finds that most of the internees have left, and the camp itself witnesses the arrival of Japanese prisoners of war, who – in the final scene – stare in surprise and disbelief at the mural depicting camp life.

When *The Dunera Boys* was first broadcast in Australia, the public reaction was mostly positive. The mini-series won four Australian Film Awards in its year of production (Best Mini-series, Best Direction, Best Screenplay and Best Actor), with the screenplay published in 1991. Three years before Australia as a nation celebrated its bi-centenary and inaugurated the view of Australia as a multicultural state, Lewin confronted the general public with a quite critical view of Australia and the United Kingdom. Although there were some critical voices in Australia – Lewin was accused of being not hard enough on the British and too hard on the Australians – [14] the harshest critique about the series was expressed in the United Kingdom:

> I enjoyed The *Dunera* Boys, the most recent Australian mini-series […]. The British, as you have come to expect now from anything Australian, were sadists and nutters, but the director, Ben Lewin, does not seem that fond of his own countrymen either. [15]

The Dunera Boys managed to agitate the British public to such an extent, that it was discussed in 'The Right to Reply', a weekly feature on Channel Four that channelled public opinion. The moderator Gus McDonald confronted Ben Lewin with angry replies from the public, especially since the depicted looting and humiliating behaviour inflicted by British soldiers caused a great stir. The most common reaction was a sense of disbelief, some of the statements showing strong emotions. The second studio guest, David Fulcher, a retired teacher who had served in the air force during the war, felt that the series portrayed the British as brutes and anti-Semites and argued that it should not have been shown on television because children who had seen it would then question the role of their fathers and grandfathers during the war. Lewin stood his ground and reassured the moderator and audience of the truthfulness of his representation, arguing: 'The truth is that the *Dunera* incident was much more brutal than it is portrayed – I bent over backward not to appear too anti-British'.[16] While most comments referred to the historical content of the series, the moderator Gus McDonald at one point also questioned the format of *The Dunera Boys*: 'Should you not have given us these facts and we would have shared your sense of shock rather than wondering what kind of drama this was?' At this point Lewin did not take the chance to talk about cinematic aspects of the movie and his choice of genre, but merely passed over the question, replying: 'It is impossible for a filmmaker to prepare for the special sensitivities of people viewing a film.'[17]

The controversy within Great Britain highlights the explosive nature of the historical narrative of *The Dunera Boys*, but also points to the element of surprise which the transgression of genres evoked. The audience expected an evening of entertainment and not a confrontation with an unpleasant aspect of the British and Australian past. Despite Lewin's own silence about his cinematic style, the audience picked up on the transgression of genres. This was the case because Lewin used various documentary-like features in his series. First of all Lewin portrays the historical events fairly accurately, although he sometimes skips historical occurrences, such as the internment of refugees in the United Kingdom or the arrival of the *HMT Dunera* in Melbourne. While this might not have been obvious to the viewer this notion was reinforced by the strictly chronological nature of the storyline. Lewin avoids any dramatic flashbacks or previews, reinforcing the sense of following the sequence of real events. Furthermore he uses actual weekly newsreels from the 1940s to create a sense of authenticity in three scenes. In the first part we see a short clip featuring the British declaration of war and another on fifth columnists and their activities in the UK. The latter is shown as a preview in the cinema, which Engelhardt visits and which is shortly after evacuated because of an air-raid warning, the scene hence highlighting the hardships of war and the growing climate of distrust. Lewin makes the most extensive use of this method in the third part at the arrival of the *Dunera* in Sydney. We first see historical news coverage showing the military welcome ceremony at the harbour, with focus on the military band.

After a rather unobtrusive cut the whole scene is continued by actors, hence integrating historical news coverage with fictitious scenes and creating a sense of authenticity that pushes cinematic boundaries. This kind of transgression not only functions on a 'superficial' level, but also shows in the way Lewin fuses different accounts and character traits into one character. For example Hans Lippe shows traits of the Olympic sportsman Franz Stampfl, who in the camp was not connected to the theatre scene.

Despite the manifold references to the documentary genre, *The Dunera Boys* is undoubtedly a drama and was broadcast accordingly as TV entertainment. In contrast to 'ordinary' documentaries, a dramatic version of events allowed Lewin a certain amount of artistic freedom, especially when it came to the depiction of characters. The following observations will compare the depiction of women and gender roles in *The Dunera Boys* with Judy Menczel's *When Friends were Enemies* (1991), a documentary of the fiftieth anniversary reunion of the '*Dunera* Boys'. One of the most striking features of the *Dunera* experience was the absence of women. Neither on the *Dunera* nor in the Australian internment camps in Hay were women present. Obviously this did not mean that the deportees did not have mothers, wives, girlfriends or daughters, but it does show the effect of the gendered politics of internment. In her documentary *When Friends were Enemies* Judy Menczel skilfully describes the story of the *Dunera*. The fiftieth anniversary and a joint journey to Hay form the central point of reference around which the film is constructed. Added in are historical features and many interviews with surviving members of the *Dunera*. While the documentary gives an accurate and emotive description of the events and features interviews with the ageing survivors, due to its focus on facts and interviews it fails to describe the yearning of most refugees for their families, not to speak of the sexual deprivation the men experienced in the camps.

Lewin on the other hand has the artistic freedom to include female actors and female gender roles in *The Dunera Boys*. As a consequence, questions arise as to what means he used to integrate women in his film. The leading female role is a young Jewish working-class woman named Naomi Mendellsohn. She falls in love with Alexander Engelhardt and gets into a fight with her brother Morrie over her 'unruly' desire for a musician, a bourgeois foreigner, albeit a Jewish one. Like the other women in the film she is sexually forthcoming and willing to transcend boundaries of class and/or nationality, and hence to a certain extent symbolizes the welcoming part of the respective nations she belongs to. Furthermore she is building a bridge between Morrie and Alexander who become an odd couple on the ship and later in the camp. Both relate to Naomi quite strongly, despite her physical absence. Her photograph, rather carelessly sold off for an apple by

Morrie to Alexander, represents the 'world of yesterday': for Morrie a (relatively) intact family life and for Alexander love and passion in exile, hence capturing the longing for wives and girlfriends quite accurately. The point comes when Morrie wants his picture back and slowly realizes that Alexander was the first lover of his sister. Whilst still in London he probably would have beaten Alexander up without hesitation, in internment the two men start fantasizing that Naomi might be pregnant. The concocted pregnancy and its consequences – Alexander agrees to marry Naomi – make the two home-sick men feel closer, and is an emotional peak in the TV drama.

Lewin's inclusion of women and female gender roles also allows him to bring to life a genuine moment of camp life usually neglected, the cabaret and theatre life and especially the cross-dressing scenes.[18] In the fourth episode Australian authorities come to visit the camp. They are not overly impressed with the neatness and the different occupations present in the camp, only when they attend a cabaret show and see a Marlene Dietrich-impersonation on stage are they really excited by life in the camp. They stare in disbelief at 'Marlene' when she sits down at their table and slowly unmasks 'herself' in front of them, denouncing their politics while 'she' removes her make-up bit by bit. It turns out that Marlene is really Hans Lippe, who is the only non-Jewish internee and was an acclaimed sportsman, who participated in the Berlin Olympics before he disengaged himself from German politics and emigrated. Hans has always been an outsider among the internees because the others, especially Alexander, doubted his real reasons for emigration and internment. The cross-dressing scene allows him to finally voice his political opinion, and at the same time shifts his outsider status to another, physical level, implying that he might be gay, another issue rarely touched upon in primary and secondary sources.[19]

If the dramatization allowed unusual aspects of the '*Dunera* experience' to be addressed, the question arises: how accurate is the portrayal of camp life in the movie? The most obvious differences between fact and fiction can be seen in the depiction of ethnicity and human dignity. For Lewin *The Dunera Boys* essentially represents a Jewish experience in the course of which Eastern and Western Jews gradually grow closer. Whereas the first part of the series focuses on the world of acculturated Viennese Jews, much of the second part is devoted to the sense of connection among the orthodox Jews and their strong will to obey Jewish laws even in the most adverse circumstances. Rabbi Aronfeld represents a strong leader in times of turmoil and despair, who stands up to the authorities, firstly on the boat, where he hits a soldier who insults him, and again in the camp where he challenges the commander to provide the necessary instruments for the kosher butcher. His sense of pride is highlighted when he walks down the gangway with the Tora, touching Australian soil as though arriving in the Promised Land. This portrayal of the rabbi as a type of Jewish 'hero', who manages to fight for the human dignity of the refugees, is of a metaphorical nature. In the description given by survivors of the *Dunera* voyage the fact is highlighted that even religious authority figures such as rabbis and priests were mistreated by the soldiers.[20] When Rabbi Ehrentreu, one of the actual rabbis on board the *Dunera*, who might have served as a model for Rabbi Aronfeld, stood up to the regime on board, he was unable to hit the soldiers with impunity as Aronfeld does in the second episode. On the contrary, after he had made too many demands, '[t]he Captain once threatened to hang him by his beard from the ship's mast and then throw him overboard.'[21]

Lewin not only uses the character of the rabbi to create what is seen as the first groundbreaking contribution to Australian Jewish film in the post-war period,[22] but also employs the assumed Jewishness of the refugees as a means to create tension between the oppressed and their Australian environment. Dunstan, the most forthcoming in the group of soldiers, is a Christian and is utterly fascinated by the Jewishness of the refugees. He quite comically tries to befriend the rabbi, who ignores his amateurish interpretations of the bible. Christian characters are not part of the camp community, the only non-Jewish character is the sportsman and cross-dresser Hans Lippe, whose only religious involvement amounts to celebrating Passover with his fellow internees. Again the differences with the realities of camp life are striking. The position of the Christians in the camp community was controversial. Although they formed a minority of approximately ten per cent and comprised different denominations including Catholics, Protestants and Lutherans,[23] they had considerable influence. The Christian communities within Australia were quite forthcoming to the Christian internees and provided them with moral support and substantial material assistance, such as the piano for the entertainment hut.[24] There were also complaints about ongoing conversion activities. For example Rabbi L. A. Falk from the Great Synagogue in Sydney urged the Jewish Welfare Society in a Report in 1940 to visit the camps more frequently, since the internees 'place the blame at our door for not having visited them as regularly as the religious leaders of other denominations'.[25]

The question remains how Lewin's generalization concerning the Jewishness of the '*Dunera* experience' can be contextualised. Needless to say, his generalization is not the only one in the film, although other 'misrepresentations' seem to have been largely a consequence of a fear of repetition, e.g. Lewin omits the representation of British internment. In the case of the portrayal of Jews the above-mentioned urge to have clear-cut boundaries between perpetrators and victims plays an important role and would also explain why Lewin omitted the fact that the *Dunera* also transported National Socialists and Italian fascists. There are two more reasons why Lewin chose to portray the *Dunera* experience as a Jewish experience. First of all, the 1980s saw a shift in the portrayal of the Holocaust as well as the rise of Jewish entertainment in the United States. The documentary *Genocide* (1981) was one of the first to portray the Holocaust as a Jewish experience, popularising scholarly approaches like Raul Hilberg's *The Destruction of the European Jews* (1961). At the same time, Jewish sitcoms, responding to a need for ethnic entertainment, began to flourish particularly in New York.[26] Although, for a variety of reasons, the 'marriage between Jews and film did not occur in Australia as it did for instance in the US',[27] an interest in entertainment that referred to everyday Jewish culture and was set within the Jewish community can also be seen in Australia from the late 1960s onwards. When for example the émigré theatre groups in Melbourne and Sydney performed plays tailored for the Jewish community, they would always perform American plays. This can be seen in the performances by the Sydney *Viennese Theatre*, which performed Elick Moll's comedy *Seidman and Son* in 1964, Arnold Perl's stage adaptation of Scholem Aleichem's *Tevya and his daughters* in 1966, Leonard Spigelglass's comedy *Dear me the Sky is falling* in 1970 or, on a more serious note, Eli Wiesel's *Zalmen or the Madness of God* in 1977. Jewish cabarets like the Melbourne based *Showmen* (later *Showmen & Friends*) flourished, particularly in the 1970s.[28] Hence it can be argued that, influenced by the United States, Jewish entertainment in Australia began to develop.

The second reason which furthered Lewin's perception of the *Dunera* affair as a Jewish experience was a consequence of contemporary politics. In the 1980s multiculturalism became the new political basis for ethnic affairs, and brought about a new understanding of Australian national identity.[29] This, in turn, increased interest in the history of ethnic communities and community cultures within Australian historical scholarship. For example, in 1988, on the occasion of the 200-year celebration of white settlement in Australia, a point of celebration for multiculturalism, James Jupp published the first edition of the major work *The Australian People: An Encyclopaedia of the Nation, its People and their Origins.*[30] Most publications on the history of the German and Jewish communities within Australia were published in the same year or shortly before.[31] With few exceptions Jewish studies neglected the religious diversity of the émigré community in Australia, partly because the émigré community had undergone a change, voicing its Jewishness more openly than it had before 1960.[32] Additionally, considering that the percentage of Jews brought out on the *Dunera* was higher (approximately 90 percent) than that among the rest of the Australian émigré community, of which, at a conservative estimate, 56 percent identified as Jewish, 33 percent as Christian and 11 percent of no denomination,[33] Lewin's representation of the *Dunera* experience as particularly Jewish does not seem that exceptional.

However, Lewin's engagement in the matter cannot merely be explained by contextual factors, but has to be seen as a deliberate choice and it entails more than just the representation of Jews and Christians in the internment camp. Lewin must have been quite aware of the fact that the *Dunera* experience was not merely a Jewish one, since the conflict features prominently in Benzion Patkin's *The Dunera Internees*. Lewin was familiar with the book and had used it on several accounts as an inspiration for scenes in the film. To name but one example: Patkin gives an account of Kurt Fischer's crossing of the German-Belgian border:

> Looking through my hand luggage, the SS man found an English text-book. He asked me whether I thought England was more beautiful than Germany. I answered that I had never been to England before and therefore could not express an opinion. He was apparently satisfied with my answer because he passed me on to the Customs officer for a body search.[34]

In the film this scene appears transformed, but can be clearly traced back to its source as this extract shows:

> Engelhardt's clothing and his open suitcase are on the table: everything is being turned out and searched by the Gestapo sergeant (...). He finds a small book near the bottom of the suitcase and waggles it ominously.
>
> GESTAPO SERGEANT: What is this?
> ENGELHARDT (pausing to speak): A dictionary. (...)
> GESTAPO SERGEANT: So you think England will be more beautiful than Austria?
> ENGELHARDT: No, Austria is more beautiful.[35]

The scene also illustrates how Lewin changes the original, in making the contrast bigger and at the same time breaking and ironizing the situation. In the opening scene this is done through Engelhardt's violin playing: He plays a song titled 'I'm in love with Vienna' (to the melody of 'Yes, we have no bananas'), with the people in traditional Austrian costumes on the platform dancing. Lewin himself connected this kind of humour to the European Jewish comic tradition, which had dominated his earlier work, including *The Dunera Boys*:

> I know that in my earlier stuff it was kind of full-on folksy with European
> like symbols. You could sort of say "Well, here's Lewin trying to be a bit
> like Sholom Aleichem."[36]

The reference to Sholom Aleichem captures the underlying principle of
Lewin's humour accurately: Aleichem's hyperbolical heroes always fail, but
are, at the same time, always hopeful and try to cope with their often harsh
everyday life with humour and melancholy.[37] In Lewin this principle is
visible in the overall film, but also in many scenes, for example in the
depression of Morrie and Alexander. Differently from Aleichem's stories,
however, the absurdity of life in *The Dunera Boys* is further highlighted and
transformed into the constant notion of people missing one another. Morrie
misses finding Alexander in Naomi's bedroom in the first episode, Morrie
never has his love affair, Naomi misses Morrie and Alexander in Australia
etc. The gender roles form another example of this principle: when the men
dress as women or appear effeminate as in the case of Friedkin, they will
never be real women. Additionally the humour in Lewin often seems more
bitter than in Aleichem, for example with the lawyer Baum slowly going
mad in the course of the internment. But even when addressing mental health
issues Lewin clings to a notion of the absurdity of life, e. g. when in the very
end Naomi shows Baum a photo of Morrie he tells her that he had already
left for Italy, leaving her at a loss what to do. Thus humour is often
combined with a further alienation effect.

Lewin's principle of ironic inversion, always combined with a sense
of absurdity, can be seen as the underlying principle of *The Dunera Boys*.
Producer Bob Weis describes the innovative moment of the mini-series thus:

> [F]or me, it is a sort of breakthrough in Australian television drama,
> because it works on the level of drama and irony. There are lots of
> situations set up, which [...] would be melodramatic, but which, in fact,
> have an ironic content.[38]

If we think about the questions of genre transgression raised at the beginning
of this article, it becomes clear that the latter also can be seen in Lewin's
interpretation of the comic tradition of European Jewry. In creating a
documentary style TV drama Lewin mocks the tradition of the genre and
convinces his audience to believe in the factual content of the story. At the
same time a close viewing of the movie reveals how he uses music and in
particular signs as meta-comments to highlight the absurdity of the *Dunera*
experience. For example, the looting of the refugees' luggage aboard the
Dunera is accompanied by a waltz, or the deportees enter the internment
camp in Hay and are greeted by a welcome sign in Italian (!).

For Lewin *The Dunera Boys* was a Jewish film and his own inspiration lay within a Jewish tradition. Lewin not only captured the incidents on the *Dunera* for the first time with a film camera, but also incorporated a Jewish tradition within Australian cinema. This allowed him to create a new perspective in terms of form, by situating the film at the border between TV drama and documentary. At the same he was able to address new aspects of the *Dunera* experience, which were neglected in later works, while at the same time generalizing and simplifying others. Perhaps the biggest irony of his attempt was that in reinventing a Jewish tradition he simplified the complexity of the Jewish experience.

Notes

[1] *The Dunera Affair: A Documentary Resource Book*, ed. by Paul R. Bartrop with Gabrielle Eisen (Melbourne: Jewish Museum of Australia and Schwartz & Wilkinson, 1990), p. 19ff.

[2] Ronald Stent, *A Bespattered Page? The Internment of 'His Majesty's Most Loyal Enemy Aliens'* (London: Deutsch, 1980), p. 53ff.

[3] *The Dunera Affair: A Documentary Resource Book*, p. 20.

[4] Cyril Pearl, *The Dunera Scandal: Deported by Mistake* (London/ Sydney/Melbourne: Angus & Robertson, 1983), p. 137ff.

[5] *Ibid.*, p. 190.

[6] http://www.afc.gov.au/GTP/mrrateminisalltime.html 21/06/2004.

[7] *Jailed by the British: BBC documentary.* Part 1: *Internment of Enemy Aliens*, Part 2: *German Prisoners of War* (1983); Judy Menczel, *When Friends were Enemies* (1991); John Burgan, *Friendly Enemy Aliens: Documentary* (forthcoming 2005).

[8] Ben Lewin, *The Dunera Boys* (Melbourne: Nelson, 1991), p. 2.

[9] *Ibid.*   •

[10] *Ibid.*

[11] Benzion Patkin, *The Dunera Internees* (Sydney/Melbourne: Cassell, 1979); Cyril Pearl, *The Dunera Scandal* (London/Sydney/Melbourne: Angus & Robertson 1983).

[12] Lewin, *The Dunera Boys*, p. 2.

[13] *Ibid.*

[14] 'The right to reply', in *Channel Four* (18.10.1985), 19:50.

[15] 'TV Reviews: The terrorist's new clothes', *Sunday Times*, 20 October 1985.

[16] 'The right to reply', in *Channel Four* (18.10.1985) 19:47.

[17] *Ibid.*, 19:48.

[18] For the treatment of theatre see: Patkin, *The Dunera Internees*, p. 73ff.; Pearl, *The Dunera Scandal*, p. 201ff.; for a photograph of a cross-dressing scene: *The Dunera Affair: A Documentary Resource Book*, [illustrations p. 47].

[19] For an autobiographical account of homosexuality in the internment camp, see Werner Pelz, *Distant Strains of Triumph* (London: Gollancz, 1964), p. 78ff.

[20] Patkin, *The Dunera Internees*, p. 38.

[21] *Ibid.*, p. 52.

[22] Jan Epstein, 'Jews and Films in Australia: The Impact of the Holocaust', in *Westerly: Shmooz Downunder: Australian/Jewish Writing* 41, 4 (1996), p. 69.

[23] Patkin, *The Dunera Internees*, p. 83.

[24] *Ibid.*, p. 84.

[25] *The Dunera Affair: A Documentary Resource Book*, p. 240.

[26] Jeffrey Shandler, 'At Home on the Small Screen: Television's New York Jews', in *Entertaining America: Jews, Movies, and Broadcasting*, ed. by Jeffrey Shandler and J. Hoberman (Princeton/Oxford: Princeton UP, 2003), p. 246ff.; see also: Vincent Brook, *Something Ain't Kosher Here: The Rise of the "Jewish" Sitcom* (New Brunswick: Rutgers UP, 2003), p. 36ff.

[27] Jan Epstein, 'Jews and Films in Australia: The Impact of the Holocaust', in *Westerly: Shmooz Downunder: Australian/Jewish Writing* 41, 4 (1996), p. 66.

[28] Birgit Lang, *Inszenierungen zwischen den Kulturen. Deutschsprachiges Exiltheater und -kabarett in Australien* (Vienna: PhD thesis, 2001), p. 113.

[29] Mark Lopez, *The Origins of Multiculturalism in Australian Politics 1945-1975* (Melbourne: Melbourne UP, 2000), p. 457ff.

[30] *The Australian People: an Encyclopaedia of the Nation, its People and their Origins*, ed. by James Jupp (London/ Sydney/Melbourne: Angus & Robertson, 1988).

[31] To name the most important: *On Being a German-Jewish Refugee in Australia. Australian Journal of Politics and History (Special Issue)*, ed. by Konrad Kwiet and Joseph A. Moses 31, 1 (1985); *Strauss to Matilda. Viennese in Australia 1938-1988*, ed. by Karl Bittman (Sydney: Wenkart Foundation, 1988); Marlene Norst and Johanna McBride, *Austrians and Australia* (Sydney: Athena Press, 1988); Suzanne D. Rutland, *At the Edge of the Diaspora: two centuries of Jewish settlement in Australia* (Sydney: Collins, 1988).

[32] Birgit Lang, *Inszenierungen zwischen den Kulturen,* Vienna: PhD thesis, p. 224.

[33] Ursula Wiemann, *German and Austrian Refugees in Melbourne 1933-1947* (Melbourne: M. A. Thesis, 1965), p. 301.

[34] Patkin, *The Dunera Internees*, p. 2.

[35] Lewin, *The Dunera Boys*, p. 6.

[36] 'Ben Lewin: Interviewed by Andrew L. Urban', in *Cinema Papers* 101 (1994), p. 41.

[37] 'Yiddish literature.' Encyclopædia Britannica. 2005. Encyclopædia Britannica Online 2 Mar. 2005 http://search.eb.com/eb/article?tocId=234158.

[38] Nick Roddick, 'History Lessons', in *Cinema Papers* 54 (1985), p. 24.

J. M. Ritchie

Exile, Internment and Deportation in Norbert Gstrein's *Die englischen Jahre*[1]

The novel *Die englischen Jahre* is superficially a mystery, in which the narrator investigates the biography of the writer Hirschfelder, a Jewish refugee in Britain. Previous critics have discussed the novel's interrogation of identity. This article seeks to assess how far it succeeds as a depiction of exile, internment and deportation. While the early chapters evoke a convincing picture of wartime London, those depicting internment on the Isle of Man sketch the background more lightly, concentrating on the (fictional) events which drive the plot.

Norbert Gstrein's novel *Die englischen Jahre* confronts the reader with many puzzles. Gstrein does not narrate the story directly, but instead tells the story through the persona of a doctor, the ex-wife of a writer. Because of her husband's admiration for a Jewish exile, Gabriel Hirschfelder, she sets out on a quest to discover the truth about this exile, especially since he claims to have committed a murder. Because of the frequently changing perspective, considerable doubt develops in the novel about the identity of the central figure and this identity question, more than exile and internment, is what first attracts the attention of the reader. Not surprisingly this is also what has caught the attention of some of the novel's critics, who have tended to place the work in that special tradition of the identity novel stretching from Max Frisch's *Stiller* to W. G. Sebald's *Austerlitz*.[2] Literary echoes indeed abound. The novelist husband is called Max, the name Sebald preferred for himself. Hirschfelder decides, like so many other exiles, not to return to the German-speaking world, and instead settles in Southend-on-Sea, not far from Sheerness-on-Sea, where Uwe Johnson settled. Hirschfelder becomes a librarian like that other long-term Austrian exile in Guildford, Theodor Kramer.

     Hirschfelder, the central figure of the novel, is a literary puzzle and hence there are various questions to be explored. How much does Gstrein, the author of Austrian 'Dorfgeschichten' (p. 10),[3] really know about exiled Jewish refugees in England; how successful is he in conveying for his readers a picture of life in England during the early war years; and how successfully has he researched the realities of exile, internment and deportation? In this connection much might be said about the unusual construction of the novel. As has been noted, it is not Max, the novelist, who pursues 'genauere Nachforschungen' (p. 11), but his ex-wife, a doctor who has no experience of literary research. In effect, as will be seen, she readily admits her general ignorance of exile, internment and deportation and is constantly confronted with gaps in Hirschfelder's life story.

Essentially, too, from the very first pages of the novel, the story of this Austrian man in exile in England is told from a woman's point of view. Though the doctor later has access to Hirschfelder's fragmentary diary and to his autobiographical novel, she mainly has to piece together his existence in exile from what she is told by the four women in his life. Four of the chapters in the novel explore his identity through the women he knew: Margaret, Catherine, Clara and Madeleine. Significantly too the dating of these chapters further limits the range of the novel to the first years of the war. Chapter two is headed 'LONDON, 1. MAI 1940', chapter four is headed, 'DOUGLAS, ISLE OF MAN, 21. JUNI 1940', chapter five 'DOUGLAS, ISLE OF MAN, 29. JUNI 1940'. Such precise dating means that the action of the novel focuses on a particular point in the progress of the war. Only two chapters focus specifically on the internment of refugees from Nazism on the Isle of Man. The penultimate chapter of the novel changes perspective to focus on the *S. S. Arandora Star* on 2 July 1940, just before it was sunk by a Nazi U-boat with the loss of life of hundreds of Italian, German and Austrian internees who were being deported from Britain to Canada.

The first chapter ('MARGARET') is set 'im vergangenen Sommer in London' in the Austrian Cultural Institute in Rutland Gate, when the narrator meets Margaret, the last of Hirschfelder's three wives, at the preview of an exhibition of portraits of exiles. The description of the Institute reads as if based on reality, down to the grand piano in the middle of the main room, though here, as elsewhere in his work, Gstrein shows that he has little time for the official representatives of Austrian culture. Once the two ladies have met, they spend evenings together, e.g. at Bailey's in London's Gloucester Road. Margaret, one gathers, had got to know Hirschfelder by putting a personal ad in a newspaper. Various candidates responding to the ad had been rejected as unsuitable and Hirschfelder, aged by then sixty-five and Jewish, had been accepted. They had married within three months of meeting. She had moved into Hirschfelder's house in Southend-on-Sea, which turns out to be a typical example of post-war English shabbiness. Thanks to his new wife's connections Hirschfelder had managed to get a job as a librarian, but had worked only mornings. He spent the afternoons (writing perhaps?) in a rented room in the Palace Hotel in Southend-on-Sea, once a luxury establishment, now nothing more than a 'Billigabsteige' (p. 23). All exile researchers look for a *Nachlass* (p. 26) and fear that the exiled author may have destroyed his manuscripts before his death. These possibilities are raised only to be dismissed. There is no trace of the 'Panorama des Jahrhunderts', the exile autobiography (*Die englischen Jahre*) which Max has suggested Hirschfelder might have been working on.

Not all is shabbiness and decline in England, however. The narrator's next meeting with Margaret in the Austrian Cultural Institute leads from there to the Hyde Park Hotel, to a café in Sloane Square, to Bailey's in Gloucester Road again, to the banks of the Thames at Richmond, to the museums in South Kensington, and later there is even mention of the Goethe Institute in Exhibition Road in which Margaret tries in vain to find a copy of Hirschfelder's book, *Die Lebenden leben und die Toten sind tot* (p. 28). One Sunday she buys newspapers in Piccadilly Circus before travelling to Southend-on-Sea, where she visits the library Hirschfelder had worked in until retirement, sees his rooms and hears how he died. Before she leaves London she goes to the Tate Gallery to see Hirschfelder's favourite picture, Turner's *Snow Storm*, a picture with the unusually long sub-title: *Steam-Boat off a Harbour's Mouth making Signals in Shallow Water and going by the Lead* (p. 49). By the end of the first chapter Gstrein has demonstrated that he has moved a long way from the hills and valleys of his native Austria and has researched the London scene intensively.

The second chapter ('LONDON, 17. MAI 1940') starts in the school mentioned at the end of the first chapter with Hirschfelder flanked by two men, 'der Blasse' and 'der mit der Narbe', who will be his close companions for the rest of the novel. The policy of mass internment, confirmed at the time by Winston Churchill with the words 'Collar the Lot', has started and refugees from National Socialism have been rounded up before being taken to a more permanent internment camp on the Isle of Man. But this chapter shortly moves back in time to take in Gabriel's arrival in England and even further back in Gabriel's mind to the conditions in Vienna which made his departure for England necessary to escape the anti-Jewish terror of the Nazis. As an exile in England, Gabriel has been found a place with the family of a judge in Smithfield and teaches German to the judge's children. There is little in this chapter about the exile experience apart from a brief mention of the tribunals to which refugees from National Socialism were subjected, here with a rather stereotypical ex-colonial officer as chairman (p. 96). The description of the immigration officer in Harwich is equally stereotypical (p. 109).

Chapter three ('CATHERINE') starts with more local London colour. Catherine, the reader learns, had got to know Hirschfelder a few days before his internment, when they had literally bumped into each other in the black-out in St Martin's Lane, although he, as an 'enemy alien' subject to curfew, should not have been there. Their next contact, she reveals, came only two months later in the form of the twenty-four line letter 'enemy aliens' in internment were permitted by the censor. What follows is a passage from Hirschfelder's autobiographical novel – a passage that conjures up a picture of the exile's view of London. Once contact had been established and Catherine knew where he was interned she sends food parcels to him on the Isle of Man. What happens to Hirschfelder after his release from internment is also typical of the time: he joins the Pioneer Corps of the British Army, 'enemy aliens' not normally being allowed to join combat units.[4] The uncomfortable position of the 'enemy alien' and former internee in wartime is further made clear when talk of internment on the Isle of Man tends to be dismissed by the man in the street or the man in the pub as a cushy holiday far from the dangers of the nightly bombings in London. Any former internee also stands out by reason of his faulty English and German accent, something which can lead to misunderstandings, for, if the exile explains that he is a German Jewish refugee the English response may well be to blame the Jews for occupying the best houses in Belgrave Square and Grosvenor Square and for profiteering on the black market (p. 128).

Not surprisingly for a novel dealing with the life of an exile in London the personal loneliness and isolation of Hirschfelder is stressed. Hirschfelder has been one of the early refugees to find asylum in England thanks to family connections. At first the numbers were small, but what had been a trickle after Hitler's accession to power in 1933 had by 1939 become a flood, necessitating the hurried setting up of organisations to deal with the problems of new arrivals, organisations such as the Free German League of Culture and the Austrian Centre. These organisations are never mentioned in the novel, for Hirschfelder avoids 'die organisierten Treffen mit anderen Flüchtlingen' (p. 132). In terms of the identity problem of the novel there may be good reason why Hirschfelder avoids contact with other refugees in exile organisations, if he is not who he claims to be. Gstrein, the author of *Die englischen Jahre*, does know about Bloomsbury House (p. 139),[5] the central body through which all exile arrivals were channelled, but because of Hirschfelder's avoidance of his fellow exiles, there is no mention in the novel of the Austrian Centre in London which would eventually have 3,000 members, offering the Austrian community in Britain a much needed meeting place, a wide range of cultural, political, educational and social activities, a restaurant, a library, a small scale publishing house and a weekly newspaper. Hirschfelder, the cantankerous outsider and loner, never uses the German language libraries of the exile organisations, never visits an exile theatre, never meets famous fellow writers like Alfred Kerr or artists like Oskar Kokoschka, the president of the FDKB. He does, however, share some of the common experiences of all wartime Londoners, such as the stifling atmosphere of an underground shelter during an air-raid, enemy aircraft dropping their bombs on the city or strafing the streets with their machine-guns, and the frightening arrival of the 'Wunderwaffen' V1 and V2 rockets, when the war is nearly over (p. 142). The narrator returns to the Austrian Institute seeking information about Austrians in the internment camps, something that it does not have. The chapter then finally closes with the arrival of a parcel containing Hirschfelder's attempts to write about his time in internment and also fragments of a diary, all of which promises a possible insight into the internment experience – but closer inspection reveals great gaps. From Hirschfelder's notes no personal picture of internment is available. The narrator-researcher then decides to find out about internment for herself by going to the Isle of Man.

Instead of offering readings from the fragmentary diary, chapter four of *Die englischen Jahre* ('DOUGLAS ISLE OF MAN 21. JUNI 1940'), startles the reader with an abrupt change of narrative perspective. The female narrator has vanished, the time is now June 1940, and the place, the Isle of Man, seven days after the arrival of the internees from the horrors of the transit camp in Liverpool (p. 164). The reader is now inside an internment camp, seen through the eyes of an unnamed second-person narrator (who appears to be Hirschfelder). Left behind is the 'Übergangslager am Stadtrand von Liverpool' (presumably the Huyton Camp, though Gstrein does not name it). The new place of internment is identified by barbed wire and the rails left from the famous Isle of Man horse-tram system on the promenade at Douglas. The state of mind of all the internees in the camp is one of boredom and resignation.

Thereafter daily life in the camp, after the trumpeter blows reveille at seven, is quickly sketched in. Barbers have set up shop, shoemakers repair shoes, watchmakers repair watches. There is a Viennese Café, there are regular lectures on an incredible range of topics, and learning and speaking English is important. But this is all dealt with in a page and a half. The rest of the chapter focuses on the Camp Commander (another rather stereotypical figure) and his interview with Hirschfelder about 'Das braune Haus' and the presence in the camp of pro-Nazi internees. The co-existence of politically opposing groups was a problem for the authorities organising internment. Fascists and Italians were interned at Peel and in Ramsey, the camp was sectioned off to prevent different groups from fighting, something which was very necessary when pro-British German and Austrian Jewish refugees and pro-Nazi prisoners were being billeted together.

Here once again Gstrein does not mention the name of the camp, although such conditions existed, for example, at Mooragh, where the authorities had to make separate sections for the inmates. There were also similar problems in the women's camps where pro-Nazi internees had to be kept apart from the Jewish majority. All this comes as a surprise to the female narrator/researcher: she later raises the matter with her landlord, who is surprised by her naiveté. When she discusses it with Leo, a former internee, however, he dislikes the word *Nazisympathisanten* and blames the Communists for causing the trouble (p. 272).

As the plot proceeds, it becomes increasingly an interrogation of Hirschfelder's true identity. The fifth chapter ('DOUGLAS ISLE OF MAN 29. JUNI 1940'), which takes place eight days later, contains little information about daily life in internment, but is crucial to the narrative, focusing on a card game, which will result in an identity switch (and later loss of life). Where previous chapters had charted the 'Collar the Lot' hysteria which resulted in the internment of 'enemy aliens' in camps such as those on the Isle of Man, this chapter details the next phase of British government policy: deportation to Canada or Australia (p. 223). The events are recounted by the same shadowy narrator, who plays cards with 'der Blasse', 'der mit der Narbe' and 'der Neue' – and loses. He will be the one to leave the island on the ship for Canada or Australia, and 'der Neue' will stay behind.[6]

The sixth chapter ('CLARA') moves back to the first-person narrative of Max's wife, who has made her way to the Isle of Man to continue her researches into the mysterious life of Hirschfelder. She has spent her first two nights in the Imperial Hotel on Central Promenade in Douglas, almost certainly, according to Hirschfelder's diary, part of the camp he had been interned in. This chapter bristles with information about the Isle of Man, from the horse-tram system already mentioned, to Castle Mona, Ramsey, Derby Castle, Port Erin, the Sefton Hotel, Hutchinson Square, Laxey, the electric railway, Snaefell, Port St Mary and Castletown. The internment camp in Ramsey is mentioned but not named (p. 262) and in the Sefton Hotel (also a former camp), the researcher meets up with Leo, a former internee, who provides her with various *Stacheldrahtlegenden*. She later returns to Port Erin, where the women's camps were. There is no indication at this point that the women (and children) were housed in two camps at Port St Mary and Port Erin (p. 260). She visits the famous Manx Museum and reads the contemporary newspapers like the *Daily Mail* which had supported Oswald Mosley and the British Union of Fascists in the Thirties and which then led a campaign to have all aliens in Britain interned. Later, from her landlord, she learns about the government's change of policy and the details of the release of internees in a government 'Weißbuch'.[7] Her research in the newspapers then leads her to newspaper stories about women in internment (p. 271) seeming to have led her (and Gstrein) to newspaper headlines like 'Pleasures of Internment: Aliens' Holiday in the Isle of Man' in the *Daily Telegraph* of 6 June 1940 and to reports of statements in the House of Commons about considerable public resentment,[8] but do not lead her (or Gstrein) to the opposite of such *Hetzartikel*, namely to the press campaign led by journals like *The Spectator* which helped to bring internment to a quick end, nor to the speeches against internment in the House of Commons by Major Victor Cazalet, who coined the phrase 'a bespattered page', nor to the campaign by H. G. Wells, who accused the Home Office of being run by Nazi sympathisers. Despite all the anecdotes and *Geschichtchen* she is fed by her landlord, local residents and former internees, the nameless researcher still ends up, like the reader of this novel, with only a vague idea of what internment was like (p. 282). There is further enlightenment regarding the exile experience from Hirschfelder's diary, which the doctor is reading and clearly his opinions are not necessarily a reflection of the reality of internment; she finds his views distressing and disturbing.

The internment newspapers (which the novel does not identify), and which for obvious reasons were cyclostyled, did appear in German and in English.[9] The literary standard was perhaps not always of the highest and the English of the English-language newspaper not always of the purest; nevertheless the very existence of the newspapers was a vital element in the exile life of the time, just as the various other cultural and educational elements in the internment camps (e.g. the *Vorträge* by an internee professor on his special subject, which Hirschfelder despises) were essential for the well-being of the inmates. Here, as elsewhere in his novel, Gstrein is very selective and perhaps not quite accurate. Hirschfelder in his camp could probably not have seen both English-language and German-language newspapers. So, for example, *The Camp*, founded in Hutchinson Camp, where Hirschfelder is interned, was by and large an English-language paper with few literary but many fine art contributions. *The Onchan Pioneer*, on the other hand, (and the novel never mentions Onchan), was a mainly German language paper with a high literary content. Hutchinson Square is identified in the novel as Hirschfelder's later place of internment, but there is no mention of the art shows there, nor of the famous artists like Kurt Schwitters, who were involved. Nor is there any mention of the excellent quality of the musical life of internment on the Isle of Man – the Amadeus Quartet was formed there – apart from the fact that Hirschfelder is sarcastic once again and applauds, when 'ein Gefangenenenorchester im Derby Castle ein schon lange angekündigtes, öffentlich zugängliches Grand Concert geben sollte und es wegen der anhaltenden Luftangriffe auf London abgesagt wurde' (p. 283). In this chapter, as elsewhere, the main impression left by the Isle of Man in particular (though famous for its 'Motorradrennen im Mai, der berühmt berüchtigten Tourist Trophy') (p. 260) and England in general, is a negative one of shabbiness and decay.

Before she leaves the Isle of Man the researcher wanders around for the last time and visits the Manx Museum, which despite what Gstrein says in this novel, has a superb collection of Manx books, publications and archives on Manx history, of which civilian internment on the Isle of Man is recognised as an important part and not simply something to be lumped together with tourist attractions as the novel claims. This chapter is headed 'CLARA', but in fact only some four pages out of nearly fifty are devoted to her, the former maid in the house of the judge, the girl with whom Hirschfelder had slept, and with whom for his own reasons the writer of the exile novel avoids all contact. When the narrator eventually finds Clara she is in a home in a wheelchair and is incapable of speech. Once again a possible source of information about the real Hirschfelder proves inadequate.

The seventh chapter ('S. S. ARANDORA STAR NORD-ATLANTIK 2. JULI 1940') represents yet another dramatic narrative leap. The female narrator has once again disappeared and the reader is back inside the thoughts of the shadowy contemporary narrator as he is awakened by two Italians shaving near him. These two Italians, the reader gathers, were not exiles, refugees or dangerous Fascists but simply Italians who had chosen to work in Britain and who had been arrested and interned along with all the other Italians in Britain as soon as Italy entered the war. There were Fascists among them, as this chapter indicates, but for the most part the Italians were, like the two Hirschfelder hears talking, Italians who had been working in places like a restaurant in London's Fitzrovia. Many of these Italians, the reader further gathers, had been interned in Warth Mills in Bury, where they had been herded together in appalling conditions (p. 303).

The narrator (the real Hirschfelder?) has been transferred by ferry, together with others from the Isle of Man, to the dockside in Liverpool, where the ship is waiting for them. Nobody has checked his identity. He immediately recognises the ship from his days in London as one for which he had seen advertisements in a shop window. Later, when the female narrator talks with Madeleine, she is presented with a brochure for the luxury vessel, so in one way or the other the reader is given a great deal of information about the ship on which Hirschfelder now finds himself together with other internees, German, Austrian and Italian, being deported to Newfoundland. (p. 349) In fact the *Arandora Star* was not the first such ship to be designated by the War Cabinet to deport internees to Canada and Australia. The *Duchess of York* had been the first to sail for Canada with

2,500 internees on board, twice the normal capacity for passengers. This ship is actually mentioned in the novel, but only as part of the mystification surrounding the Hirschfelder/Harasser identity switch. There was also such a ship as the *Arandora Star* and on 30 June 1940 this prison-ship sailed, carrying two-and-a-half times as many people as it was designed for, and was attacked and sunk off the west coast of Ireland at 6 am, on 2 July 1940 by U47 under the command of Günther Prien, the man who sailed into Scapa Flow Naval Base and sank the *Royal Oak* (p. 352). Within half an hour of the torpedo attack it had sunk with the loss of 682 lives.[10]

This incident caused an immediate uproar and, following an investigation, the British government subsequently reversed the policy of deporting 'enemy aliens', but this decision took time and as Madeleine points out in the novel: 'Der Skandal daran war, dass die meisten Überlebenden schon eine Woche später nach Australien geschickt worden sind' (p. 351). Here once again Gstrein avoids all detail, but the next great scandal of the time was what happened on the SS *Dunera* carrying 2,400 internees to Australia. Following this scandal forced deportations ceased.[11] Through the mind of Hirschfelder the reader experiences in this chapter the explosion when the torpedo strikes the *Arandora Star*, the subsequent panic, the struggle in the water till rescue ships arrive and the presumed death among many others of Hirschfelder himself, though nothing is definite in this novel.

The final chapter ('MADELEINE') returns to the doctor and her quest for Hirschfelder. She had known little about internment and the Isle of Man at the start of her quest and she knows equally little about the *Arandora Star* tragedy. She had returned to her work in Vienna and had given hardly a thought to her *Nachforschungen*, until she comes across a report in the newspaper Madeleine works for, an article about the role of the Channel Islands in wartime during the German occupation. The two women meet in the Café Griensteidl am Michaelerplatz in Vienna and what follows is an account of their conversation, though once again the doctor proves a less than reliable researcher. Nevertheless her final startling revelation is that the mysterious fourth man had taken Hirschfelder's identity and Madeleine had been knowingly married to an impostor for years. This answers the main riddles of the novel, but the reader is still left with many unanswered questions. If this is true, it means that the famous exile novel had not been written by an exiled Jew from Austria, that the real Hirschfelder had died on the *Arandora Star* in 1940, and that the non-Jew Harasser had lived on in his place. This means further that the successful exile autobiographical novel is yet another example of Wilkomirski-type false memory. Binjamin Wilkomirski's *Fragmente* came out to great acclaim in 1995 as a Holocaust memoir, but was later shown to be pure fiction, a novel. It emerged that Wilkomirski was one Bruno Doesseker, who was not of Jewish origin and had never been interned in a concentration camp.[12] In *Die englischen Jahre*, Gstrein further complicates the situation by having Max, the novelist, reappear to make his wife an offer to use her material to write a novel about Hirschfelder instead of her. He would use an assumed name, with the aim of baffling the hated 'Wiener Bande' (p.388) who will not be able to work out from the changing narrative perspectives and the mixture of imagination and reality who has actually written the novel.

Coming back to the question of the presentation of exile, internment and deportation, it has to be said that Gstrein's four years of work have resulted in a remarkable *tour de force*. He knows his London and in the first part of the book especially he is completely successful in conjuring up the atmosphere of the city in wartime with its barrage balloons, ack-ack guns, petrol rationing, black market, blackout, air-raid warnings and the effects of the blitz. As far as exile is concerned, the real Hirschfelder is restricted to life in the judge's house and apart from errands to various parts of London's East and West Ends he has little or no experience of the later famous exile institutions like the Free German League of Culture or the Austrian Centre. Harasser, the false Hirschfeld, lives out the many remaining years of his self-imposed exile (he dies fifty years after the end of the war) in the post-war shabbiness of Southend-on-Sea. Only two chapters in the novel are devoted to internment, but unlike Max, the exile expert in his novel, who works only in archives, Gstrein has certainly visited the Isle of Man and explored the actual sites of the island's internment camps. Moreover, the chapter devoted to the tragic sinking of the *Arandora Star* forcefully highlights the horrors of the forced deportation of internees. More than ever before – and perhaps for the first time for a German reading public – the exile, internment and deportation of Jewish exiles have been brought to life on the page.

Notes

[1] Norbert Gstrein, *Die englischen Jahre*, Frankfurt am Main: Suhrkamp, 2001; page numbers in the text refer to this edition. For the English edition see Gstrein, *The English Years*, translated by Anthea Bell, Harvill and Vintage 2003.

[2] See, for example, J. J. Long, 'Intercultural Identities in W. G. Sebald's *The Emigrants* and Norbert Gstrein's *Die englischen Jahre*' in *Journal of Multilingual and Multicultural Development*, Vol. 25: 5 & 6, 2004, pp. 512-28.

[3] Gstrein's earlier novels, dealing with life in Austrian ski resorts and the effect of backward-looking provincialism, include: *Einer* (1988), *Anderntags* (1989), *Das Register* (1992), *O2* (1993), *Der Kommerzialrat* (1995), all published Frankfurt am Main: Suhrkamp.

[4] Yvonne Kapp and Margaret Mynatt, *British Policy and the Refugees, 1933-1941.* With a foreword by Charmian Brinson, London 1997, p. 138.

[5] See the contemporary brochure for refugees – 'While you are in England. Helpful Information and Guidance for Every Refugee' [n. d.], ed. by German Jewish Aid Committee (Bloomsbury House) & Jewish Board of Deputies (Woburn House).

[6] At first sight the identity switch in *Die englischen Jahre* may appear improbable, but contemporary accounts suggest that it was not only possible but did indeed happen. See Kapp and Mynatt, *op. cit.*, p.116.

[7] The "Weißbuch" refers to the government White Paper regarding the release of internees. In fact there was more than one and, as a result, more than eighteen categories for release. See Kapp and Mynatt, *op. cit.*, p. 138 ff.

[8] See Charmian Brinson, '"In the Exile of Internment" or "Von Versuchen aus einer Not eine Tugend zu machen": German-speaking Women Interned by the British during the Second World War' in *Politics and Culture in Twentieth Century Germany,* ed. by William Niven and James Jordan, Camden House 2003, pp. 83-84. Professor Brinson has many examples of the negative aspects of internment for the women and children in the Isle of Man camps. See also Brinson: 'Autobiography in Exile: The Reflections of Women Refugees from Nazism in British Exile, 1933-1945' in *German-speaking Exiles in Great Britain. The Yearbook of the Research Centre for German and Austrian Exile Studies,* vol.3 (2001), pp. 1-22.

[9] For a survey of all the camp newspapers see Michael Seyfert, *Im Niemandsland. Deutsche Exilliteratur in britischer Interniernung. Ein unbekanntes Kapitel der Kulturgeschichte des Zweiten Weltkriegs* (Berlin: Das Arsenal 1984). For an analysis of two newspapers, one German-language and one English-language, see Jörg Thunecke, 'Die Isle of Man-Lagerzeitungen *The Camp* und *The Onchan Pioneer*: Kultur im Ausnahmezustand', in *German-speaking Exiles in Great Britain. The Yearbook of the Research Centre for German and Austrian Exile Studies,* vol.3 (2001), pp. 41-58.

[10] Kapp and Mynatt, *op.cit.*, p. 112 ff.

[11] Kapp and Mynatt, *op. cit.*, p. 121ff.

[12] See Sue Vice, 'Benjamin Wilkomirski's *Fragments* and Holocaust Envy: Why Wasn't I there too?' in *Immigrants & Minorities,* vol. 21 (March/July 2002), Special Issue on *Representing The Holocaust,* London 2002, pp. 249-268. See also Philip Gourevitch, 'The Memory Thief', *New Yorker,* 14 June 1999, pp. 47-58.

Index

Abraham, Gerhard, 87, 90
Ackerl, Katherina, 110
Adomat, R., 90
Aleichem, Sholom, 187, 189
Alexander, Major P., 142-44
Altmann, H. C., 73
Anderson, Sir John, 12, 19, 153
Asquith, Herbert Henry, 29, 85, 94

Bach, Johann Sebastian, 71
Baddiel, David, 15
Bahrs, Emil 90
Baily, James T., 48-49, 51-52, 54-56
Baneleur, E. de 69
Banholzer, Josef, 71
Barnes, James and Patience 102
Bassett-Lowke, W. J., 51
Baum, Max, 133
Becker, Alfred, 172
Beckmann, H., 89
Beethoven, Ludwig van, 68-69, 71-72
Behrens, E., 89
Bell, George, Bishop of Chichester, 12, 108, 144
Bene, Otto, 101
Beu, E., 89
Biesen, C. van, 89
Bird, John C., 18, 84
Blessing, Bertha 107-08, 110-11, 113
Blume, August 87
Blumenthal, Oskar 73
Bock, Johannes 85-86
Booth, Mary 113

Borneman, Ernest 167-68
Bowman, Major 89-90
Boyd, Christopher 115
Bracey, Bertha 102
Brainin, Norbert 15
Braun, Ernie 109
Brecht, Bertolt 122, 128
Bredow, G. A. 73

Cazalet, Major Victor 12, 146, 199
Cecil, Lord David 146
Cesarani, David 19-23
Chappell, Connery 21
Chisholm, Sir Samuel 93
Chopin, Frédéric 71
Churchill, Winston 19, 143, 146-47, 153, 195
Cohen, Israel 63
Cohen-Portheim, Paul 18-19, 36, 58
Colpi, Terri 22
Corvin, Michael 140, 147
Cossmann, Paul 36
Crown Princess of Sweden 57
Cruickshank, Dame Joanna 102, 104-05, 139, 141, 148-49
Csavojatz, A. 70
Cuthbert, Inspector C. R. 105

Daniel, Captain H. O. 142
Davies, Brigitte 109
Dawidowicz, Lucy 20
Deutsch, Otto Erich 122-23, 133
Dewar, Lord 92
Dittmar, Henry Gustav 140
Driesch, Wilhelm 89

Dudow, Slatan 122
Duwe, Gustav 89
Dvořák, Antonin 71

Edward VII, King 68
Ehrentreu, Rabbi, E. 186
Elgar, Edward 68
Elias, Norbert 134

Falk, Rabbi, L. A. 186
Farrant, Deemster 158
Farringdon, Lord 103
Fehle, Bruno 114
Fischer, Kurt 188
Fleischmann, A. 69
Foa, Bruno 155
Forster, E. M. 104
Franz Josef I, Kaiser 70
Friedenthal, Richard 14
Frisch, Max 193
Fulcher, David 183

Gál, Hans 14, 121-24, 126-28,
    130-35
Gellhorn, Peter 15
Gerhardt, Elena 75
Gillman, Peter and Leni 11, 21
Gleitsmann-Wolf, Friedrich 68,
    72-74
Goehling, Oskar 72
Goethe, Johann Wolfgang von 91,
    175
Goldberg, W. 70
Göritz, Andreas 169, 177
Greene, Sir Wilfrid 104
Gross, Otto 52, 55
Gstrein, Norbert 14, 193-97, 199-
    202
Gyoeri, Emil 68, 70, 73

Haake, Herr 70

Hanway, Louis 92
Harrison, Rev. J. Benson 103
Hasenclever, Walter 148
Heartfield, John 121
Heber, Karl 69, 71-72
Heckelmann, M. 73
Heilig, Bruno 145, 149
Hennings, C. R. 18
Hilberg, Raul 20, 187
Hirschfeld, Gerhard 21
Hitler, Adolf 102-03, 108, 139,
    196
Hoffmeyer, F. 89
Höllering, Georg 13, 121-28, 130-
    35
Holmes, Colin 21-22
Hopf, Herr 71
Huber, J. J. 111
Humpoletz, Paul 127, 132
Hutmacher, Herr 71
Hutter, Richard 132-33

Jennings, Gertrude 112
Jochmann, Sister Anna 109-12,
    114
Johnson, Lieutenant 141
Johnson, Uwe 193
Jupp, James 187

Kachmarck, Herr 50
Kadelburg, Gustav 73
Kadisch, J. M. 73
Kalmer, Joseph (i.e. Josef
    Kalmus) 139
Karg-Bebenburg, Hans 132
Karlowa, Otto 101-02
Kerr, Alfred 196
Kerr, Sir Michael 14-15
Ketchum, John D. 91
Ketterer, Georg 92
Keun, Irmgard 148, 152

Kleist, Franz Rinteln von 37, 42
Koch, Eric 21, 165-66, 168-69
Kochan, Miriam 21
Kokoschka, Oskar 196
Koenen, Emmy 103
Kramer, Theodor 193
Kreutzer, Konradin 89
Kreisel, Henry 14, 166, 168, 173-
    75
Kruse, Herr 71
Kushner, Tony 19-23

Lafitte, François 11, 19
Lamprecht, Robert 167
Lang, Andreas 54
Lauer, O. 69, 71
Laurenz, F. 92
Lehmann, Leopold 141
Lehmann, W. 69
Leibfried, Mrs. 92
Leimer, Herr 71
Leopold, Herr 71
Lewin, Ben 179-90
Lewinson, Herr 72
Lissauer, Ernst 75
Liszt, Franz 69, 71
Looker, Elizabeth 107-08
Loraine, Sir Percy 153, 155
Luce, Claire Boothe 112
Lytton, Lord 146

Mackay, Robert 23
Mackintosh, Charles Rennie 51
Madoc, H.W., Chief Constable
    Lieutenant Isle of Man 64, 68
Mann, Heinrich 148
Mann, Thomas 148
Manz, Stefan 19
Marguiles, Hans 148
Markel, Dr. 74
Markel, Karl E. 90

Marsh, Major C. R. C. 142, 149
Matt, Charles 51
McDonald, Gus 182-83
McDougal, Mrs 92
McKellar, Elizabeth 109
McKenna, Reginald 94
McKinnon Wood, Thomas 93
Meidner, Ludwig 121
Menczel, Judy 180, 184
Meyerbeer, Giacomo 68
Moll, Elick 187
Mollwo, Alfred 69-70
Momigliano, Arnaldo 157
Mosley, Oswald 198
Mosse, Werner E. 21
Mozart, Wolfgang Amadeus 68,
    112, 158, 199
Muck, Karl 75
Murray, Professor Gilbert 12
Mussolini, Benito 14, 153-54, 163
Mutzke, Martha 92

Naftel, Theo 104-05
Necker, Wilhelm 140, 144, 148
Nelki, Erna 103
Neumann, Robert 139, 142-44,
    150
Newmark, John 166
Newton, Lord 30, 40
Novotny, Johann 69

Olden, Rudolf 148

Pacitti, Guglielmo 161
Pacitti, Maria 161
Paganini, Nicolò 70
Panayi, Panikos 11, 18, 84-85
Paolozzi, Sir Eduardo 14
Paterson, Alexander 165, 168,
    174
Patkin, Benzion 181, 188

Peacock, Frau 90
Peake, Osbert 146
Pearl, Cyril 181
Perl, Arnold 187
Perutz, Max 15
Pietzner, Carlo 140
Planer, Rev. C. 89
Plüschow, Gunther 30, 36
Pol, Otto 148
Pollak, Ernest 167, 169, 171
Probst, Hans 149
Pult, D. W. 32-33, 41

Quayle-Dickinson, Major 56

Raimund, Ferdinand 89
Rathbone, Eleanor 12, 146
Reichenfeld, H. F. 165
Reinholz, J. F. 141
Reizenstein, Franz Theodor 122
Rischowski, Ira 104, 109
Rocker, Rudolf 18
Rosenkranz, Albert E. 90
Rothschild, Alfred Charles 68, 79

Sachs, Walter 141
Sachse, Fritz 36
Sarasate, Pablo de 70
Sargeaunt, B. E. 67
Scheller, Walther 33
Scheuffler, Hans 69, 71
Schiller, G. W. 142
Schmidt-Reder, Bruno 30
Schmieder, W. 73
Schnitzler, Arthur 73
Scholten, A. 72
Schönberger, Gustav 102, 109
Schreiber, Fritz A. 83-85
Schubert, Theo 71, 112
Schultzen, Herr 90
Schulz, W. Fr. 89

Schulze, Hans 140
Schumann, Robert 71
Schwarz, Freimut 140
Schwenger, Herr 70
Schwitters, Kurt 121, 199
Scott, W. P. 179
Sebald, W. G. 193
Seyfert, Michael 121
Sibelius, Jean 69
Simion, Erna 103-04, 107
Simon, Sir John 94
Singewald, Arno 85-86
Slatter, Lieutenant-Colonel S. W.
  141
Snell, Lord 154
Spalding, Keith 14
Spier, Eugen 102
Spigelglass, Leonard 187
Spindler, Carl 34
Sponza, Lucio 22
Stampfl, Franz 184
Steiner, Friedrich 145
Stent, Ronald 21
Sterbal, Rudolph J. H. 68-69, 72
Stettenheimer, J. M. 73
Stoffa, Pal 18

Talbot, Henry 181
Trombetti, Luigi 158-59

Ullrich, Hermann 122, 134-35

Vaughan Williams, Ralph 104
Vischer, A. L. 37, 42

Wagner, Richard 69, 71-72
Warschauer, Heinz 167, 175
Wasserstein, Bernard 21
Watterson, Brenda 108, 117
Watzlaff, Otto 89
Weber, Karl Maria von 37

Wedgwood, Colonel Josiah 12,
146, 152
Wehrhan, Fritz 102, 106, 108,
113, 115, 149
Wehrhan, Gisela 106, 113
Wehrhan, Isolde 106, 112-114
Wehrhan, Wanda 101-02, 104-11,
113, 115, 149
Weinlich, Th. 69
Weis, Bob 180, 189
Weiselberger, Carl 14, 166, 168-
71, 173-75
Weiss, Erwin 122
Wells, H. G. 12, 199
Wellesz, Egon 121
Werfel, Franz 148
West, Margery 13, 64, 68
Wiegand, Friedrich Bernhard 83,
86
Wiesel, Eli 187
Wilhelm II, Kaiser 70
Wilkomirski, Binjamin (i.e. Bruno
Doesseker) 201-02
Willinger, E. 87-88
Winder, Robert 15, 77
Winter, Herr 69
Wolf, Herr 70, 72
Wolff, E. 33
Wolmer, Viscount 146

Yarrow, Stella 19

Yearbook of the Research Centre for German and Austrian Exile Studies, Volume 8 (2006)

Volume 8 will publish a selection of the Papers from the Conference 'Austria in Exile', held in London 14-16 September 2005, which are listed below:

- **Anthony Grenville**: The Emigration of Austrians to Britain after 1938 and the early Years of Settlement
- **Brigitte Mayr/Michael Omasta**: Fritz Rosenfeld, Filmkritiker
- **Charmian Brinson**: Eva Priester as a Propagandist for Austria in British Exile
- **Jörg Thunecke**: Die vollständige Fassung von Ludwig Winders Exilroman *Die Pflicht* in *Die Zeitung*
- **Tobias Hochscherf**: Austrian émigré Film-makers in London 1928-45
- **Christian Cargnelli**: Images of Vienna: Paul L. Stein, Richard Tauber and British Cinema
- **Andrea Hammel**: Austrian Women Exile Writers and the Historical Novel
- **Jutta Vinzent**: Images of Austria in *Die Zeitung*
- **Deborah Vietor-Engländer**: Imagining Austria: Kohlröserl, Alpenglühen und Patisserie
- **Colin Beavon**: Images of Britain in the Work of Georg Kreisler
- **Renate Feikes**: Exil der Wiener Medizin in Großbritannien
- **Paul Weindling**: Austrian Medical Refugees in Britain 1938-45
- **Jennifer Taylor**: Bruno Adler's 'Kurt und Willi' Dialogues
- **Tatiana Liani**: Stefan Zweigs Exil in England
- **Matthias Würz**: The Struggle of Emigration: the Austrian Conductor-Composer Karl Rankl
- **Maximiliane Jäger**: Zur literarischen und publizistischen 'Remigration' Robert Neumanns 1946-65
- **Anthony Bushell**: Many Happy Returns?
- **Anne Peiter**: Veza und Elias Canetti
- **Margaret Ives**: 'Cousins in Exile': An Anthology of Poems

The editors welcome contributions relating to any aspect of the field of German-speaking exile in Great Britain, not limited to the refugees from Hitler in the mid-twentieth century. Articles should be sent on disk and in hard copy to: the Hon. Secretary, Research Centre for German and Austrian Exile Studies, Institute of Germanic and Romance Studies, Senate House, Malet Street, London WC1E 7HU. A style sheet is available from the Hon. Secretary.

Call for information

Database of British Archival Resources Relating to German-speaking Refugees, 1933-50

In proportion to its size, Britain received more refugees from Nazi-occupied Europe than any other country, the majority of whom were German-speaking and from a Jewish background. This Arts and Humanities Research Council-funded project will inaugurate a new era in migration research by recording the variety of archival resources relating to German-speaking refugees who arrived in Britain between 1933 and 1950 and whose papers are located in public and private British collections.

The objective of this three-year project which started on 1 March 2004 is to create a comprehensive database. The rich holdings of institutional archives and personal collections are widely scattered through the British Isles, and there is currently no research tool that can be consulted. Both German and English-language resources will be included to provide access to the cross-cultural influences of the refugees and the cross-fertilizations between continental and British culture. To reflect the growing interest in Life History and Oral History, the database will include information on collections of audio and audiovisual autobiographical narratives. The database will record the names of individuals and the location of their papers along with brief biographical descriptions. The outcome of the project will be a valuable facility for researchers to enable them to locate archival material. The database will be available via the Internet and thus accessible from all over the world.

During the first year of the project we have included details from public archives and a small number of private collections in our database. We have managed to include well-known institutional collections such as the files of the Society for the Protection of Science and Learning in the Bodleian Library, Oxford, as well as individual life stories such as the tapes and transcripts of 'The Life of Else Rosenfeld', consisting of 23 programmes as broadcast on BBC Midland Home Service in 1963, which are now kept in the Birmingham City Archive. The size of the collection varies from a one page letter written by the former member of the Kindertransport Paul Hart to the Reunion organiser Bertha Leverton, now part of the 'Reunion of Kindertransport Documents, 1987-2002' collection at the Wiener Library, London, to a vast collection such as the Karl König Archive. König was the founder of a worldwide movement of international therapeutic communities for children with special needs established in 1940 in Camphill House near Aberdeen. Many questions remain open: we are, for example, looking for papers relating to Norbert Brainin of the Amadeus Quartet.

Besides internet research and archival visits, our search for private papers has been aided by a call for information in the Association of Jewish Refugees Journal. We would also welcome suggestions from the academic community and other interested readers. Please contact the project's Research Fellow below. If you would like to be kept informed about the progress of the project, please contact us and we will put you on our mailing list to receive three-monthly updates on the project by post or email.

Dr Andrea Hammel
a.hammel@sussex.ac.uk
Centre for German-Jewish Studies
Arts Building B 120
University of Sussex
Falmer, Brighton
BN1 9QN, UK

Libuše Moníková in Memoriam.

Edited by Brigid Haines and Lyn Marven.

Amsterdam/New York, NY 2005. IV, 320 pp.
(German Monitor 62)

ISBN: 90-420-1616-7   Bound € 68,-/ US $ 85.-

The novelist and essayist Libuše Moníková (1945-1998) made a unique contribution to German, Czech and world literature, writing in German from a distinctly Czech perspective in a manner which can best be described as encyclopaedic and highly intertextual. Positively received abroad, particularly in Germany and the US, her works remained until recently relatively unknown in the land of her birth.

This volume, whose appearance marks what would have been the sixtieth anniversary of her birth, is the first in-depth study of the work of this truly European writer. It contains specially commissioned articles by Czech, German, US and British scholars, as well as an appreciation by her friend and fellow writer F.C. Delius, an English translation of one of her last interviews, and the first comprehensive bibliography. The essays range from close readings of a single text, in particular the satirical, picaresque novel *Die Fassade* and the posthumously published *Der Taumel*, to surveys of themes, techniques or motifs within her *œuvre*, for example nation, exile, history and myth, and studies of Moníková's intertextual references, particularly to film and the work of Arno Schmidt. The contributions emphasise the comic, the personal and the ambiguity in her works, as well as the sheer breadth of Moníková's interests and sources.

USA/Canada: 906 Madison Avenue, UNION, NJ 07083, USA.
Call toll-free (USA only)1-800-225-3998, Tel. 908 206 1166, Fax 908-206-0820
All other countries: Tijnmuiden 7, 1046 AK Amsterdam, The Netherlands.
Tel. ++ 31 (0)20 611 48 21, Fax ++ 31 (0)20 447 29 79
Orders-queries@rodopi.nl   www.rodopi.nl
Please note that the exchange rate is subject to fluctuations